FROM BATO TO KULIN BAN
THE HIDDEN HISTORY OF BOSNIA

EMIR MEDANHODŽIĆ
SUAD HAZNADAREVIĆ

SARAJEVO, 2025

Čuvari baštine Bassania Foundation expresses its thanks to Emir Medanhodžić, President of the Management Board, who financed the translation and publishing of this book.

Emir Medanhodžić Suad Haznadarević

FROM BATO TO KULIN BAN – THE HIDDEN HISTORY OF BOSNIA

Publisher: Emir Medanhodžić

Co-publisher: Čuvari baštine Bassania Foundation

For the publisher: Emir Medanhodžić

Editor: Nihad Filipović

Assistant Editor: Nedžada Bisić

Proofreader: Amazonclassicpublisher.com

Reviewer: Nihad Filipović

Abdulah Sidran

Cover page: Adna Medanhodžić

Title page: Adna Medanhodžić
Printing: Amazonclassicpublisher.com
Translation: Lingua Leads

Number of copies: Print Per Order

Copyright © 2025

Čuvari baštine Bassania Foundation© Sarajevo, 2025

All rights reserved. No part of this publication may be reproduced, distributed, or transmitted in any form or by any means, including photocopying, recording, or other electronic or mechanical methods, without the prior written permission of the publisher, except in the case of brief quotations embodied in critical reviews and certain other noncommercial uses permitted by copyright law.

CONTENTS

Foreword 1

Introduction 6

1   Searching for the truth about Bato of the Daesitiates 19

2   Romanisation of the Illyrian area until the III CENTURY .. 29

3   Arianism in Illyricum 55

4   From Arianism to the Bosnian Church 83

5   Gothic heritage in Bosnia 98

6   Contacts between Arianism and Islam in Illyria 112

7   The theological approach to Jesus/Isa a.s. and the relations between Arianism and Islam 129

8   Avars in Bosnia 146

9   Bosnia And Illyrian Banates Between The Franks And Byzantium 164

10 The relationship between Bosnia and Raška IN THE EARLY MIDDLE AGES 185

11 The emergence of the Banate of Bosnia and ITS FIRST BANS 208

12 Ban Borić 231

13 Dominus Bosnae – Kulin, the Great Bosnian Ban 240

14 Arian basilicas in Bosnia and Herzegovina from the IV to the VI century 257

15 Arian Bosnian churches IV–XIV century 293

Afterword/review by academic Abdulah Sidran........................314
Bibliography..317

FOREWORD

"The first step in liquidating a people is to erase its memory. Destroy its books, its culture, its history. Then have somebody write new books, manufacture a new culture, invent a new history. Before long, the nation will begin to forget what it is and what it was. Honest (fair) history is liberating".

(American historian Arthur Schlesinger)

History, as scarcely any other discipline of the spirit here in Bosnia and Herzegovina, and more broadly in the countries of former Yugoslavia (in addition to the literatures, of course), especially since the middle of the XIX century, and continuing to modern times, was the servant of the ideology of nations in culture (meaning also in politics), before all in the construing of the nation, and afterwards also in the spreading of such constructs in space, so that literally all generations of our people in those times, which lasted almost to the end of the XX century, were deprived of a deep historical knowledge of the ancestors, people and peoples that populated our Region before us, of the specific culture which has and upon which was formed the mentality of that world, and then also of its successors, us, those of today, as we are.

That, of course, as all tardiness and ignorance, has its price, because, as per some unwritten default (pre-destined, predetermined function in a computer system), the lie and perverted historiography is transferred from generation to generation, is ultimately adopted as knowledge, and then that has far-reaching consequences. Focusing on the Bosniak people (Bošnjani, Bošnjaci), today, those consequences of continued historical lying and distorting of the truth about us are primarily felt as an identity problem, as a problem of a rooted awareness of origin. Because the historic path of the Bosniak people, by the force of historic destiny, was exactly such: it is a people that all but lost the entire history of the pre-Ottoman, Late

Antiquity, and Early Christian periods. And, referring to the thought of the historian Schlesinger from the beginning of this text, if Bosniaks ignore it, if they marginalise it in their awareness (of identity), or if they do not want it, there is someone who does.

What is the average knowledge among people in the region of former Yugoslavia, and, specifically, what is the average knowledge among Bosniaks about those times and cultural and historical phenomena, occurrences, happenings, and persons of those times? How much do we know about motifs of the Assyrian goddess Ishtar on stećci, the Egyptian goddess Isis, the motif of Vedic swastikas (hooked crosses) on stećci, Celtic goddesses, Illyrian snakes and dragons? How did the same ones find themselves in Mesopotamia and in Egypt? And how did they find themselves in Bosnia? Where did they originally appear, and where were they brought to? How is it that in Bosnia, on stećci, there are more motifs of the Indo-Iranian Zoroastrian deity of light – Mithra, than can be found in Iran? How did that similarity in the names of the highest-ranking ancient Egyptian priests and the highest priest in the Bosnian Church, both were called – *did*? What is it that the Illyrian hillforts (gradine) around Jablanica are telling us? What do we know and how much do we know about the Arian basilicas of Bosnia, about the contact between Arianism and Islam, about the Bosnian Church and the tradition on which it appeared? What do we know and how much do we know about the earliest appearance of the entity Bosnia, about the first forms of, put into the terminology of today, state-like formations in that area, about the first rulers and Bosnian bans of the period before Ban Borić in Bosnia, about Ratimir (in Franciscan annals *"region Ratimari ducis"*), by all indications the first Bosnian Ban, and what do we know and how much do we know about such regional rulers of Raška, Duklja, and so on? It is a whole extensive history about which generations upon generations of our people learned almost nothing or really nothing in schools. And it concerns the key connections on the historical path of Bosnia and its people.

Works with which we are met in the book by Suad Haznadarević and Emir Medanhodžić – *From Bato to Ban Kulin*, are focused exactly on that "lost" history; they are chock full of many forgotten, in the average consciousness suppressed or unknown historic facts, and in that regard this book is a rare and significant contribution to Bosnian studies. Without knowing the facts (and facts are the light of truth in societal relations), which are, without any spin, objectively, in the context of circumstances and relations in time laid out and analysed in these works, it is impossible to properly consider Bosnia and its people, of yesterday and today.

I am certain that from that impossibility, from that and from such deep ignorance of our people about themselves, also partly stems the tragedy of the more recent history of Bosnia and the Bosnian people. They are people and a people, as they say "beaten into submission", flummoxed, split in terms of identity between the feeling and the "folkloric" knowledge that they carry from home – that they are their own, on their own land – and the falsified "knowledge", imposed by education, about themselves and their history, it is a people which still, despite the finally publicly articulated consciousness about their own specialness as a people, is partially adrift in terms of identity, and as such is susceptible to the propaganda of the ill-intentioned, who still dispute its right to a country (and language), and thus also to a history.

A few words about what I personally expect as a reaction of some to the appearance of Haznadarević and Medanhodžić's book; namely, this book is the work of an amateur duo in historiography, and so some methodological complaints about the approach and processing of the topics which the authors deal with in their contributions. Some may notice that this is more of a journalistic, rather than a scientific approach and that, except for the references, there is no deep analytic-synthetic comparative insight and the like.

However, history is a science dealing with studying the past, people, occurrences and facts of the past as they are, and not how they should be. History reveals, it does not cast judgment, especially not cast judgment by the decisions of modern-day values. According to our understanding and the highest historic standards, historic authors, based on their own insight, can contextualise in time the facts that they found, but should not omit them, should not uncritically adopt them and especially reduce them to the measures and judgements of today. For example, based on the uncritical reception of Constantine Porphyrogenitus about the Sclaviniae or the records of the Priest of Duklja about the "Croatian rulers" of Bosnia, it is wrong to draw a postmodernist conclusion about the Serbianness or Croatianness of Bosnia.

Haznadarević & Medanhodžić, with their contributions in the book *From Bato to Ban Kulin*, in an argumented, presentational and logically convincing way demask exactly those and similar mythologems of Yugoslav historiography, revealing to us the earliest history of Bosnia in a new light.

The contributions in this book are chock full of historically well-founded, yet lesser-known or to the average person completely unknown facts, which I personally (because I too am one of the generation schooled in the time of national- opportunistic lies about Bosnia and its history), and I'm certain so will everyone who delves into the reading of them – collected, presented and understood in the context of the time in which they appear – perceive them as an explosion of truth in a sea of ignorance, omission, and blatant lying about the historic entity Bosnia and its people – the Bosniaks. Truly, these contributions are as a light in the deep darkness of the tunnel of history through which the people and peoples of the Western Balkans, and specifically of Bosnia and Herzegovina, have passed and still are passing. And that's a quality that rises above any possible complaint about the methodological approach.

Finally, amateurism is usually understood as something supplemental, of lesser worth, the result of mundane curiosity, not to say something pejorative. However, in modern times, the technological and overall civilisational breakthrough of humanity opens up new possibilities, creates new content and interactions on the relation between professional work, free time and the culture of idleness.

In those relations today, also inverted is the traditional understanding of professional and amateur contributions in matters of the spirit, i.e., of science and culture, especially when talking about public services (e.g., the school system, healthcare, social services, etc.) and social sciences (e.g., History). Individuals who are involved in research work, or the subject of their interest, as amateurs, without being burdened by the shackles which sometimes follow professional employment (salary, status, prestige, etc.), out of passion, out of love, and out of an emphasised interest for certain topics, open up new possibilities and envision new approaches based on different conceptions of expertise.

The book by S. Haznadarević & E. Medanhodžić – *From Bato to Ban Kulin*, truly indicates new possibilities and envisions a new approach in reading and understanding the earliest history of the people and area in which the entity known in history under the name Bosnia (in modern times with the addition – and Herzegovina) originated, lasted through time, and exist today.

The contributions which we encounter in this book aim at one thing: with the light of truth about a forgotten history, to liberate us. Therefore, I believe it is not an overstatement to say that this reading is worth reading for all who want to know what Bosna is, and who the devil that people called Bošnjani – Bosniaks – Bosnians.

Nihad Filipović

INTRODUCTION

This book, „From Bato to Kulin", Suad Haznadarević and I have been writing together for three years, while our contemplations and research have been ongoing for much longer, almost 30 years. We wrote it for a few basic reasons. The first and fundamental reason is that we love Bosnia and Herzegovina, as our motherland, and that we love history, which we are reading and researching our whole lives, as we are conscious of the Latin maxim "historia magistra vitae". Additionally, we like researching lesser-known and unknown facts and terrains in Bosnia and Herzegovina, and more broadly in the region of Illyricum. Also, we do not aspire to give any final solutions, but leave the book open to further studies, conclusions and theses.

One of the reasons is that some historiographers from our surroundings are writing falsities, ill-intentioned conclusions and some fabrications, for now more than 150 years, and all to appropriate our history, divide and destroy our country, and that action is still ongoing. The aim of this book is to confirm or even change the findings up until now with scientific facts, and to raise awareness about that problem and encourage younger historiographers to openly and courageously advance towards new research, analyses and interpretations of our older history. Of course, we were mindful not to fall into the trap of interpreting history from the perspective of today, in addition to citing as many primary sources of data as possible, so that our theses would be founded in historical documents.

However, the immediate cause for our writing is the non-existence of a complete book dealing with the theme of Late Antiquity and the Early Middle Ages, except for the separate work by Muhamed Hadžijahić: *Bosna u 9. i 10. stoljeću* (*Bosnia in the 9th and 10th century*). Living through time with understanding is something that is greatly lacking in the people of Bosnia, and, to cite George Santayana:

"Those who cannot remember the past are condemned to repeat it".

That the Bosnian-Herzegovinian people are culturally and educationally neglected, and that it does not sufficiently understand their history, was clear to me when I first visited the royal city of Bobovac in 1987. I saw unmarked trails, unmown knee- height grass, everything around the mausoleum – the tomb of kings, overgrown by thorny shrubs and weeds. The most painful thing was when I opened the door of the mausoleum, the tomb of the last Bosnian kings, and saw that someone had a bowel movement inside it.

Two years later, in 1989, I was present on a celebration of 800th anniversary of the Charter of Ban Kulin, which was organised in a well-known traditional restaurant "Aeroplan" in the heart of Baščaršija in Sarajevo, where there were only about thirty people in attendance, mostly artists, public service workers and journalists. They looked like political agitators, like some secret conspiratorial sect on some mysterious mission. Only a few years later, in 1992, the long-prepared large military aggression against Bosnia and Herzegovina occurred.

The period that this book is concerned with begins with Bato's revolt (6–9 CE) against the Roman occupation of Illyricum, and ends with the first written traces of the Bosnian Bans Borić and Kulin. Records exist of the many problems that Roman emperors had in conquering Illyria, and the fact that the Illyrian military leader Baton (born in what is nowadays called Breza) spent the rest of his life as a guarantor of the peace accord between Rome and Illyricum in Ravenna, Italy. From Bato to Ban Borić or Ban Kulin, the events from that period related to Bosnia are not sufficiently researched. Many artefacts and documents were destroyed by Avars and Slavs, as well as by Rome, Vatican, and Byzantium, the conquering peoples of that time, and the Ottomans also took with them the remains of the heritage of the ruling dynasty Kotromanić, which certainly additionally complicates access to this millennium-long period.

What can be seen in Bosnia with the naked eye are stećci, Illyrian forts, medieval cities, the cultural and historical heritage of Bosnia that yearns for our attention and respect for those who built them. Those are our ancestors, the old Illyrians and the Good Bosniaks. They, and many questions tied to them, played a decisive part in our ever-deeper commitment to the research of Bosnian history. What can be found in the literature are interpretations in which we, on multiple occasions, using the comparative method, came to understand that there exist two theses about one historical fact, those being the Croatian and the Serbian thesis. It has forever been believed that the history of Bosnia, according to the literature, only begins with the Middle Ages, with the fall of the Bosnian Kingdom and the arrival of the Ottomans. The period about which we wrote in this book has been called a "unclarified period" in historiography. We do not know what problems some Bosnian historians have with the interpretation or a liberal approach to the understanding of historical facts. There likely exists a fear of the academic community that could ridicule them or call them by derogatory names, as is the case with some historians that attempted to write about the history of Bosnia, about the fall of the Bosnian Kingdom and the arrival of the Ottomans, as did, for example, Dr. Ibrahim Pašić and others.

I began my involvement with the stećak, as one of the most significant historical monuments which only Bosnia has, in the early 2000's; out of curiosity, out of love for history and stećci, I visited many locations (more than 2000) in which necropoleis are found and read almost everything there was to read about that.

Reaching most of the locations was laborious, often trodding along kilometres of impenetrable undergrowth and forests, some of which even the local populace was not aware of.

Visiting those numerous locations, I am once again saddened by that cognisance that the relationship towards history has not changed much. In most locations, I could see that the stećci were destroyed, neglected, moved, built into the foundations of houses and religious buildings, garages, barns, chicken coops, as well as bisected by roads, etc. Hundreds of stećci are bisected by roads, even the most beautiful amongst them in Radimlja, Mile, the Wedding Cemetery in Morine, etc. By disturbing the stećci, the spiritual world is disturbed as well, retaliating against all these horrors of the material world.

Imagine what the level of consciousness among the ruling political structures in Bosnia and Herzegovina is, that the entire necropolis is moved from Donji Čevljanovići to Bijambare, where tourists visit it and pay their entry fee, without previously having provided for the bones of the buried, nor archaeological research being conducted. They do not understand that those stećci are the spiritual anchors of our past and our future.

We want to leave the door open for all further discussions about whether stećci are a classic medieval creation of Bosnian history and headstones, or a continuation of previous periods of Illyricum or the Early Middle Ages under Arian and Gothic influences.

Always upon reaching a location, I feel a special energy which makes me happier and more fulfilled, I feel a special inspiration which is hard to explain, but I know that it keeps pushing me to visit some new locations. Sometimes I seem to the people around me to be an eccentric who, well, purely out of love, spends his time, money, and energy just to find and visit some location where there are stećci.

However, that strange and beautiful feeling always drives me forwards. Some messages I may see clearly, and some I may think about for months and years. It is obvious that the stećci are telling us something, we just have not yet figured out – What?

The first thing that comes to my mind is: How good that they wrote it down on a big stone, so it cannot be easily destroyed, and so that information may be transmitted across thousands of years.

The second thought that crosses my mind is how good it is that they hid that knowledge in symbols, so it cannot be abused. A symbol is "a visible mark of something invisible". The word associated with the symbol, symbolism (Greek: *symbolikos*), is "the use of conventional or traditional signs in representing divine beings and spirits".

The third thought, or question, is: How did they build those necropoleis on elevations from which there is a clear view on all four sides, and there is almost always an oak tree in the middle?

Contemplating and analysing those phenomena, it seems that they knew of some energy nodes on which they then placed them for a reason. For what reason and how? We still haven't found that out, and for now, I am only following my feeling. It is interesting that almost always, as though by rule, above them, there is also a historic hillfort or some cave constituting one whole. Examples: Boljuni near Stolac, Petrovići near Sarajevo, Gojčin near Kladanj, Bečani near Šehovići, etc.

The inscriptions on the stećci were added subsequently as medieval graffiti, which is evident from them always being on the margins or in free spaces of the drawings' composition.

Of course, there's the question: When were the stećci made and who placed them there?

Mostly, around 90% of them are found on the territory of Bosnia and Herzegovina and its borders, in Croatia (Imotska krajina and Cetinska krajina, Konavle), in Serbia (Bajina Bašta, Prijepolje, Priboj, Sandžak) and Montenegro (Durmitor, Pljevlja, Šćepan Polje, Nikšić). There are none around Belgrade, Zagreb, or Podgorica. Meaning, only in the "real Illyricum" (Latin Illyria proper).

If the Bogomils built them, how come there are none in the Bulgarian homeland of the Bogomils? If they are Arian monuments, how come there are none in Asia Minor or the Near East? If they are Cathar/Patarene monuments, how come there are none in France and Italy? If the Illyrians built them, how come there are none among the Veneti, Histri, Liburnians, Pannonians, Mazaei, Dardanians, etc?

So many questions are waiting for answers! The answer is that in Bosnia, an Illyrian-Roman and Arian-Gothic synthesis was created, which resulted in a material form, the stećci.

There are many in the scientific field who believe the stećci to be a medieval construct. But, if they are from the Middle Ages and if, in the opinion of historians, they are headstones, then why are there no biblical, New Testament symbols on the stećci: where is Jesus

Christ, Saint Mary, the Apostles, Saint Peter or Paul, angels, the Apocalypse, heaven and hell – there is absolutely none of those. In the Ragusan archives of the Middle Ages, there is not a single document describing the carving of stećci, and it is well-known that Ragusans were detailed and comprehensive in their descriptions of their surroundings.

The association of stećci with the Middle Ages is based only on the inscriptions in Bosančica (Dr. Lejla Nakaš), but those are mostly graffiti subsequently added in corners or places where there remained some free space, and absolutely do not fit in with the complete composition of the decoration on the stećci. Besides that, only 0.5% of all stećci have inscriptions on them. Is that enough for a conclusive definition? The question also arises: Why is there not a single document mentioning the building of stećci? My thinking and assumption is that stećci are much older in origin! On them are found pre-Greek, pre-Roman, and pre-Illyrian symbols. Where did the Phoenician goddess Ishtar, the Egyptian Isis, the Celtic goddess, and the Vedic swastika come from?

Were these symbols brought into Bosnia, or were they taken from Bosnia to there? My humble opinion is that Bosnia was one of the genetic centres in Europe and that people in the Mediterranean and the world communicated across Bosnia and exchanged knowledge and experiences. In the Library of Alexandria, I found an inscription that high Egyptian priests were called "djed", and it is known that Egyptians were coming to Epidaurus (Cavtat) to Konavle and paid in gold for the plant mandragora which was used in Egyptian rituals, and which grows only in that area and exists nowhere else in the world. How come there are more temples of Mithra in Bosnia than in Italy or Iran?

Stećak from Brtonjica, Konavle, with a motif of the Phoenician goddess Ishtar (Ištar /ˈɪʃtɑːr/). The first engraved mention of the Illyrian Dardani tribe in Karnak/Luxor in Egypt, 1296 BCE.

Also, my contemplations lead me to conclude that the stećci are ritual sites, and that they subsequently also became grave sites. With time, beside them emerged Muslim, Orthodox, and Catholic graveyards.

Why do I think so?

Because on most necropoleis all elements for a ritual are found, those being: The largest stećak in the shape of a slab in the middle as an altar, then a hollowed-out stećak (possibly for ritual washing), followed by circumferential stećci serving as the boundary of a sacred space, etc.

Suppose one considers the attire of our ancestors of the Brygian/Phrygian tribe on the stećci. In that case, they are dancing the Bosnian ritualistic silent dance, they are wearing Brygian caps of wisdom, they are holding lilies in their hands, on their feet are *opanci*, they are wearing *gunj* coats, it is all reminiscent of an Illyrian *ganga* song. So, at that time, all of it had a religious ritualistic character which, with the passage of time, was transferred to current folklore.

One of the oldest sanctums of the Proto-Illyrian Pelasgian tribe (allies of the Trojans), "Dodona", is in Epirus (nowadays on the border between Albania and Greece), where the head priest foretold future events by listening to the leaves of the large oak tree and writing them down on lead tablets. Over 3000 lead tablets were found buried under that large oak tree, at the centre of the circular sanctum. What kind of knowledge of nature and spiritualism was it that led the Illyrian tribes to come to all more important decisions in rituals surrounding an oak tree, which symbolised strength and wisdom, as well as its connection to the underworld and the overworld?

See the photograph of the sanctum of the Pelasgian people named "Delphi" with its megalithic circular structure reminiscent of the sanctums of Proto-Illyrian tribes. Also, the same Pelasgian people founded the town of Pelasgion (nowadays Athens) on Mount Acropolis, where to this day the megalithic stones in the foundations of the Acropolis can be seen.

Megalithic foundations of the Acropolis in Athens and in Delphi as Illyrian heritage of the Pelasgian tribe. The Illyrian symbol of a pinecone at the entrance to the Vatican Museum in Rome.

Trojans created their script (King Cadmus, 1313 BCE had a large library in Thebes (potentially Old Klek near Neum)). The Greeks/Hellens subsequently adopted the entirety of Illyrian heritage, incorporating it into myths and legends, and they translated Homer's Iliad and Odyssey into Greek only 400 years after (around 800 BCE) it emerged on Illyrian land around 1200 BCE. In the Acropolis Museum in Athens, I found a few reliefs depicting snakes, and it is well-known that the most important symbol for the Illyrians was the snake (*zmija*), dragon (*zmaj*) in the masculine form.

In the descriptions of the Battle of Kadesh in 1296 BCE, fought between the Egyptians under the leadership of pharaoh Ramses II and the Hittites under the leadership of King Muwatalli II, the Illyrian tribe of Dardanians, which fought on the side of the Hittites, is mentioned for the first time in written sources. That is the first written evidence that Illyrians came into contact with the greatest empires of that age. That text mentions the "Sea Peoples", who haven't been identified by science, and the question arises: Could they have been the Illyrians?

Is Svevid, as the supreme god of Illyrians, actually the Egyptian all-seeing eye of the Egyptian god Horus?

Is the "ankh" an anthropomorphised lily?

There are many similarities and evidently common sources of all these symbols. When I visited the Roman Forum and the Vatican Museum and photographed the old Illyrian (Bosnian) symbols: the lilly, the tree of life, the Illyrian star and crescent moon, in my mind the final decision to begin writing formed. What did the old Greeks, Romans, and the Vatican know about us, and we don't? What are they hiding from us? Is it knowledge or material wealth?

Furthermore, to understand the symbolism of stećci, we should dive deeper into the spirituality of the people that created them. How did they live, what did they believe in, what knowledge did they have?

Those distant ancestors of ours, freely called "Trojans", with their megalithic civilisation had an exceptional knowledge of nature, history, space, the sky, plants and animals, or, they lived in accordance with that. They knew intuition to be stronger than knowledge and that the entirety of knowledge rests with the Creator. Because of that, their entire life was spiritually oriented towards the sky. That spiritual knowledge is forgotten and covered in thick layers of counterfeiting, distortion, and total destruction.

When looking at some subsequently made geographic maps, in the area of Bosnia there is always depicted a large emptiness, when the area of Bosnia was actually teeming with life. If we know that there is hillfort after hillfort, and that almost 10,000 Illyrian hillforts is documented on the territory of Bosnia, then why has a real map of those Illyrian hillforts of ours never been made?

The ancient Illyrian motifs of a snake and a dragon on Bosnian stećci are waiting to be decoded.

If it is known that the Trojan prince Enea is the founder of the Roman Empire, then it should logically follow that he brought his language and his script, known as the Etruscan language and script, which is similar to Bosančica, as per the book *Goti u Bosni* (Goths in Bosnia) by Bisera Suljić Boškailo? In the Roman museum "Ara Pacis", dedicated to the Roman emperor Augustus, in their documentary film about the emergence of Rome, they mention that Rome was founded by the Trojan prince Enea, after the fall of Troy. As the saying goes, the wise will understand!

How is it that, exactly in Bosnia, Wulfila the Ostrogoth bishop came up with the Gothic alphabet, which has a stark resemblance to Bosančica, and translated the Bible into the Gothic language, which was in use in the Arian Bosnian churches? How is it that the first Bible, the Vulgate, was compiled and translated into Latin by a man from Bosnia, Hieronymus (St. Jerome), born in Stridon near Duvno?

There are too many coincidences which are not well-known, and which point towards the continuity of knowledge and spirituality of people from the Bosnian area.

My thoughts and above-stated assumptions arose from the basis of me visiting numerous historic locations domestic and foreign, locations with stećci, hillforts, the history books I have read. My efforts are but a humble attempt, contribution in approaching the described topics with the intent to waken the curiosity in enthusiasts like myself, and, of course, the incentive and encouragement among younger generations to think and draw conclusions freely.

The time has come to write the real history of Bosnia!

Emir Medanhodžić

1 SEARCHING FOR THE TRUTH ABOUT BATO OF THE DAESITIATES

Bato, as the embodiment of bravery and courage of the people from this area, deserves to have monuments across Bosnia, to admonish and remind us of who and what we are, to be a confirmation of this people having distant ancestors and roots, that it is proud and indestructible, and somewhat stubborn and defiant because of a dream.

Bato was probably born between 35 and 30 BCE in the area of "upper" Bosnia. He belonged to the Illyrian tribe of Daesitiates which lived on the areas in what is nowadays central Bosnia and Herzegovina. Since 33 BCE, the Daesitiates were under Roman rule, having a semi-autonomous status of *civitas peregrini* (the name for populace which had some administrative and territorial autonomy, but did not have the status of being citizens of Rome). In said times, the territories of the Daesitiates were part of the Roman province Illyricum, whose capital was in Salona, close to Split, on the shores of the Adriatic Sea. It is thought that Bato's family was influential and that he was a political and military official of the Daesitiates (a princeps).

Why is it that so little is known about Bato of the Daesitiates, our greatest military leader and hero of the old world, who is being compared to Hannibal, and why is he not mentioned in the broader public discourse? In the ninth year CE, at the end of the Great Illyrian War, almost the same day, Arminius from Germany (Germania), their greatest hero, defeated three Roman legions (around 15,000 soldiers) in the Teutoburg Forest, using Bato's tactic of ambushes in river canyons.

If we take as a starting point the fact that, to quell Bato's Illyrian revolt, Rome sent around 200,000 well-trained soldiers gathered from the Netherlands to Iraq, then we have to ask ourselves:

How did Bato resist such a force and wage war for 4 years? What was behind his power? As we are great history enthusiasts and have some degree of knowledge of it, while visiting and researching the terrains on which "antiques" are found, we tried to create a, in our opinion, logical mosaic of the arrangement of those ruins, or "old hillforts" from that period, and tried to answer said questions.

Primarily, it was the economic might that the Illyrians sourced from gold, silver, iron and other metal mines, which are concentrated around Vareš and Vranica. Of course, there was also livestock, wildlife, fish, forests, horses, agriculture, water, grazing fields, etc., that is to say, great natural resources which Bosnia had were of great importance for the logistics and might of Bato's warriors.

Second was the skillful strategic use of the terrain configuration, because they built all their hillforts on inaccessible hills, so that they were visually connected, without any enemy being able to go unnoticed on the corridor form Sarajevo to Vareš and from Zenica to Travnik or Bugojno (it is interesting that already in those times the Illyrians knew about strategically important nodes, because 2,000 years later, in all of those locales, mobile telecommunications repeaters were set up).

The third important element is the strength and courage of the Daesitiates, intrepid warrior's adept in warfare, who, thanks to the ores we already mentioned, had the best swords, spears, shields and helmets made from that Bosnian iron. Imagine such a Daesitiate cavalry, all of them tall and strong, with glistening weapons which they coated in fat to make it shine as much as possible, and with helmets on whose tops horse-hair tails whirled whiled they moved. Their appearance alone must have inspired fear in any army; (I believe that is a tradition since antiquity – similar cavalrymen were employed by Alexander of Macedon, the Khalifs of Al-Andalus, the Hussars, etc.; but, the well-known helmet with a horse-hair mane is a hallmark of the Illyrians, and not of Sparta, as modern Greeks try to present it). That army was given a special quality by Bato himself, with his closest staff, who showed great determination, agility, bravery, oratory skills with which he motivated the entire army, and leadership by example, because he was always at the spearhead of the army. His determination is described as well by the datum from Roman sources, which says that, once Bato of the Breuci surrendered and when he was captured as a traitor, Bato brought him before the entire army asking whether to kill him or spare his life, to which the army unanimously decided for the traitor to be killed, which Bato did himself.

The fourth element was the strong spirituality of Illyrians, or the tribe of Daesitiates, which was safeguarded by djeds/druids, their spiritual leaders which possessed knowledge of connection to the spiritual world and the Creator.

The Illyrians are the only people of the old world which had no slaves, because to them freedom was the most valuable thing, which was inherited by the Good Bosnians, who also never had slaves in the Middle Ages.

Where does the search for Bato begin?

Let us begin from the "Roman stela" of the familial tomb of Bato of the Daesitiates, found in some later period in the village of Župča, in the Breza municipality. Having come out to the hillfort named Podgora above the village of Župča, I asked myself where the town of Hedum could have been. Roman sources mention it and write that by way of milestones, it is 124,000 Roman paces away from Solin, which roughly fits the territory on the line from Sarajevo to Vareš, and with Breza, or the village of Župča, in the middle. According to all that, the city of Hedum could be exactly there, above the village of Župča.

THE HIDDEN HISTORY OF BOSNIA

The tombstone of the familial tomb of Bato of the Daesitiates

Supposedly, when Tiberius asked Bato and the Daesitiates why they had revolted, Bato replied: "You Romans are to blame for this, because you send as the shepherds of your flocks, not dogs or shepherds, but wolves." Bato spent the rest of his life in the Roman city of Ravenna.[1]

Was Bato born there, did he play as a child by the waterfall behind Hedum, did he herd sheep on Očevlje, where there is one of the most beautiful stećci, with a depiction of a man reading a book, and from where the neighbouring hillfort of Dubrovnik can be seen, did Dubrovnik protect Hedum's back and control the river Misoča? Where did Bato spend his youth, and where did he go to school? Perhaps in nearby Moštre in Visoko?

Those are all questions that remain unanswered and are waiting for historians, archaeologists and other scholars and experts to answer

---

[1] Smith, Dictionary of Greek and Roman Biography and Mythology Archived June 7, 2008, at the Wayback Machine - He sent Bato to Ravenna.

them. The Podgora hillfort spans a very short distance, about 100 meters; no significant archaeological excavation took place there. From it "stretches" a view of the Breza valley and the neighbouring towards Ilijaš and Visoko. But its main drawback is that, unlike other hillforts which are unconquerable thanks to tall cliffs on three sides, it can easily be approached from the flanks and the valley. Maybe that is the already Romanised city of Hedum, a Roman fort that monitors the passage through the Breza valley on the shores of Stavnja river towards Vareš, and protects the Early Christian Arian Basilica in the centre of the city.

At a distance of around 5 km as the crow flies it is connected with the hillfort Crkvina in the village of Košare, Gornja Breza, which is followed by the hillfort of Kapica, the hillfort of Križ and the hillfort of Dabrovine in Vareš, as well as the hillforts in the municipality of Visoko – Čajangrad, Vratnica, Visoki; and in Kakanj – Crnač, Vrana, etc. That interconnected system of hillforts at a distance of 5 km is simply an impenetrable defence system.

After connecting, or realizing, discovering that web of old hillforts, it becomes clear how strong of a defence system the Illyrians had and why for 250 years they waged war with the Romans, the greatest global power of the old world. It saddens us to see that on maps, our historians did not mark our old Illyrian hillforts, as though it were an empty area, and in the field, it is clear that these areas teemed with life.

What did those hillforts protect?

They protected gold, silver, and iron mines, and they safeguarded the hidden knowledge about nature and the spiritual world with which select and initiated ones communicate in the caves nearby those hillforts. That continuity extended through the ages, from the Illyrians to the Good Bosnians, and then by way of Sufi sheikhs to the present day. Spiritual people recognized each other, and so the druids passed the staff of wisdom and the tree of life to the Bosnian djeds, and they passed it to the Mevlevi sheikhs. Bato, as a prince of the Daesitiates, certainly was raised on those traditions and knew of the spiritual secrets.

The Romans, after conquering the Dalmatae, did not enter further into the interior, so Daesitiates recognised the central Roman rule, but with certain rights and freedoms. From that, it can be concluded that Bato served in the Roman army, where he acquired military knowledge and techniques, and fought in numerous global battlefields. There is a possibility that he maybe met Arminius in that time, and that they forged their plans to revolt together.

In Bato's revolt, on the Roman side, 15 out of a total of 25 legions in the entire empire were engaged, plus the additional allied forces (20,000 Thracians), and on Bato's side, 120,000 soldiers and 9,000 cavalrymen. Emperor Augustus in his panic demands additional mobilisation and releasing captives and slaves, warning them that Bato will attack Rome.

How great that force must have been, to strike at Solin and Sirmium! However, because of inexperience and unfamiliarity with siege tactics, they did not manage to capture these fortified cities. In the siege of Solin, Bato was injured, likely by a stone from a catapult. He retreated to the territory of the Dalmatae, into the fortification of Andetrium near Split, to recuperate. When the Romans attack Andretium, he leaves and retreats onto his territory, of the Daesitiates, which is the only logical solution, to lead the decisive defence from his territory. Some Croatian historians suppose that he surrendered in Andretium (Muć near Split), but it makes no sense for him to surrender on the territory of the Dalmatiae in an unimportant fort, which the Roman historian Cassios Dio also confirms in his notes.

The question arises: Where did the decisive battles take place?

Roman sources claim that the decisive battle was fought near Arduba. Once again, a question: Where is Arduba? Many place Arduba in Vranduk, based on descriptions in Roman sources which say that in that place, where Arduba is, a surging river coils around the fortification, as is the case with Vranduk. But Vranduk is a small fortification, it could not shelter thousands of refugees, and it is also on the periphery of the Daesidiates' territory, which extended to Zenica, which refutes the suppositions about it being Vranduk. Such a city, for security and defence, should be somewhere in the interior. And the datum that the river coils is unreliable, since the river Bukovica also coils around Bobovac, Misoča near Dubrovnik, the river Zgošća near Crnača/Kakanj, the river Miljacka near The White Fortress, and many other examples of the same exist, because important hillforts were built exactly in such places. Such a city needs to be defended with several rings of defence.

If you look at the hillforts around Bobovac, on the entrance into the canyon of river Stavnja, there are the hillforts Dabrovina and Križ, one across the other, the canyon is narrow and impassable for an army, and it may be attacked with rocks from atop the crags. By way of upper Breza and via the old road to Vareš, on the east side by way of Brdo, Striježevo, and Radonjići, there are the hillforts of Babe and Brda, Jukino brdo, Gradac near Ostrlje, and Planinice. On the north side, above Bobovac there are Borovice, Nažbilj, two hillforts Crnača/Kakanj and Gradac above Zgošća, and further to the east we find Desetnik, Vrana towards the hillfort of Visoki, and to the south, the hillfort in the village of Poljani, in front the entrance to the river Bukovica canyon.

Since the river Bukovica coils around Bobovac, and that it was hard to conquer, surrounded by those numerous hillforts as it was, a possible supposition is that Arduba was in fact Bobovac.

Bobovac used to be a large hillfort and fortification which covered a large area, from Mijakovići, Dragovići, Lješnice, Poljane, and other places, but it was probably torn down, only to be restored in a reduced capacity in 1350 by Stipan (Stephen) II Kotromanić, when he moved it from Stipan-grad to his capital, Bobovac.

Bobovac is the most important (royal) city in medieval Bosnia. It was erected on a steep, terraced crag of the southern slopes of the mountain massif of Dragovske and Mijakovske poljice above the river mouth where the Mijakovska river flows into Bukovica, to the south-west from Vareš. It is located nearby the villages of Mijakovići and Dragoići, in the municipality of Vareš. In the opinion of the author of this interesting contribution, Bobovac was erected in the location of the ancient Illyrian hillfort of Arduba. Nowadays, little is left of the famous royal hillfort of Bobovac.

The supposition that Bobovac is in the location of the former hillfort Arduba, besides its strategic positioning, is also based on its size, because only a large fortification could accommodate a larger number of refugees.

That not only the men were strong and brave is proven by the magnificent patriotic act of Daesitiate women, who wouldn't allow their husbands to surrender, but insisted for them to fight to the last one, while they, with their kids in their arms, threw themselves into the more than 100-meter-tall river Bukovica canyon. That act is in the same class of the world-renowned Jewish Masada in 70 CE, when women threw themselves from the Masada fortress, on the Dead Sea coast. Whether Bato was there at that time is hard to know.

What is possible and most likely is that peace negotiations took place, and that some peace accord was signed, because it is unusual that the Romans gave Bato a villa in Ravenna for him to use, and that they did not execute them, as they did with all their significant captives (the Gaul Vercingenotrix or the Dacian Decebalus, for example). Perhaps the negotiations happened in some of the Illyrian hillforts in Sarajevo, since, according to historical sources, that is where the last pockets of resistance remained. As a gesture of trust, Bato gave his eldest son to the Romans, as a pledge of sincerity and responsibility, as was the custom in those times. (The most interesting part of that is that, after the death of the first Roman emperor Augustus in 14 CE, 25 Roman emperors have their origins in Illyricum and that Sirmium (Sremska Mitrovica) was declared one of the capital cities of the empire in 249 CE).

According to Roman written accounts, not having understood what freedom meant to the Illyrians, or the tribe of Daesitiates, they asked Bato why he started the revolt, and he replied: "You sent wolves instead of dogs to guard sheep".

As we already said, for these ideas to be confirmed, expert evidence is needed, for the engagement of whom the state should provide by prioritising and enabling investing into archaeology and modern multidisciplinary research. Until then, we may only attempt to reach the distant past and keep visiting those old stone hillforts. But, the stone remains silent...

Bato, as the embodiment of bravery and courage of the people from this area, deserves to have monuments across Bosnia, to admonish and remind us of who and what we are, to be a confirmation of this people having distant ancestors and roots, that it is proud and indestructible, and stubborn and defiant because of a dream.

2 ROMANISATION OF THE ILLYRIAN AREA UNTIL THE III CENTURY

In a fierce three-year war between Rome and Illyria, in which on the side of Rome 15 out of the existing 25 Roman legions were employed (plus auxiliary forces that amounted to almost the same number of soldiers as those fifteen legions), and a tenacious Illyrian army which was gathered around Bato (Baton) of the Daesitiates (the Daesitiates are an Illyrian people or tribe from the area of modern day central Bosnia), Illyria was devastated.

Bellum Batonianum (Bato's or Baton's War), artist – Besjan Behrami, 2005, displayed in the Skanderbeg Museum in Krujë, Albania

Naturally, in this war, as in all other imperial wars, the motivation for the Romans was to occupy new territories and spatial expansion and through that, to amass wealth, increase power through the agrarian economy and through exchange of goods, i.e. trade (which is the dominant form of economic sustainability of human societies, up until the industrial revolution in the XVIII century in Great Britain, continental Europe, and USA) and the strengthening of their military factor by incorporating members of the occupied peoples in the Roman armada, or in short – an overall increase of the Roman Empire's might. And Bato and the Illyrians resisted occupation because of the treatment they were subjected to. Allegedly, when Bato was captured and the revolt was quashed, he said: "You hounded sheep, and brought out the wolf".

A statue of Bato of the Daesitiates, National History Museum in

FROM BATO TO KULIN BAN

Tirana, Albania

After he crushed the resistance in 9 CE and entered into the centre of Illyria, the area of modern-day Bosnia, Tiberius Ceasar Augustus (16/11/42 BCE–16/03/37 CE) plundered and took as spoils of war, as the expression goes – everything that could be carried away – to Rome. According to legend, Rome shone in gold and silver captured in Illyria. What happened in the lands of Illyria was severe devastation of an area and of people: the Illyrian tribal people were decimated – the material and cultural wealth had been plundered, the written records were destroyed – many hillforts and settlements that emerged in the millennia-long period of Illyrian life, from Istria to Macedonia.

A precarious peace commenced, which lasted for 300 years. This was a period that the Romans used to reinforce their rule over the newly occupied province, to Romanise the peoples of that area, to exploit the resources of that area, and to strengthen the army with the aim of further conquests.

Solin (or Roman Salona) originally was a fortification built by the Illyrian tribe of Dalmatae. Dalmatae, along with the Liburnians, were excellent sailors and controlled the sea routes from this fortification. Solin was strategically important because it is located on a crossing of roads which connected the Adriatic coast with continental Illyria.

After defeating the Illyrians, a triumphal celebration for Tiberius was held in Rome. Left, a slab found in Trilj, nowadays it is kept in the Archaeological Museum in Split. The lower part of the slab depicts shackled Illyrians – a Daesidiate and a Breuci.

Around the 1st century BCE, Gaius Julius Caesar, the Roman military leader, politician, and writer, made Salona a Roman colony and the centre of the Roman administration for the entire province of Illyria. That province will later be split into Pannonia and Dalmatia (which was named after the Dalmatae tribe). In the times of Emperor Diocletian, around 300 CE, a large palace was built in Salona, which today is a rare material testament to Roman splendor in Dalmatia. Diocletian's Palace was a luxuriously furnished residence and consisted of a series of villas and buildings of court, military, sacral, and urban architecture. Croatian historians, without any data, claim Diocletian to be from Salona, from the Dalmatae tribe.

However, the future emperor Diocletian was born in Diocleia, which is modern-day Podgorica in Montenegro (the Illyrian Duklja).[2]

Diocletian, Istanbul Archaeological Museum

Besides Salona, Narona, located in the village of Vid, near the mouth of Neretva into the sea, is also an Illyrian fortification, which is confirmed by archaeological findings from the 7th century BCE. It served as a trade centre connecting Illyria with old Greece. Narona enters the sphere of Roman interest in the 2nd century BCE. From

---

[2] Vučinić Stevo, *Prilozi proučavanju ljetopisa popa Dukljanina i ranosrednjovjekovne Duklje*; Fakultet za crnogorski jezik i književnost, Cetinje 2017, p. 18.

that time on, the Roman military had a base in Narona, but it was made into a Roman colony only in 33 BCE by Octavian. In Roman times, a forum, a temple and baths were built in Narona.

From these two centres, Salona and Narona, the Romans controlled parts of Illyria. They established their military garrisons, which were supposed to secure peace, free communication and exploitation in the entire area. Illyria had to remain docile because any unrest would have meant tectonic disruptions in the whole empire, as it happened during the 250-year-long and exhausting Illyrian-Roman war and revolt. In parallel with that, the process of integration into the Roman Empire began. The process of Romanising Illyria started to. Although contact between the two cultures, Illyrian and Roman, had been made long before, only with the definitive conquest of Illyria did the process of Romanisation begin.

First, let us see: What is Romanisation?

Simply put, Romanisation is understood to be the subsuming under the influence of ancient Rome, or the influence of the Catholic church, those peoples whom the Roman Empire conquered, and the spreading of Latin amongst those peoples. Romanisation is a very complex term, as is the term culture itself – broad and all-encompassing. In that sense, it is hard to specify and distinguish what the original cultural content of the Romanised Illyrians was from what was introduced into their cultural identity.

So, the term "Romanisation" is broad, and it is not completely clear what being Romanised means. Some authors think that the degree of Romanisation can be examined through the degree of admittance or of adoption into Roman citizenry. We believe that this manner of access of the Illyrians to the structure of Roman rule cannot yield adequate answers as to the success of Romanisation of the indigenous Illyrian population. Because it is a fact that Illyria, after Bato's War, became a Roman semi-autonomous province in a very short period, this leads us to the conclusion that the granting of such a status to the Illyrians was caused by some other reasons, and not the Romanisation of that population. Human identity and way of life cannot be changed that easily. That requires many generations living under certain cultural principles, in this case, Roman cultural traditions and rules. The Roman concept was the dominant culture at that time, but Rome itself was in cultural interaction with others, for example, Mithraism and Christianity. Finally, it is a culture that appeared and developed on the seeds of Hellenism with the adding of new contents which are born from a new civilisation, of which the most important are Roman (civil) law and architecture.

Those are two fields in which the Roman Empire left traces in civilizational contents which remain to this day. Roman viaducts, plumbing, spas, reinforced roads, mosaics (which were brought to perfection in Ravenna by Arian Goths), amphitheatres, etc., are well-known. And Roman civil law is to this day the foundation of the civic law in modern Europe.

After Christianity, by adoption of the Edict of Milan in 313, became the state religion of the Roman Empire, the barbaric act of burning down the Great Library of Alexandria in 391 (which was a treasure trove of knowledge in the world of antiquity), and the division of the Empire into the Eastern and the Western Roman Empire in 396, a new cultural era began.

The new Christian religion overtook many segments of cultural tradition, gave them a new sheen with its criteria, and thus became the measure of a new world-view, which will additionally shape the relations within Roman society. This course progressed very slowly. Although Christianity was the state religion, through the constant raids by non-Christianised peoples from the north, many parts of the Alpine region and Illyria, although relatively close to the centre of the empire, remained de facto non-Christianised, i.e., outside the official (or state) interpretation of Christian religious law. Thus, the Arian Goths were dominant in Illyria for almost 200 years, and for 200 years after them, the Avars as well, up until the Franko-Avar War in 791, after which they were more extensively Christianised.

Meaning, only with the re-establishment and unification of the Frankish Empire, and the collapse of Avar domination in Illyria, did a more extensive process of christening and Christianisation of parts of Illyria and Western Europe begin.

Romanisation through the prism of Christianity in the area of Illyria had the most success on the islands and coastal cities of Istria and Dalmatia. However, knowing that coastal Liburnia and the city of Zadar are heretical even in 1202, and that the pope, not by chance, named the Neretvan Banate Pagania, because it was under the influence of the Bosnian Church, then we can conclude that Romanisation through the prism of Christianity in the newly emerged duchies and banates of Illyria became widespread only at the beginning of the Early Middle Ages. That is the time in which the banates that would later constitute Croatia fell under the rule of the Ugric peoples.

Although the Roman Church had its organisation, there remains the question of its efficacy. We said that Zadar and the Banate of Neretva were strong heretic centres (or, in other words, they were under the influence of the Bosnian Church). The Republic of Poljica, which is located near Omiš, refused to be under the influence of the Split diocese until the reign of the Bosnian King Tvrtko. Data about that is found in the document by Pope Honorius III from 1221, where he sent the bishop Acontius to Bosnia, because there "falsities against the Lord's faith are preached publicly". Bishop Acontius earlier spent time in Dalmatia, in Split and Omiš, where he found that for a year, no "God's service" was held in Split. He fought against the population of Omiš, and he had to leave Split because his life was threatened. At the same time, wealthier people from Zadar adopted Patarian beliefs en masse. That was mostly the influence of the Bosnian Church.

Coinage with a depiction of the Illyrian King Gentius, 180 to 168 BCE, from the dynasty (tribe) of Ardiaei.

So, the process of Romanisation progressed very slowly, in coastal and more easily accessible areas, and especially in the interior and central parts of Illyria (or the province of Dalmatia) and its mountainous regions (Bosnia). Indigenous Illyrians rejected foreign influences; thus, the Romanisation in the area of modern-day Bosnia was not successful. The only segment in which Romanisation, so to speak, "took" is within the government. The native populace, because of existential advantages, sent their children into the Roman army, and the rare few that could, at the apex of the Roman Empire, when educational institutions (schools) were beginning to be established, which, of course, was paid, would send their children into education. Those children, after finishing their education, would return to their birthplaces and, with the benefits and privileges that they had, would become a part of the Roman administrative (governing) apparatus. However, the overall percentage of "Romanised" Illyrians in the area of modern-day Bosnia was low relative to the overall population.

We had the opportunity to read much about Romanisation in the literature, and to get the impression, with the absence of data and through the terminology used in historiography, that there is an effort to present Illyria as an undeveloped, backwards, and incompetent civilisation. However, it is not so. By mostly destroying material evidence of the Illyrian way of life (the already mentioned burning of the Great Library of Alexandria, which certainly held knowledge about the Illyrians as well; finally, to this day artefacts written in Bosančica can be found in Egypt, which is a sign that contact between the two cultures existed), the view of the courses of Romanisation as a process of pacification, cultural elevation and connection to civilisation, became and remains prevalent to this day. The devastation and material destruction of a culture and civilisation older than the Roman was erased from the collective consciousness, and instead, through the term Romanisation, primarily through the prism of Christianisation, such a perverted understanding stayed alive, it can be said, to this day.

The tomb of the Illyrian King Gentius in the Italian city of Gubbio, defeated and captured during the Third Illyrian War, he was taken to Rome, where he died.

As a consequence of historic occurrences and circumstances it came to be that what happened in the area of modern-day Croatia, without any critical approach, has been transferred as valid for Bosnia as well, even though we know that Bosnia, its aristocracy and people, through their fondness of the Arian version of Christian religious law, and later through the teaching of the Bosnian Church, did not accept anyone's influence, up until the arrival of the Ottomans, when, together with the Bosnian Kingdom, that church and its understanding of the belief in Christ disappeared from the historic stage.

In light of the most recent discoveries about the Illyrians and Illyrian contents in the elements of the identities of the people which today inhabit the areas of what was centraln Illyria and Dalmatia, we are obliged to examine, research and confer to future generations the Illyrian, pre-Roman period and contents of that culture in that new optic. More so because in the consciousness of the average person from those areas, the Illyrian character of their (our) ancestors has been lost. Yet, regardless of the Romanisation and later Slavicisation of that area, that consciousness is still alive in many forms, especially in Dalmatia and in Bosnia.

Coins of the Illyrian king (3) Monunius or Monounious (Greek Μονούνιος; Latin Monunius; regined 290–270 BCE)

Roman legacy in Bosnia

We find material cultural legacy from the Roman period near military garrisons, villas (houses or domus) in which administrators lived, and Roman cemeteries. After completing their military service, veterans would receive estates on which they built villas. Those are houses with auxiliary buildings. Villas were closed off from the outside world by tall walls, and inside them, in the villa courtyard, the entirety of life took place. That is where baths, kitchens, auxiliary buildings, workshops and warehouses were located. The three main types of Roman villas are the villa rustica, villa suburbana, and villa urbana. On the territory of Bosnia, there are over 150 locales on which Roman villas have been confirmed to exist, and the most well-known one is the villa rustica in Mogorjelo near Čapljina.

Besides the remains of Illyrian hillforts of the Daesetiates in Ilidža, thermal waters were one of the reasons for the Romans to build their settlement in this location. In a place called Panik, near Bileća, archaeologists found two villas: a villa urbana in the locale of Crkvina–Parežani, and a villa rustica on Dračeva Strana. Unfortunately, all these locales have been flooded by the water from the artificial lake Bilećko jezero

A larger archaeological site is in Bankinci, near Laktaši. Sites with artefacts from the period of the Roman Empire are also found in Mali Mošunj (Travnik), Proboj and Zličani (Ljubuški), Majdan (Mrkonjić Grad), Novi Šeher (Maglaj), Višići (Čapljina), Strupnići and Lipe (Livno), Mala Rujiška (Bosanska Krupa), Stup (Sarajevo), Ilidža, Bihovo and Putovići (Trebinje), Donji Šepak (Zvornik), Tišine (Zenica), Suvaja and Kijevci (Bosanska Gradiška).

Mozaic, Skelani, the legacy of the Roman municipia, which were administrative centres, in this case, the administrative centre of Podrinje.

Bosnia, rich with various minerals and ores, was of great interest to the Roman Empire. Thus, in Skelani, near Srebrenica, a municipium (administrative centre of central Podrinje) was discovered, which, in the opinion of archaeologists, is the largest finding in the Western Balkans. It was a mining centre for extracting silver, which is abundant in eastern Bosnia. The municipium was in use until the 4th century. Stelae, urns, headstones, excerpts mentioning important figures in the Roman Empire and those with import for the province of Dalmatia, and Roman milestones, are part of the material legacy.

It can be concluded that, besides trade relationships, through which the Romanisation of the Illyrians was conducted, legions of Roman soldiers, and settlements and homesteads of military veterans played the main role in this slow process.

After Baton's war was lost in 9 CE, the Illyrians were granted the status of civitas peregrinus, (translated literally, or put in today's terms, those living abroad), with a degree of territorial and administrative (governmental) autonomy, and Bato himself, as a guarantor of the status granted to the Illyrians and that no further revolt would occur, was taken to Ravenna where he lived out the rest of his life until his death. However, the key moment in integrating the Illyrians in the Roman Empire was a move by emperor Marcus Aurelius Antoninus – nicknamed Caracalla – who in 212 issued the decree Constitutio Antoniniana, with which civic rights were granted to all free inhabitants of the empire, including women. The only exception was dediticii, i.e., persons captured in wars and enslaved people. Until that point, only Romans, i.e., the inhabitants of the city of Rome, of the Romance language area (modern-day Italy), and inhabitants of Roman colonies and fortifications in the provinces had the status of Roman citizens. The Illyrians, after this event, made a big entrance in the scene of global and European history, so we find them even in the highest governmental position in the empire, that of the emperor.

Caracala's idol was Alexander of Macedon, and that move, of granting civic rights to all free inhabitants in the empire, was dictated above all by the attempts first, to increase the income of the empire through taxes (which earlier were levied only from a limited category of citizens of Rome; in the entire empire, according to the last five-year census we know of, in 47 CE, there were a little over 6 million inhabitants with the status of full citizens of Rome, which is only about 9% of the approx. Seventy million total population in the empire, and second, to strengthen the military even more, as the key factor in further conquests and strengthening of the Roman Empire.

This is one of the indications that, to acquire civic rights, no altruistic motivations nor Roman cultural values were important. On the contrary, the motivation is to strengthen the power of the Empire and the ruling elite. As always in history, the state (empire, here the Roman Empire) aspired to increase material wealth; the Empire needed a strong army and able military leaders, and all of that was achieved through efficient tax policy. Meaning, the greater the number of taxpayers, the greater the income in the state coffers, and therefore the stronger the military and the overall state administration are. The process of Romanising Illyria progressed slowly. That was the case as much because of the strong spiritual self- awareness of the Illyrians and their disinterestedness, as because of the geographic characteristics of the Illyrian province: tall mountain massifs, and karstic and impassable terrain, and the relative distance from stronger Roman centres in Dalmatia, Salona and Narona, and in Pannonia, Naisus and Sirmium. Even so, that process continued inexorably, and the distinct Illyrian spirit and pragmatism is demonstrated in the fact that Rome, impressed by its stout resistance in the revolt against the Roman colonisers, during Bato's uprising, granted to the Illyrians the status of civitas peregrini (meaning selfgovernance and a degree of autonomy), and, on the other side, Illyrians joined the Roman army.

It is a historic fact that many Illyrians advanced in the service, and 19 of them became emperors of the Roman Empire. Those are: Decius, Hostilianus, Claudius II, Quintilius, Aurelian, Prorus, Diocletian, Maximanus, Constantine the Great, Constantinus II, Jovian, Valtinianus I, Valens, Gratian, Valentinianus II, Maricianus, Anastasius I, Justinian I, and Emperor Justinian the Great.

Meaning, that view of Illyrians as inferior subjects of the Roman Empire, which occurs for who knows what reason, is a distorted perspective and de facto does not correspond to the real situation, position, and influence of the Illyrian factor in the Empire. The Illyrians are, already from Bato's uprising and resistance to Roman occupation, and definitively from 212 CE and being granted civic rights, from the first emperor Decius, who came to power in 249, until Justinian the Great in 565, an important factor in societal trends in the Roman Empire.

Emperors of the Roman Empire of Illyrian descent

In literature, the Roman building of roads is emphasised, so almost every road used in this period is called Roman. The Romans did build roads; however, the streets of antiquity in the mountainous parts of Dalmatia, in this case, Bosnia, are not Roman-built roads.

Why does historiography neglect the possibility that Illyrians had their road infrastructure?

In Bosnia, many Illyrian hillforts, of which many kept continuously existing, meaning being used, in the Middle Ages as well, so it is logical for them to have had road infrastructure connecting these hillforts and settlements. High mountain massifs and a krastic and impassable terrain do not mean that the people inhabiting that area did not communicate. That would be illogical and absurd by the definition of human societies, which never remain isolated, but are directed towards mutual contact and interaction.

Map showing some Illyrian hillforts and roads in the area of modern-day Bosnia, Herzegovina and Dalmatia.

Therefore, it is absurd that the Romans built the roads in Illyria to the extent presented in literature. The Illyrians did not have aviation to fly over Illyria. And, logically, they did communicate. Meaning, what the Romans could have done is using, and then adapt and adjust some of the Illyrian roads according to their needs. Actually, in Bosnia, only fragments of so-called Roman roads were found, and what was found does not correspond to the standard of Roman road building (is not paved and does not have a protective area on each side of the road). That means that the Romans used Illyrian routes of road communication, and, where it was necessary, adapted them by the Roman standard of road building.

An example of Illyrian roads, which are called "Roman," can be found in central Bosnia. One so-called "Roman" road extends in two directions, one from Bugojno to Rama, Prozor, Narona and Ragusa. The other one towards Duvno and Solin, and on the north, crossing Rostovo, towards Novi Travnik (Kaštel on Rostovo) and Zenica (Arduba, later Bobovac–Vranduk), then, from Bugojno, crossing Gornji Vakuf and Fojnica, towards the Bosna river basin. Those roads are called Roman, but they connect Illyrian hillforts. So, they connect old, pre-Roman Illyrian hillforts, and we are of the opinion that they could have been created only in the centuries-long movements of the natives, and as such are not the product of Roman craftsmanship.

That the Illyrians were good builders is evidenced by many demolished hillforts. To this day, many have been discovered and mapped, but there exist other Illyrian hillforts waiting to be discovered, such as the one which one of the authors of this book, Emir Medanhodžić, found with his team of researchers in the vicinity of Jablanica.[3].

Regardless of which direction one heads towards through Bosnia, everywhere, at a short distance, they would encounter two or three Illyrian hillforts, grouped or at a distance of a few kilometres from each other. One of the reasons for the closeness of the hillforts around Jablanica is the protection of the river Doljanka, which contains gold. The Illyrians panned gold from this river. The same is the case with the rivers Lašva and Fojnica. Bosnian King Tvrtko Kotromanić knew that gold existed in these Bosnian waters, so he invited experienced miners, the Saxons, to mine and survey

---

[3] It took two years for us and our group of researchers, consisting of 5–6 people, to find and document on the map 16 Illyrian hillforts which we named. Pavao Anđelić documented only a few in Jablanica, and, unfortunately, none of them have been archaeologically investigated. All of it is overgrown with brushwood and shrubbery, so we had to carve our way with a machete. A logical question arises: What was being protected by this circular defence around Jablanica, behind these 16 hillforts? Maybe a roadway along the river Neretva or some mines? We also charted all of these hillforts on the map (we express our gratitude to our friend Meris Šehić) to demonstrate how life was flourishing in that area, because on maps Bosnia is always depicted as an area almost without any civilisation. And Jablanica was the centre of the most powerful Illyrian tribe (or dynasty that was the namesake of the tribe), the Ardiaei; from that area they moved towards the coast of the Adriatic sea, where they fromed a kingdom.

these areas. Many medieval hillforts kept the continuity of Illyrian hillforts, were upgraded, repaired, and new ones were built as well.

In the period from the 4th century before the current era to the 1st century of the current era, when Rome was, so to speak, in its inception, the Illyrians were in contact with the Hellenic culture. On many artefacts, vessels, jewellery and other items, archaeologists found ornamentation and symbolism which evidences the intermingling of these two cultures.[4]

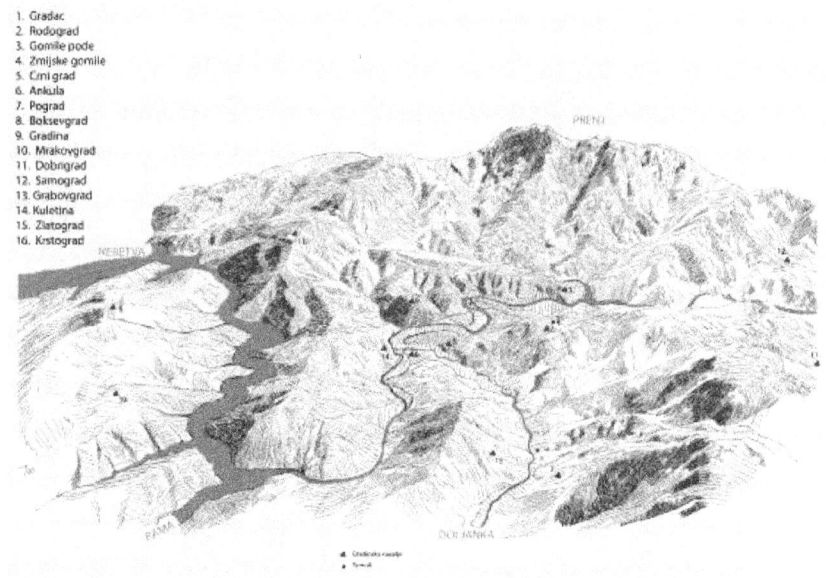

Map of Illyrian hillforts along the stream of the river Neretva, the Jablanica part.

---

[4] https://www.jutarnji.hr/kultura/art/arheoloska-senzacija-na-korculi-ove-grobnice-nisu-bile-poznate-na-jadranu-otkrice-drevnog- blaga-koje-mijenja-povijest-285625 Croatian archaeologist Dinko Radić: "I believe that the findings in Kopila will change the way in which we regard history in this area. We often perceive the Illyrians as marginal, especially in relation to the concurrent Greek settlers, however, our research showed that the role of the Illyrians in this are was much greater than was thought and presented until now, even in political life. The Illyrian society, at the time to which the graves are dating back, was rich, powerful, and certainly also dominant in this are." The graves are from the 3rd, 2nd and 1st century before Christ, and the population of this location perished only in the age of old Rome, when Octavian, the future emperor Augustus, sent the army which dealt harshly with the local Illyrians.

Regarding the discovery of Illyrian tombs in Kopila, island of Korčula [5] (graves from the 3rd, 2nd and 1st century before Christ), Croatian archaeologist Dinko Radić said: "I believe that the findings in Kopila will change how we regard history in this area. We often perceive the Illyrians as marginal, especially about the concurrent Greek settlers; however, our research showed that the role of the Illyrians in this area was much greater than was thought and presented until now, even in political life. The Illyrian society, at the time to which the graves date back, was rich, powerful, and certainly also dominant in this area."

The Germans have a proverb which says: "Wer schreibt, der bleibt" – "He who writes, stays". This can be applied to the Romans and the Illyrians in the process of destruction or appropriation and "drowning" of elements of Illyrian culture after Roman occupation, especially knowing that the Illyrians had their original "Messapian script", of which almost nothing remained, except for some artefacts discovered in Sicily.

---

[5] https://www.jutarnji.hr/kultura/art/arheoloska-senzacija-na-korculi-ove-grobnice-nisu-bile-poznate-na-jadranu-otkrice-drevnog- blaga-koje-mijenja-povijest-285625 The graves are from the 3rd, 2nd and 1st century before Christ, and the population of this location perished only in the age of old Rome, when Octavian, the future emperor Augustus, sent the army which dealt harshly with the local Illyrians.

Photo M. Vuković, aerial photograph of the necropolis in Kopile, Korčula island, source: scientific paper by Dinko Radić and Igor Borzić – The island of Korčula: Illyrians and Greeks, PDF, 284912.

Latinisation of the Illyrian area

Think Latin, write Croatian – a formula which has been applicable since the 18th century, and through which, by inertia, Romanisation in Croatia is discussed in Bosnia as well. The question is: How justified is it for such a view, which is certainly valid for Croatia, to be applied to the Bosnian situation as well?

Justinian's Roman Civic Law Act from the 6th century was written in standard Latin. This standard (usage of Latin) was applied in Christian theology, philosophy, natural sciences, law and government during the next two millennia, up until the 19th century. That standard, i.e., phrases, concepts, and terms, are used in Latin to this day in political, scientific and professional communication and literature. That is not only the case in our language area, but in the entirety of Europe, because the languages are derived, among others, from Latin linguistics and tradition. The languages that stem from Latin are Italian, Spanish, Portuguese, French and Romanian. Where Roman rule was strong, local variants of Latin arose (nothing is known about them), which, with time, brought about a suppression of the native language.

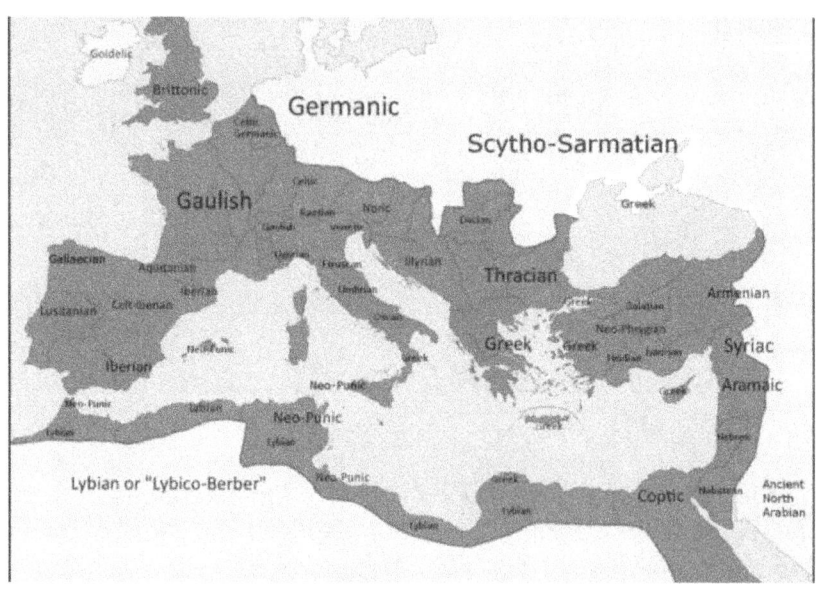

Provincial languages in the Roman Empire, circa 150 CE; author Javier Fernandez-Vina, 2014, used source: "Landscape of Languages – The position of provincial languages in the Roman Empire" by M.S. Visscher

The percentage of the literate population in the culture of antiquity never surpassed approximately—thirty percent. Thus, in the Roman Empire, huge masses of illiterate and semi-literate people did not speak in the official "urban language", but in their popular languages, which had their paths of development. Knowing that these areas were inhabited by different peoples, as would be expected, a symbiosis of other cultures and languages arose, based on which specific forms of language emerged and developed further through time.

The main source for learning Latin today is not living speakers (as in modern languages), but preserved old texts. Between the literary and the popular language, as well as the language spoken by educated strata of the Roman population in everyday communication, differences exist. Traces of this spoken Latin can be found in Plautus' comedy, Petronius' novel, and some epistolary works.

Although in this text we endeavour to speak about the Romanisation of the geographic area of modern-day Bosnia until the III century, we do not find it as an achieved project in the sense of the cultural Latinisation and Christianisation of the area even in the XIII century. It is similarly noted by Bosnian historian Dubravko Lovrenović: "Up until the XIII century, there are no traces [in Bosnia, author's note] of a wider scope of Romanisation and Latinisation".[6]

We will be so free to claim that until 1247, when the Ugric Dominican priest Ponsa was named the bishop of Bosnia, with the task of Catholicising and Latinising the Bosnian Arian diocese, there are no traces of a wider scope of Romanisation, and therefore Catholicisation and Latinisation in Bosnia. The disinterestedness of the population in the Bosnian diocese in the mission which bishop Ponsa set out to accomplish, we believe, is one of the reasons why the Vatican decided to move the seat of the diocese to Đakovo.

The djeds of the Bosnian Church, future men of the Church (at that time practically the only literate people), it is assumed, knew Latin, but did not speak it. Because there was no need to do so: the people had adopted the teaching of the Bosnian Church, which was perceived as of the people and which in many aspects diverged from the Latin Catholic Canon, so there also were none who would

---

[6] Dubravko Lovrenović http://www.prometej.ba/clanak/vijesti/predavanje-povodom-550-godina-od-pada-bosne-1137

advocate for the Latin agenda, nor any were ready to accept it. And if missionaries did appear (like bishop Ponsa), they encountered resistance.

The new, Catholic teachings were not accepted in Bosnia even in the XIII century; meaning, the Romanisation and Latinisation through church teachings was not successful even in the XIII century, let alone the III or VI century. By temporarily "giving up" on Bosnia, the Vatican and Hungary opened the space for the de-Catholicisation of the already poorly accepted Catholicism and strengthening the banate of Bosnia and its Bosnian Church. Favourable conditions for the spreading of Christianity among the immigrant groups of the Slavic population emerged with the appearance of Cyril and Methodius and the script they established. However, the immigrant Slavs also refused the use of Latin in prayers. Also, knowing that the members of the Bosnian Church used the Bosnian language and the Bosančica script, Latin also had no usage among the native Illyrian population. This question is very broad and will be sporadically thematised in the book. There are many answers to it in the texts that follow.

In Blidinje, there are several necropoleis with stećci. The largest one is in Dugo Polje. Here, 150 of them were preserved to this day, so this necropolis, named after the plain it is located in, is also

categorised as large by their numerousness. According to shape, most are slabs. 72 are documented. Next in order are chest-shaped stećci, of which there are 59, 14 tall chests and five gabled ones, of which four are with a pedestal.

32 stećci are decorated, and of the decorations, the most common are rosettes, which appear 34 times in total. Certainly, the depictions of figures are the most interesting, among which the ones that appear on three monuments and nowhere else on stećci stand out the most. The first one is found on the south-eastern face of the now partially damaged chest. On the left side of the slab a man is standing. Next to him stands another one, with his arms raised at an angle towards

the head of the first one. Behind him are two or three men with their arms raised in the same manner.

THE HIDDEN HISTORY OF BOSNIA

Blidinje, Dugo Polje

3 ARIANISM IN ILLYRICUM

To find out about the emergence and development of Arianism, a special form of Christianity in the Roman province of Illyricum, and thus the area of modern- day Bosnia and Herzegovina, it is necessary to consider a wider geographic area. Southern Austria, Italy, Slovenia, Dalmatia, Pannonia are all areas which, with prolonged war and struggle, ever since 250 CE, were gradually settled by eastern Goths. In the period of 250–550, the eastern, Arian Goths, settled the Roman province of Dalmatia, becoming the second most numerous populations in Bosnia, immediately after the Illyrians. They had their Goth state which acted within the Roman Empire, and they managed to achieve cultural and religious influence over the local Illyrian population.

Arius (Areios, Arios), detail from a Byzantine icon showing the First Council of Nicaea.

Goth rule lasted until the year 550, when they were defeated by the army of Emperor Justinian. However, the Goths and the native Illyrians were not two isolated, separate worlds. The Illyrians, as the bearers of the old civilisation of antiquity, and the Goths, who endeavoured to rule that area and for a time were the rulers of the country, lived in symbiosis. Although of different ethnic descent, those people, living and sharing the same space, exchanged different knowledge and traditions.

The mountainous highland areas of modern-day Bosnia and Herzegovina provided the Goths with a special defensive protection. The period of 300 years of Goth domination was enough for them to achieve significant influence in the area in which they lived. In parallel with the breach of the Goths into the Roman Empire, Arianism gathered great momentum in its spreading, exactly from its centres in Constantinople and Alexandria.

The Goth bishop Wulfila (Little Wolf, or Wolf Cub), 311–383, for political reasons, with strong support from Emperor Constantinus II, was sent as a missionary to the Goth barbarians, in a mission to work on their Christianisation and integration into society. He converted many Goth tribes – the eastern Goths, Vandals, Longobards, and Burgundians – to Christianity, that is Arianism. Wulfila lived and worked in the area of the Balkans and, together with the Illyrian bishops, preached the Arian teaching in which Jesus is not equivalent to God.

The script that was used by Goths was Gothic runes. Wulfila's greatest merit was the development of a new Gothic script and the translations of parts of the Bible into the Gothic language. His Gothic script, as shown in the works by Professor Bisera Suljić Boškailo[7], is equivalent to Bosančica, which is comparable to the Messapian script, which is evidenced by 300 discovered documents.

---

[7] Bisera Suljić Boškailo. (2017). Univerzitetska misao - časopis za nauku, kulturu i umjetnost.

The Arian bishop Ulphilas, also known as Orphila, which are Latinised form of the Gothic name Wulfila, teaching the Goths the gospel; illustration from some German history book – Wikipedia. en

It naturally follows that Bosančica is older than Wulfila's script, because it appeared on those Illyrian territories before Wulfila.

The fact that the Illyrian bishops knew, that is, worked with Wulfila, shows that they most likely participated in the creation of Wulfila's alphabet during the translation of the Bible into the Gothic language.

Wulfila's Gothic Bible (so-called Codex Argenteus) also contains the Gothic translation of the "Our Father" prayer. Thus, Arianism becomes the primary belief among converted Germans.

Wulfila died in Constantinople in 383 CE, and at the time, already, the majority of Germanic tribes that settled the area of the Mediterranean had already accepted the Arian faith. The rapid spreading and acceptance of Arianism in our area, even in the time of Wulfila, is evidenced by the fact that in 351 and 359, four synods were held in Sirmium (Sremska Mitrovica), which adopted the so-called Sirmian Arian Formula. Thus, the Arian bishops used the period from the IV to the VI century for the rise and mass expansion of Arianism.

As an adherent of the Arian faith, King Theodoric ruled over the province of Illyricum from 474 to 526. In the Gothic kingdom, special attention was paid to the organisation of the church. During the rule of Theodoric, there were no religious persecutions. His rule is characterised by peace spanning multiple decades. He was tolerant, while simultaneously promoting, wherever possible, the Arian creed, and he built and expanded Arian churches. Thus, the Goth tribes accepted Arian Christianity and, with their presence, influenced the rest of the population.

In all places where two Early Christian basilicas appear, one near the other, one of them was built by Arians for their needs. So, in that time of the expansion of Christianity, a part of the Illyrian population accepted the Arian interpretation, and a part the Orthodox one.

Theodoric treated Orthodox and Arian Christians the same. He built a baptisterium for the Orthodox Christians as well as for the Arian Christians, and maintained cooperation and friendly relations with Catholic Rome. In his letter to the Hebrews, he says: "We cannot order and prescribe religion, as no one will believe contrary to his will". Thus, he granted full freedom of religious expression to the Hebrews as well.

Theodoric established the centre of the Gothic state in Ravenna, where he built an Arian church, San Apollinare Nuovo. The Church at Piazza Vittoria in the small

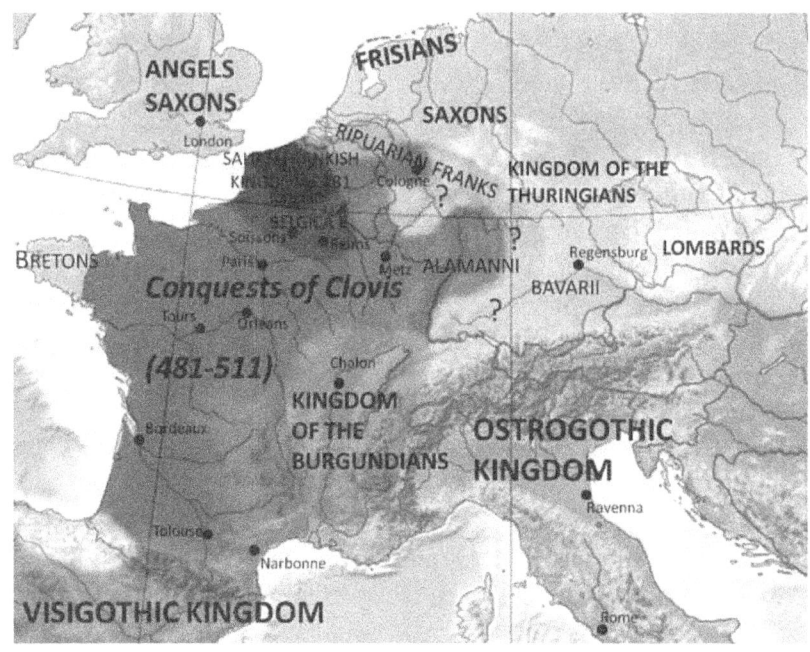

The Gothic Kingdom at the time of King Theodoric's death, 526 CE.

The Italian city of Grado is Arian as well. One written account says that after a fire, bishop Macedonius rebuilt this church (539–557) in Grado in Italy, and dedicated it to St. John the Evangelist.

Wulfila's magnificent Codex Argentus, a valuable manuscript of the Gothic translation of the Bible, was created during his reign in Italy. The Goths used the period of Theodoric's rule to recover from the wounds of prolonged wars and upheavals within the Roman Empire. He established Gothic rule in all areas where these newly arrived people settled. The eastern border of the empire was on the river Drina, and the administrative centres for Illyria and the area of modern-day Bosnia and Herzegovina were in Salona (Solin near Split) and Sirmium (Sremska Mitrovica).

The Libellus Gothorum or *Genealogy of Bar – Chronicle of the Priest of Duklja* is a source that cites that the Goths, even after the Gothic-Byzantine War in 536 did not emigrate from these areas, so they, together with the Illyrians, given the political and war turmoil in the Byzantine Empire, could rule over the area of the province of Dalmatia from the VI to the VIII century.[8] Supporting this historical source is the latest genetic research showing that the native "I2" haplogroup, popularly termed the Alpine-Dinaric haplogroup, constitutes more than 50% of the genome (DNA image) of modern-day inhabitants of Bosnia and Herzegovina. The German anthropologist, lawyer and historian, Theodor Mommsen, who in 1902 received the Nobel prize for his work *The History of Rome*, considers the Muslims of the north-east Balkans to be direct descendants of the Ostrogoths.

According to the *Chronicle* of the Priest of Duklja, on the territory of modern-day Bosnia and Herzegovina, the Goths established a political centre from which the Gothic dynasty ruled. The state was divided into banates, and the ruler held the title of king. Bosnia was divided into upper or mountainous Bosnia and lower or flat Bosnia.

Therefore, it could be concluded that from the 7th century up until 1166, Bosnia was independent from Byzantium. In the X century, Bosnia is mentioned as comprising the area of Uskoplje, Luke and Pljevlje to the west, with the Drina county to the east, which was under the rule of the holder of authority – the Ban.

Arius and his teachings

Arius (Areios) was born around the 260s CE in modern-day Libya, and he died in 336 in Constantinople. His family was of Hebrew descent; they were rich and followers of Early Christianity. Arius was very educated and familiar with the science of his time. Who his teacher was cannot be said with certainty, but it is believed that it is likely he was a student of Lucian of Antioch. Arius earned the trust of scholars and was named the bishop of Alexandria during the rule

---

[8]"Libellus Gothorum" The Chronicle of the Pope of Duklja; Matica Hrvatska Zagreb 1950.

of Emperor Constantine the Great. Arius' teaching about Jesus shook the foundations of the Holy Trinity. He taught that Jesus from Nazareth was not and cannot be God, but was created by God. Only God is since ever and forever, without a beginning.

Jesus has his beginning and by that alone cannot be God. The Holy Spirit Gabriel, who is the Word and a creature created by God, is the true Word of the true God. For Arius, God does not have a beginning or an end; thus, Jesus and the Holy Spirit (Gabriel) are created by God. Only God has eternal wisdom and existence.

The church fathers Hieronymous and Gennadius communicated the Arian form of baptism for new believers and those Christians who converted to Arianism: "I baptize you in the name of the unbegotten Father, in the name of the begotten Son, and in the name of the Holy Spirit begotten as the Son".

Arius developed his teaching into a document named *Thalia* (Feast). This teaching was supported by many religious authorities, bishop Eusebius of Caesarea, Eunomius, antipope Felix II, the Gothic bishop Wulfila, and the patriarchs of Constantinople: Macedonius (342–346, 351–360), Eudoxius of Antioch (360–

370), Demophilus (370–379) and Maxentius (380)

By the Edict of Milan (313), Emperor Constantine, as a follower of Arianism and a friend of Arius, abolished the religious persecutions of Christians and made Christianity the state religion of the Roman Empire. Because of the constant conflicts with the Goths who already invaded the borders of the Roman Empire and a large part of Illyria, "Emperor Constantine designated Sirmium (modern- day Sremska Mitrovica) his residence in 316. He stayed in Sirmium up until 328, until the situation with the Goths had calmed down".[9] In these times, which meant the dissolution of the Roman Empire, he saw in the Goths a great political and military potential and interest.

---

[9] ISTORIJSKI INSTITUT CRNE GORE; Monumenta Montenegrina; Book II, Arhiepiskopije Duklja i Prevalitana; Scriptores ecclesiastici, Podgorica 2001, page 7.

He worked on imposing the ideas of Christianity on the Goths.

The Ecumenical Council of Nicaea and the exile of Arius

The synod of Egyptian bishops first denounced Arianism, so Arius hid in Asia Minor, where he found many new followers. Thus, Arianism deeply entrenched itself in Syria and Armenia, and in different societal strata in the other parts of the Roman Empire.

Due to these two approaches to teaching about Jesus, the Church was split, and one of the greatest schisms in Early Christianity emerged. As Emperor Constantine fruitlessly tried to pacify the dissension, he convened the Ecumenical Council of Nicaea, 325 (also known in the science as the First Ecumenical Council of Nicaea). At that council, Arius' postulates were denounced. It was ordered that all Arian books be burned, and the propagation of the Arian understanding of the nature of Jesus, i.e., of the Christian faith, was banned.

Arius was exiled (or fled, hid) in Illyricum (Illyria), together with his followers, the bishops Secundus of Ptolemais and Theonas of Marmarica. Knowing that Arius, because of his teachings, was excommunicated and exiled to Illyria in 325 at the Council of Nicaea, we see that Emperor Constantine and Arius were in Illyria at the same time. Although at the Council he was forced to exile Arius to Illyria, it is obvious that during these years they were together in a holy mission of arianisation of new peoples. Arius got the opportunity to, with his numerous followers and bishops, finally reckon with the Illyrian bishops and metropolitan bishops, followers of Nicaean Christianity who voted at the Council for his excommunication. So, not only were Arius and Emperor Constantine engaged in the arianisation of the Goths and Illyria, but bishop Wulfila also translated the Gospels into the Gothic language.

Emperor Constantine and the burning of Arius' books (scripture) at the First Ecumenical Council of Nicaea, from a Code of Canon (Church) Law, northern Italy, around 825.

During his exile in Illyria, Arius garnered many followers. There were many Arian bishops who, out of political reasons, even with the help of Rome, administered Illyrian dioceses; Photinus, the bishop of Sirmium, spread Arius' teaching with all his might. After him, Rome supported the Arian Germinius, who would be the bishop for decades to come. In Naissus (Niš), the position of bishop was held by the Arian Bonosus of Naissus. In Singidunum, Ursacius was replaced by an Arian, bishop Secundanius, and bishop Paladius, an enemy of the decisions made in Nicaea, spread Arianism throughout Dacia. The situation was the same in Dardania and Dalmatia.

"The decisions from Nicaea were not enforced, that was not demanded by Constantinople, nor by Rome, which allowed Arius' teaching and doctrine also in Italicum. Illyrian bishops would participate, aside from regional councils, in all major church council assemblies across Western Europe, propagating and trying to impose Arius' teaching as canon, truth be told, in a more moderate manner".[10]

Arianism spread despite the condemnation, and was supported by Emperor Constantine himself, who, after meeting Arius in 326 in Sirmium (Sremska Mitrovica), rehabilitated him, granted him the approval, full right and agreement in his beliefs.

Arius died in Constantinople, steadfastly fighting and advocating for his teaching.

After the death of Arius (336) and the death of Constantine (337), and after the division of the Roman Empire into the Eastern and the Western Roman Empire, Arianism experienced new momentum during the time of Arius' successors. Arianism was in no sense a small sect or heresy. It is a monotheistic religion that entered our area and grew into a large Church that presented itself as the only true one. The Bosnian Church was founded on the Arian truth of the oneness of God. It will be the standard-bearer of monotheism in the area of Illyricum, at first the Banate, and later the Kingdom of Bosnia, up until the appearance of the Ottoman Empire.

A significant number of people in the Near East, the Balkans, and Western Europe were followers of Arianism, which was especially popular among the nobility. The presence of Arianism in the area of Bosnia is evidenced as well in the Arian basilicas which were inherited from Gothic Arians, such as the Basilica in Cim near Mostar, the basilica in Turbe near Travnik, as well as many tombs across Bosnia. The most famous tombs of the old Bosniaks, which contain Arian elements, are in Turbe near Travnik, Oborci near Donji Vakuf, Stranjani near Zenica, and Vrdolje near Konjic.

How extensively Arianism had spread in Bosnia is also evidenced in a letter from the Pope from the beginning of the 15th century; it mentions Bosnian Arians, and calls for the Hungarian King Sigismund to lead a crusade against the heretics, followers of the

---

[10] ISTORIJSKI INSTITUT CRNE GORE; Monumenta Montenegrina; Book II, Arhiepiskopije Duklja i Prevalitana; Scriptores ecclesiastici, Podgorica 2001, p. 15

"detestable Arius". Indeed, Sigismund did break into Bosnia in 1405 and was defeated. So, that is how a faith that began in Egypt, then spread across the Near East, ended its journey in Bosnia.

What did the Goths leave as a heritage to Bosnia?

The legacy of the Goths is the many stećci in necropoleis whose graves are oriented, typical for Germanic tribes, in the direction northwest–southeast, a Gothic cross on them and the Gothic Arian basilicas.

"In historiography until now, the motif of a cross on stećci was interpreted as belonging to the Catholic or Orthodox faith of those whose earthly remains are found underneath the stećci, and the traditions of the cross, which are not only Orthodox and Catholic, were completely disregarded."[11] "Because it is a cross which came to medieval Bosnia from the east, it must be said that what is at hand is the tradition of the Arian-Greek cross. Stećci engraved with a symbol of the cross can belong to members of the Bosnian folk Church and the Bosnian "Krstjani", especially those stećci on which there is the motif of the so-called Greek cross, which in Bosnia is of Arian-Gothic provenance. That especially applies to members of the Bosnian folk Church, whose beginnings are found in antiquity and Bosnian Arian-Gothic basilicas.

The orientation of the stećci in the direction north–south, as is found in the necropolis in Vrbljani, is close to the typical Germanic orientation of graves, whose graves are mostly oriented in the direction northwest-southeast. The necropolis in Vrbljani can only be of Arian-Gothic origin. Graveyards organised in rows, as is the one in Vrbljani, is also a tradition of Gothic origin. Of the same Arian-Gothic origin are also the three Greek crosses on the gable and chest-shaped stećci, and one stećak hollowed out in the shape of a basin, which follows the traditions of Gothic funerary

---

[11] prof.dr. Ibrahim Pašić: *Predslavenski korijeni Bošnjaka: Mile i Moštre*, Des, Sarajevo 2009, p. 120.

internment customs."[12]

We noticed that many necropoleis, which are oriented in the Germanic direction of NE-SW, SW wrongly labelled, and on the information panels it says that they are oriented in the direction East–West, as is the case with the necropolis in Vinci near Jajce. The situation is the same with basilicas oriented in the direction NE–SW. Whether this oversight was accidental or intentional, to ascribe a different character to Arian basilicas, we cannot know. The oversight in determining the cardinal directions in which the necropoleis of stećci and Arian basilicas are oriented in the area of Bosnia and Herzegovina is evident.

So, the Bosnian stećak, if we follow the line of ethnicities from those who "raised" them, i.e. used them, is multinational; the stećak is a Germanic– Illyrian headstone and a grave marker of Bosnian Arian Goths, and from Gothic Arianism, the Bosnian folk Church was developed, from which emerged the Bosnian Church.

The clergy from Salona, and likely also the believers, were inclined towards Arianism during the entirety of the period of Late Antiquity. From archaeological and written sources, it can be established whether, and to what extent, Arianism was retained in the area of the province of Dalmatia after the Council of Nicaea. It was certainly suppressed, but it is impossible to claim that it was rooted out. On the contrary.

During Gothic rule over these areas, Arianism would become associated with the ruling strata of the population, while sources do not mention the presence of Arianism in the Church hierarchy.

---

[12] prof.dr. Ibrahim Pašić: *Predslavenski korijeni Bošnjaka: Mile i Moštre*, Des, Sarajevo 2009, p. 123.

Stećak is a Germanic-Illyrian tombstone and tombstone of Bosnian Arian Goths; from Gothic Arianism, the Bosnian Church developed and emerged.

As a suffragan diocese of Solin, the Bosnian diocese is mentioned at the Arian council in Solin (Salona), 15 June 530; the name of the bishop who administered the Bosnian diocese at that time is also known. In the name of his clergy, bishop Andrija complained at the council that he was in so much debt that not only was he unable to help the poor, but the clergy had no means to cover their most essential needs.

At the Second Council in Solin, in 533, the Bosnian bishop asked for his diocese to be divided into two, because it was too large in area. The metropolitan bishop found the plea to be justified and promised to divide it as soon as possible. This idea probably never came to bear, because of the imminent raids by barbarian peoples which destroyed all traces of this old Bosnian diocese. In the Arian basilica in Grudine in Čipuljić, modern-day Bugojno, a floor tile from the 2nd or 3rd century was found, bearing the inscription "Bistues", which suggests that Bugojno was a strong civil and religious centre, MUN (icipium) BISTVES, and in the 6th century, also the seat of the diocese.

The Goths left the most traces of their existence in the mountainous areas and especially in Bosnia. Thus, the following toponyms remained: Delegošta, Vogošća, Vareš, Mile, Moštre, Gudinoge, Gudelji, Konogovo, Godomilje, Gačani, and in Herzegovina: Otolež, Gacko, Hrgud, Argud, Orgošta, Otilovci, Kotezi, Gaćice – all of them are toponyms derived from Gothic roots, which were studiously written about by Dr. Ibrahim Pašić.

Ruins of the Arian Basilica near Mostar.

Even 800 years after that, Arianism is alive in our area in the "Ecclesia (diocese) Dalmatia" (which is also called Slavonia or Bosnesis) as one of seven heretical Christian Churches in Europe (among which are the Cathari and the Constantinople Church), mentioned at the council in the Cathari castle Felix de Caraman held in 1167.

The connection between the Cathars and Arians is undisputed. For example, the biographer of Bernard of Clairvaux, a Christian Doctor of the Church and the founder of the Cistercians, who fervently preached against the Cathars, called the Cathars from

Toulouse – "Arians".

In the necropoleis in which the stećci are oriented in the direction north–south, or in the direction southwest–northeast, which is a common occurrence, only an Arian–Gothic cross can be the subject of discussion, more so because the stećak is of Arian origin.

The cross, which arrived in medieval Bosnia from the east, must be said to belong to the Arian-Greek tradition of the cross. The stećci, which are engraved with the symbol of the cross, belong to the followers of the Bosnian folk Church, the so-called Bosnian Krstjani. Graveyards organised in rows, as is the one in Vrbljani and many others, is also a tradition of Gothic origin. Of the same Arian-Gothic origin are also the three Greek crosses on the gable and chest-shaped stećci, and one stećak hollowed out in the shape of a basin, which follows the traditions of Gothic funerary internment customs. Therefore, the Bosnian stećak by its ethnic belonging has a multinational character; the stećak is a Germanic gravestone, a gravestone of Bosnian Arian natives, the Illyrians, and of Arian Goths.

Ruins of the basilica in Mokro near Široki Brijeg, 5th century.

In Bosnia and Herzegovina, there are more than 50 Early Christian basilicas built in the period from the IV to the VI century found up until now. The Goths, as dedicated Arians, urged that they be built. The Early Christian basilicas which were found on the territory of Western Bosnia and cities which are located in this area: Bihać, Kotor Varoš, Banja Luka, Varcar Vakuf (Mrkonjić Grad), Ključ, Glamoč and Duvno. The ruins of Arian basilicas of central Bosnia are arranged around multiple larger settlements: Šipovo, Kupres, Donji Vakuf, Gornji Vakuf, Bugojno, Zenica, Travnik, Vitez, Kakanj, Kiseljak, Vareš, Sarajevo, Prozor. The basilica in Breza near Sarajevo is Gothic as well, where, among the decorative plaster on one of its pillars, an engraving of Gothic runes (FUTHARK) was found.

In a site in the village of Mujdžići near Šipovo, an Early Christian Basilica was found, which, by its size of 27 × 24.5 meters, belongs to the largest basilicas found in the area of Bosnia and Herzegovina. In the area of eastern Bosnia, findings are clustered in three places, those being: Srebrenica, Vlasenica and Foča. Findings of Early

Christian basilicas in Herzegovina are arranged around the cities: Gacko, Stolac, Konjic, Široki Brijeg, Čitluk, Mostar, Grude, Ljubuški, Čapljina, Posušje and Neum.

The number of basilicas found in Bosnia and Herzegovina indicates that Arianism was already widely accepted. In historic findings overall, a large number of Gothic remains are obvious, and are a confirmation of the historic significance of the Goths in Bosnia and Herzegovina.

It could be concluded that the Ostrogoths established on the territory of the Illyrian Daesitiates tribe the beginnings of the early medieval state of Bosnia. In the structure of the Bosnian-Herzegovinian population, the Goths, or Germanic peoples, are an indisputable historic fact. Therefore, the historically confirmed Germanic presence on Bosnian-Herzegovinian soil authoritatively has its archaeological, onomastic, linguistic, genetic and overall historic dimension!

Illyrian-Gothic, Arian cross on the stećak is a prehistoric Solar symbol of eternity, constant movement, the shifting of life and death (dialectics of nature).

The village of Oborci lies next to the main road from Travnik–Donji Vakuf. The late antique basilica was built on a small hill on the site of Glavica or Crkvina, in the very centre of the village.

The place is exposed to strong movements of air and noticeable oscillations in temperature during the day. In the period of Antiquity, the area was known for its intensive liveliness. The Roman Road from the valley of the river Vrbas passed through Oborci, towards Turbe and Travnik. The population mainly engaged in agriculture and iron mining. Archaeological material from one tomb chamber found in the interior of the basilica suggests that it was an area exposed to the cultural and perhaps the political predominance of the eastern Goths.

The preserved ruins of the Arian Basilica in Oborci.

Around 500 metres from the basilica, there were found ruins of Roman buildings were found, which likely belonged to some agricultural homestead. In several places, findings of iron slag was discovered. Near the basilica, an imposing necropolis of stećci is located. One of the stećci is engraved with the symbols of the moon and star. The humble furnishings of the Arian basilica are an indication that it served some rural municipality.

The site was first devastated in 1930, when the inhabitants, in search of treasure, destroyed the southeastern part of the apse and the altar place. In 1943, a bunker with deep trenches, serving the purpose of controlling the nearby traffic way, was built on the archaeological site. On that occasion, the larger part of the site was dug over, and the western wall of the basilica was damaged. In 1956, the area was again devastated by the building of a private residential building. The owner of the land on the Crkvina site, without a permit, laid foundations in part of the ruins of the basilica and the tomb chamber, and informed the relevant authorities only afterwards. In the same year, research and conservation works were conducted.

The Arian Basilica in Oborci is basically an elongated rectangle, 15.45 × 19.72 m in dimensions; its orientation is: NE–SW. It consists of an antechamber (10.67 × 4.20 m) and a nave which extends into the space of the chancel and ends in a semi-circular apse with misericords. On the south wall of the antechamber is the entrance to two connected rooms of unknown use. A similar room is on the opposite side, albeit with an entrance from the northern wing.

The northern side wall is longer than the southern wall and, together with the apse, encloses a smaller room which was entered from the north wing as well. Between the nave and the chancel stood two pillars, probably belonging to the triumphal arch of the altar screen. Of the northern pillar, only the base was preserved, while of the southern one, part of the body was preserved as well. The base consisted of a 62 cm long plinth, and, instead of a torus and scotia, there is only a conical taper towards the body of the pillar. The base and the lower part of the pillar are made of one piece of stone. This phenomenon is characteristic of construction in the V and VI centuries.

A necropolis of stećci is also located near the basilica. Of the decorative ornamentation, only one crescent moon is noticeable.

THE HIDDEN HISTORY OF BOSNIA

Crescent moon; necropolis in Oborci, in a field belonging to the Balihodžić family, some 300 metres from the Arian basilica.

The Arian basilica in Varošluk in Turbe

In Turbe near Travnik, in 1893, a basilica, quite large for this environment, was excavated. Its dimensions are 29.50 × 16.65 metres. From its outlines, it can be seen that it consisted of ten rooms, thereby exceeding most buildings of the same type in Bosnia and Herzegovina. According to the latest plotting of the layout of the building, it can be noted that this is a dual basilica. From the example of Hemmaberg, a hill in Austria, we know that in dual basilicas, one is always Arian-Gothic.

Ruins of the Early Christian dual basilica in Turbe (1).

The first person to research, describe and publish a work related to this basilica was Ćiro Truhelka. Subsequently, three vaulted tombs, with a considerable amount of materials within them, were found underneath the basilica. This finding proves once again that in most cases, a vaulted tomb can be expected to be found adjacent to basilicas. In the area of the church itself, an additional, very interesting material was found, that being gold jewellery, of which a necklace with eighteen medallions and a small cross was preserved.

Ruins of the basilica in Turbe near Travnik (2)

Truhelka dated the basilica to the IV century, citing the lamp made of red loam, which is considered to belong to the earliest period in Christianity, and he also cites the remains made of glass, from purely Roman vessels.

However, those are not sufficient reasons to place this building into said period, so the period of its construction should be placed in the V century, when Arianism exerted the most influence in this area. The northern part of the building, whose ruins can be seen to this day, was found later, in 1923. Archaeological research determined that the dual basilica was built on the foundations of an older building with a hypocaust.

Arian basilica in Otinovci, Kupres.

In Otinovci near Kupres, a basilica with three naves was found, which was more elongated than other churches, and with all of the naves ending in a semicircular apse, of which the one in the middle was the largest. In the narthex and the southern side nave, vaulted tombs were found. The length of the lateral sides was

24.50 metres, while the width was 14.15 metres. Here, along with the ruins of the church, a few epigraphic findings were discovered. From the remains of ashes, it can be assumed that the building was damaged, if not destroyed, in a fire. However, there is no additional information on this very interesting finding, and the reason for that is the lack of archaeological research. From everything discovered, it can be seen that this sacral building does not by any feature stand out from other basilicas dated to the V or the VI century, and no smaller archaeological findings which would disprove this opinion were found, therefore there is no reason not to place it in that period, until newer research determines that dating more precisely.

THE HIDDEN HISTORY OF BOSNIA

The Arian Basilica in Breza.

In 1930, another building was discovered in Breza, pointing to the Ostrogoths as its builders. It has an antechamber and a nave with a horseshoe-shaped apse, which was decorated on the outside with protomes of boars and oxen. The eastern portal is similar to the frontage of Theodoric's palace in Ravenna. One smaller pillar is engraved with the Germanic, runic alphabet, the Futhark. Adjacent to the building was a spacious courtyard, and at its end, there was a building of considerable size similar to a hospice. Because of that, it is presumed that the complex in Breza represented the residence of a higher Ostrogothic administrative officer. One of the pillars is engraved with the Latin alphabet, and the other one with the Germanic runic alphabet, consisting of 24 characters. The height of the runes ranges from 0.5 to 2.6 cm. Helmut Arntz dates the inscription to 525. Wolfgang Krause hypothesises that the graffiti stems from the middle of the 6th century and believes soldiers engraved them from some Gothic tribe which was not close to this area. Tineke Looijenga hypothesises that the Langobard tribe, which lived in the vicinity of Breza from 535 to 567, was the author of this runic graffiti.

On some fragments of pillars, Latin graffiti was found as well (the Latin alphabet, the word "mise/ricordia", the letter "P", and a drawing of a horse). A Roman inscription by Ulpius Proculus, embedded as a spolium, was found as well. The inscription mentions Valens, son of Varron (princeps Daesitiatium), that is, a noble of the Illyrian tribe of Daesitiates, and a castle (castellum Daesitiatium). During excavations, fragments of tegulae, molten window glass and an Avar arrowhead were found.

Germanic runic alphabet in the basilica in Breza

Conclusion

There are no specific architectural characteristics by which Arian churches could be distinguished from Catholic ones, except for the very important difference in the orientation of the placement of the foundations. When examining the manner of construction in Early Christian basilicas in the area of Bosnia and Herzegovina, it can be seen that almost all of them were built according to one and the same principle. According to the manner of construction, they are so-called Bosnian basilicas. Of the total of fifty-six definite findings, fifty-three of the basilicas have one nave. At the same time, the remaining three belong to the type of basilica with three naves (Otinovci near Kupres, Kumjenovići and Ustikolina near Foča). So, it can be seen that there is a lack of basilicas of the type with two naves in Bosnia and Herzegovina, and the reason for that is unknown.

Also, a very interesting fact is that in the area of Bosnia and Herzegovina, five findings of dual basilicas (basilica gemina) were discovered. The arrangement and relationship between these two sacral buildings tell of the existence of two Church organisations in one place. One belonged to the Roman Church, and the other to the Ostrogothic Arians.

Equally interesting is that "Bosnian" basilicas in a considerable number of cases have a larger width than length, and that they are built so that their sides are mostly equal, i.e., in the shape of a square. One of the characteristics of these basilicas is that the baptistries in most cases are found in the northern part of the building or outside of the building, and the orientation NE–SW, and NW–SE is an almost regular phenomenon in most basilicas in Bosnia. The most consistent addition to Arian basilicas is vaulted tombs. A large number of Early Christian sacral buildings hide within them one or more of this type of tombs, and that seems to be the norm that, when these buildings are discovered, very frequently vaulted tombs will be found as well, and vice versa.

If we examine the period when the basilicas emerged, then only one possible answer exists, and that is that more than 90% of these buildings stem from the V and the VI century, while only an insignificant number of them can be said to date from the IV century. Further, we are of the opinion that from Gothic Arianism the Bosnian folk Church emerged, from which the Bosnian Church would develop.

Genetic research, which is topical in recent years, shows that in the genome (DNA image) of the citizens of Bosnia and Herzegovina, the native, "dinaric" I2a1 haplogroup is the most represented.

Keeping in mind that aspect as well, we conclude that the foundation for a correct "reading", understanding of the early and later history of Bosnia is the era of Illyrian-Gothic domination in the area of the modern-day state of Bosnia and Herzegovina.

With the fall of the Western Roman Empire in 476, in the area of the modern-day state of Bosnia and Herzegovina, clearly, Roman rule on the soil of Bosnia and Herzegovina disappears as well. During the middle of the 6th century, after the Gothic Wars, Justinian, the Emperor of the Eastern Roman Empire (later in history called Byzantium), would only formally restore Roman rule, because that state no longer had the power to govern these areas.

After that arrived the Avars and Slavs arrived, who would finish off the traces of Roman civilisation and everything that was left as the legacy and heritage of that time. The Romanised population began retreating to the Adriatic coast or into the mountainous areas.

A period of isolation ensues, from the 6th to the 10th century, during which the area of Bosnia remained closed off to the external world and about which history has almost no data.

The decimated population, with almost no resources, continued living their traditions, but without the ability to build large and beautiful buildings, and thus also churches. During that period of isolation in our area occurred the formation of the Bosniak people and the oldest early feudal state among South Slavs, the Banate of Bosnia.

Stećak with a lilly motif, necropolis Ravanjska Vrata, Kupres.

4 FROM ARIANISM TO THE BOSNIAN CHURCH

From the first emergence and establishment of Christianity, in the first three centuries, numerous heretic movements emerged. Almost all were trying to explain the nature of Jesus from Nazareth.

The mere thought about the person and miracle of Jesus, but primarily his resurrection, for everyone who believed in his miracles, moved into the sphere of the conception of divine power which extends throughout the life of Jesus. The main fulcrum, tradition and belief of the heretic movements were strong and clear from the beginning. They taught and believed that Jesus undoubtedly was a human. He was born as humans are born, he died as other humans die. He lived as a human and was known as a human, he had close friends and a very large number of followers who listened to him and bore witness to his acts.

The Arian belief was based in Origenes (Origen – Origenes Adamantius, approximately 184–253 CE), and developed into a conclusion and unification of all other heretic movements which were opposed to the orthodox side – that is, all those movements which did not accept the complete mystery of the two natures of Jesus. Arius knew of all religious schools developed up until that time, therefore also of Manichaeism (Mani, 216–277 CE). Mani grew up in a Judeo- Christian family, and his teaching was adopted from China to the Western Roman Empire. Knowing the teaching of Mani, who was considered to be the successor of Zarathustra, Sidhartha, Buddha, and Jesus, naturally had a certain influence on Arius, which was reflected in his teaching of the categories of "good and evil".

Arianism stems from the desire to clearly and simply visualise something which goes beyond the possibilities of empirical cognition and understanding.

If Arianism, with its rationalistic tendency, had won over the entire society, that new religion and society would have been something like Islam and Muslims or perhaps, seeing the nature of Greek and Roman society, something like an Oriental Calvinism.

Arianism appeared in a society which for a long time already had enjoyed that universal social policy in which all people were citizens. The Roman Empire was one state, from Euphrates to the Atlantic, and from the Sahara Desert to the Scottish Highlands. The emperor ruled as a monarch, as the chief commander of the civil and military sector.

The emperors and the entire government which was dependent on them were anti-Christian. For almost 300 years, the Church was considered an interloper and threat to the traditions and beliefs of the Roman pagan world. During this period, it became stronger, had its chief official, bishops and own organisation, which was very developed and powerful. With emperor Constantine, it finally became the official religion of the Empire.

However, it cannot be assumed that the majority of the population adopted and adhered to the Christian religion. Many could no longer pay heed to what was left of the old gods, and could do nothing against the new Christianity. There also existed a strong group of highly intelligent and determined pagans. They had on their side not only the traditions of the rich ruling class, but also the majority of the members of the upper class, writers, artists, and government officials.

When the power of Arianism had shown itself in those first years of the officially Christian Empire and its universal rule across the Greco-Roman world, Arianism became the core or centre of many powers. It became the gathering place of many strong surviving traditions from the old world, intelectual, social, moral, literary, and all others. Old noble families which kept their old family traditions considered Arius a more sympathetic and better ally than a regular Christian. On the same side are the intellectuals who prided themselves on the cultural tradition of that world. All this strengthened the Arian movement which was destructive to

Christianity.

The large so-called Ludovisi Sarcophagus, a Roman sarcophagus from 250–260 CE, discovered in 1621 near the Porta Tiburtina gate, a part of the so-called Aurelian's Wall in Rome; also known as Via Tiburtina Sarcophagus.

There existed one more category in that world, separate from all others, one that was exceptionally important, and that is the military. Why is it important to understand the position of the military?

The military, certainly, was only a small part of society. It was the binding tissue, strength and support for the Roman Empire in the fourth century; that had been the role of the military in centuries past and was to remain so for generations. This is absolutely important, because it explains three thirds of what happened, not only in the case of the Arian heresy, that is, of several centuries before the current era to the beginning of the seventh century. The societal and political position of the military explains all of those seven hundred and more years.

The Roman Empire was a military state. Advancement in government ranks went through the army. The conception of glory

THE HIDDEN HISTORY OF BOSNIA

and success, becoming rich, in many cases, almost in all cases, achieving political power, was dependent on the military at that time.

Southeast Europe, 525 CE

In the beginning, the military consisted of Roman citizens, which were all Italian. Then, as the might of the Roman state expanded, auxiliary troops became prevalent, people who followed local leaders and joined the Roman military system, and even regular units were recruited in each province. There were many Gauls – that is, French, in the army, many Spaniards and so on, before the first hundred years of the Empire elapsed.

In the following two hundred years, up until the Arian heresy, the military was increasingly recruited from the ranks of what were called "barbarians", the term describing people who were outside the strict borders of the Roman Empire. They were more disciplined and much cheaper than citizens. They were less used to the art and benefits of civilisation than citizens within the borders. A large number of barbarian soldiers were Germans, Illyrians, Thracians, and a good part were Moors, Arabs and Saracens, and even some Mongols who came in from the east. This large body of the Roman army was strongly tied together by discipline, but even more so by professional pride. A man would be part of it from adolescence to his middle age. Nobody except the military had a monopoly on might. And its chief commander was the emperor.

The military was the main "capital" of the entire Arian movement. With the military wholeheartedly on its side, Arianism was winning and managing to be a counterbalance to orthodox Christianity.

At a moment when high society in the empire was Arian and with the emergence of the Goth bishop Wulfila (313–397 CE), all Goth troops adopted the Arian religion. In the military, Arianism was considered to be the distinctive thing which made it superior to the civilian masses, just as Arianism was a distinctive thing which made the intellectual feel superior to the popular masses.

The soldiers, whether of barbaric or civilian recruitment, felt sympathy with Arian teachings for the same reason that the old pagan families felt sympathy with Arianism. At that time the military, especially the military leaders, supported the new faith and it became a kind of trend that if you wanted to be "someone", you should be Arian. One could say that conflicts arose between the military leader on one side and the Catholic bishops on the other. There certainly existed a separation between the Christian population in cities, the Christian peasantry in the country, and the almost universally Arian soldier. The adoption of Arianism had a vast effect.

What we do know is that the Western Empire was overrun by savage tribes called "Goths" and "Visigoths", "Vandals", "Suevi", "Franks" who "conquered" the Western Roman Empire, Britain and Gaul and parts of Germany on the Rhine and the upper Danube, Italy, North Africa and Spain.

The official language of all this part of the Empire was Latin. The laws and all the acts of the administration were in Latin. There was a continuation of what had been going on for centuries, entering of people from outside the Empire into the Empire, because within the Empire they could get the advantages of civilisation.

And the military, on which everything depended was at last almost entirely recruited from barbarians.

As the Empire was enormously large, it was hard to administrate distant places, collect taxes from far away into the central treasury, or to impose an edict in remote regions. Thus the rule in those regions was increasingly overtaken by leading officers of the barbarian tribes, who were now Roman soldiers; that is, their chieftains and leaders.

Sant Apollinare Nuovo basilica in Ravenna. Built during the reign of Teodorich the Great, the basilica was originally dedicated to Christ the Redeemer, entirely in the spirit of the Arian understanding of Jesus. After the Goths were defeated, Emperor Justinian ordered the decorations in the churches to be artistically reshaped to erase any trace of the Goths and their belief. The name

of the basilica was then changed to Sanctus Martinus. (Wikipedia)

Local generals of Goth descent overtook rule, so they handed down the nominating to official posts and the collecting of taxes to their descendants. In this way, local governments were formed in France, Spain, Illyria, and even Italy itself, which, while still feeling a part of the Empire, was practically independent.

All these local governments in the West, such as the Frankish generals and their groups of soldiers in northern France, the Visigoths in southern France and Spain, the Burgunds in southeast France, the Goths in Italy, the Gothic tribe of Vandals in north of Africa, all of them were Arians. The Franks in northeastern France and what we today call Belgium were still pagans.

Theodoric (Theoderich or Teodoric; real Gothic name Thiudoric), 493–526 of the current era, was the ruler of the eastern Goths. Like all other barbarian chieftains by birth, as he was the son of one who had been taken into Roman service, he himself was brought up at the court of the emperor. By his ancestry, he belonged to the Gothic ethnic group.

Jesus, mosaic on the ceiling of the Arian monastery in Ravenna. A very rare and extremely unusual artistic representation of Jesus as an older teenager, almost a boy. But, Theodoric and the eastern Goths were Arians in their belief; that is likely the reason for portraying Jesus in this manner, keeping in mind the belief that the Son has a beginning, is begotten by the Father, and by rank is underneath the Father. The mosaic was created during the reign of Emperor Justinian the Great, by reconstruction after the fall of the Gothic Kingdom.

He managed to defeat Odoacer who was of Germanic descent as well, and with an army of 25,000 soldiers, to take over rule in Italy. Thus he became practically independent. The centre of his power was in the Italian city of Ravenna. As other soldiers and military leaders, he was a follower of Arius.

The largest stronghold of Arianism was in the Roman province of Illyricum, where it flourished exactly during the reign of Theodoric the Great.

After 300 years, Christianity definitively won the battle against Arianism. The military of the Roman Empire remained Arian and endured because it was supported by the officers in the command of the western disctricts. The military spirit was still present in Arianism, and because of that, the basic idea of Arianism – the doubt whether Jesus could truly have been God – survived after the formal cessation of preaching Arianism among the population.

It is often said that all heresies die out. That could be true, but it is not true that with time the vital principle of heresy necessarily loses power. Arianism was one of those heresies that disappeared. The same fate overcame Calvinism. That does not mean that the general moral effect or atmosphere of a certain teaching disappears from among the people. For example, Geneva in Switzerland, in this day is a Calvinist city. However, there is not one person in Geneva who accepts Calvin's highly defined theology. The teaching is nominally dead, but its effects on society remain.

The story about the disappearance of Arianism in the West is usually written and understood incorrectly. What was European Christian society in Western Europe like during the fourth, fifth, and sixth century, that is between the time at which Constantine left Rome and established the new capital of the Empire, Constantinople/Tsarigrad in Byzantium.

The substance of the Arian doctrine in the West found its continuation in different teachings of Protestant reformers. What had enormous consequences for Arianism in the East was the emergence of Islam.

Islam, which came from the desert, quickly became a contra-religion in which Jesus had the role of a divine messenger, but any form of the divinity of Jesus is denied. The disappearance of Arianism in the East meant the restructuring of the Christina Eastern Roman Empire. Faced with this catastrophe, the Christians which remained independent reacted to Orthodoxy as their only chance for survival.

Arius was the apex of the mass movement. The reason for his success lies in the momentum which he gained thanks to his previous education. To this should be added the personal characteristics of Arius. Persons of this sort, who become leaders, do so because they gathered knowledge by which they are imposed. They would have not become so if they did not have something within them beforehand. The second factor which influenced the rapid spreading of Arius' teaching is the accession of the military and the upper social strata to his teaching.

Mosaic in the Sant Apollinare Nuovo basilica in Ravenna, with a depiction of Jesus on the Sea of Galilee. It is unusual to see Jesus artistically represented as a young man, especially as a boy. However, the Goths were Arian Christians, and according to Arian teaching, the Son is begotten by the Father, so the power he has is also of the Father. The artistic representation of Jesus as almost a boy, we can speculate, represents him as a youthful boy – the Son – exactly for that reason.

Arius certainly had strong authority. Within him there was a large ambition and a strong element of rationalism. He held within him enthusiasm for what he believed to be the truth.

Arius is said to have been quite straightforward, "of common sense", which garnered the attention of the masses. He also had a driving power.

For a time, Arius lived in exile, in the Roman province Illyricum, where he bolstered the already adopted roots of his teaching and established strong foundations for the coming Gothic bishop Wulfila. Through the influence of Wulfila on the territory of the province of Illyria, which included the territory of modern-day Bosnia and Herzegovina, something like a Gothic "folk Church" emerged.

The Gothic Arian Church also had priests and bishops, although they were not determined and ordained by the Pope. However, they had to live off of their own work and they did marry. There was no Pope, no tithe, no worship of saints or relics, no cult of the Mother of God, no confession, no baptism of children, no ritual sacrament, but a "brotherly meal" after the Early Christian model.

The Gothic-Arian church or the "folk Church" had its places of worship, basilicas. In Bosnia these basilicas are typical by their manner of construction as well, and they can be said to have been a special type of Bosnian Early Christian basilica. Their attendants lived in them only "temporarily", i.e. without lifelong vows.

All the principles of the Gothic folk Church remained with its successor, the Bosnian Church.

When nowadays the term *hiža* is mentioned in Bosnia, what is meant by it is exactly this form of spaces in which prayers were held.

After losing the battle against Emperor Justinian in 554 CE, the Gothic soldiers retreated into the highland areas of Bosnia where they created a strong basis for the emergence of the Bosnian Banate and finally the Kingdom of Bosnia.

The Bosnian Church was the state religion of the Bosnian state. It is known that throughout the entirety of the Middle Ages it fought in great conflicts against the crusaders and the inquisition, which tried to destroy it because it was considered heretical.

In the example of Bosnia, as in that of Geneva, if you would ask modern-day Bosnians, regardless of their religious affiliation (until about 150 years ago everyone in Bosnia was a Bosniak), whether they have any connection to Arians or the Bosnian Church, they would categorically deny it.

However, the tolerant Gothic-Arian spirit and justness remained among this people, as in their name itself – "the Good Bosniaks".

Through Wulfila's first popular Bible, the Goths become Christians in faith, but as a people within the Roman Empire produced its own Gothic clergy and own church, they were immediately labelled as Arian heretics.

Under accusation of heterodoxy and heresy, same as the Arian heretics, the life of Ban Kulin, and thereby the state and the people, were threatened. The Ban, the chief religious elders, i.e. the djeds and other Bosniaks, in front of Roman emissaries, to avoid inquisitors and a crusade, had to sign a text by which they denounce their heresy:

„First of all we denounce the schism, because of which we are infamous, and accept the Roman Church. We guarantee in the name of all who belong to our society and come from our places, with all properties and possessions, that we will never in the future follow the perversity of heresy. In all churches we will have altars and crosses. The books, of the New as well as of the Old Testament, we will read as the Roman Church does. In each of our places we will have priests, who must, at least on Sundays and on holy days, in accordance with directives from the Church, read the mass, hear confessions, and issue

penance. We will celebrate the holy days of saints determined by the Holy Fathers and no one, whom we would with certainly know to be a Manichaean or another heretic, will we accept to reside with us. Of excellent (disembodied) head is he who thinks and says otherwise."

The question arises, why would the Bosnian Church and Ban Kulin be denouncing heresy if the first, famous Charter of Ban Kulin, issued to the Raguswans on 29 August 1189 by Ban Kulin, begins with: "In the name of the Father and Son and Holy Spirit".

Exactly because Gothic Arianism, which had deeply embedded itself in our area, does not accept the Holy Trinity as the Church of that time interprets it, but does in its vocabulary have the Father, who is the Creator, with no beginning and no end, the Son, who is begotten and has his beginning, and because he is begotten cannot have absolute divine power, and the Holy Spirit, who is only on Earth to help Jesus.

Gothic Arianism did not disappear from the territory of the Roman province of Illyria even after the fall of the Gothic Kingdom in 554. It remained on the territory of modern-day Bosnia and Herzegovina in its true form and essence, which probably caused the creation of the first state, the Banate of Bosnia, and the Bosnian Church, which for a long period was the state religion.

This period of 635 years, from 554 to 29/08/1189, when the Charter of Ban Kulin was written, because of the lack of information, is insufficiently described in historiography. However, the connection between the Arians and the Arian teaching of that period and the time in which we register the emergence of Kulin, the famous Charter of Ban Kulin and his reign, because of which, among the people called Good Bosniaks, to this day remains the proverb "since Ban Kulin and the good old days".

Stećak, necropolis Ravanjska Vrata, Kupres

The Ravanjska Vrata necropolis in the municipality of Kupres is on the list of 30 medieval necropoleis of stećci, which were declared UNESCO World Heritage in 2016.

The necropolis consists of two parts, the Lower and the Upper Necropolis. In the part termed Lower Necropolis, there is a group of 43 stećci, which are well-made and oriented in the direction northwest-southeast. In the part termed Upper Necropolis, there are 25 stećci, without a definite system in the direction east-west. Around the necropolis, in each direction, there are many larger and smaller stones, so the stećci are embedded into the environment. The most common motifs are ribbons and bordures, rosettes, crosses and crescent moons. subsequently stylised plants appear in the form of lilies, scenes of hunt and dances, an arm with a sword in hand, two women, a man with a horse, a bent vine and a spiral circular wreath. The quarry from which the stećci were sourced was in the immediate vicinity.

A number of stećci are completely sunken, part of them have fallen over. Most stećci are covered in moss and lichen, and part of them are visibly damaged by cracks.

At a distance of 800 metres there are two additional necropoleis, Trišića Njiva and Konopi, and to the west, on the hill of Crljenica, there is a necropolis with 25 stećci.

5 GOTHIC HERITAGE IN BOSNIA

Before they came to our lands, the Goths lived in Scandinavia. After leaving Gotland, they cross the territory of modern-day Poland and Ukraine, where they are first mentioned in 50–100 CE. On their journey, they come into contact with the Celts, and certainly become exposed to different influences, especially in the border regions. Thus, Germanic hisotriographers cannot draw a clear line between Gothic and Celtic heritage. Before they adopted Arianism, the Goths were followers of a mythology of various gods and demigods, which in most cases were female. Every military leader who came back with a victory on the battlefield could be considered a demigod. The tribes had their totems and gods, while families could have had familiar gods. They had a few common gods; Odin or Wodan is the chief deity in the mythology of Germanic peoples. At times, he is the god of gods, the god of war, the god of poetry and of runes (script), of death and extasy with demonic-shamanic elements.

Thor (by Mårten Eskil Winge, 1872)

Besides that, they believed in the Sun, the Moon, the mother of fertility, Holle (Terra Mater), the deity of war and victory on the one hand, and the protector of law and order on the other, Ziu (Tiw), is sometimes equated to the Roman god Mars. Thor (Donar) was the deity of storms and vegetation, then the deity Frig (Freya).

It is noticeable that pagan beliefs, regardless of which ethnic group belong to, the Roman, Illyrian, or Germanic, had deities that largely did not differ from each other.

On their long journey towards the Roman Empire established a clear hierarchy of military and civilian administration. The names of their tribal rulers are known even in the times before the Huns broke onto European soil, and they are: Berig, Gadarich (2nd century), Filimer (2nd/3rd century), Ostrogoth (around 250), Kniv (around 250).

Since the time when the Gothic tribes split into the eastern and the western Goths, the lineage of Gothic kings was as follows: Geberich (334–337), Vultulf, Ermanarich (–375), Vithimiris/Vinitharius (375–376), Hunimund, Thorismund. The kins of the eastern Goths were the following: 451–468/69 Valamir, 468/69– 474 Thiudimir, 474–526 Theoderich the Great, 526–534 Athalarich, 526–535

Amalasuntha, 534–536 Theodahad, 536–540 Witichis, 540–541 Hildebad, 541.

Erarich, 541–552 Totila, 552. Teia.

It should be noted that all the names which are listed and have the suffix "ich" in them are read as [ˈitɕ], which is certainly confirmed by the bronze plate of Theodoric the Great issued by the prefect Catulinus reads "Thloderići".

In their historic expedition, the Goths arrive in the territory north of the Black Sea in 238 at the latest, and the year in which they could have split into Terwingen (forest dwellers) and the eastern Goths is in 291. Ermanarich was the first historic and, at the same time, the last king of the Goths before the arrival of the Huns in this territory in the year 375. His death is reported by only two historians: Jordanes and Ammianus Marcellinus. According to Ammianus, he committed suicide after being defeated by the Huns. King Ermanarich was celebrated among his people because of his military skill and just rule. Because of his influence and importance for the Goths, he found mention in many stories/sagas about the Goths.

Let us at this point comment on a perplexing phenomenon;

For a long time, some Serbian historians introduce confusions and untrue information about the Gothic King Ermanarich, 375, and King Totila, 541–552. According to their theory, King Svevlad I is supposed to be the Gothic King Ermanarich, 375, who is not a Goth, but allegedly a Serb, which is, of course, ridiculous. And Samovlad, Svevlad II Svevladović, according to their theory, had three sons – Boris, Totila, and Ostroil. That would mean that the Gothic King

Heldebad, 540–541, (see the list) actually the brother of Svevlad, who is allegedly of Slavic descent, whose sons after his death allegedly continued the Slavic conquests of the Roman Empire. Boris ruled over his father's land, while the younger brother, Totila, broke into Rome.

Actually, the Gothic King Totila, originally named Baduila (little warrior) is the brother of the Gothic King Hildebad (ruled 540–541), from the Amal tribe. The name of his father is in the list of kings, and it certainly was not Svevlad II Svevladović, allegedly a Slav.

What is at hand here is a liberal translation of the name Ermanarich into Svevlad in Serbian, insertion and an attempt at Slavicisation of Illyria in the period of Late Antiquity.

Gothic kings managed to occupy Pannonia and their centre of power was south of lake Balaton, in modern-day Hungary.

When the Gothic Kingdom, that acted as part of the Roman Empire, was flourishing and in full momentum showed its power, Roman Emperor Justinian decided to re-establish control over the entire Empire and end the rule of Goths and their king Theodoric. The Emperor received various complaints about Theodoric. Although Theodoric was tolerant towards the effort of economic and cultural advancement, he could not circumvent the societal upheavals of the time. The conspiracy against the Goths was formulated by the bishops of the Roman Church, because within its ranks were people who endeavoured to reduce the rule and power of monotheistic Arianism and the Arian Goths, and, in that confusion, to seize the title of Pope.

In this conflict the Goths shortly lost several rulers. The last among them was the newly appointed king of the Goths, general Teia.

As the imperial army advanced, Teia lost control over his territories. In October of 552, he was defeated in the last battle on the hill Mons Lactarius – literally "Milk Hill" (modern-day Monti Lattari near

Naples, possibly Monte Sant' Angelo). During the retreat of the military and the people, the people crossed over into territories which were safer for their survival. A part of the remaining army sided with the Langobards and the Franks, and a part of the Alemanni tribe, which was under the protection of Theodoric, found sanctuary in the territory of Illyricum, modern-day Slovenia, Croatia, and western Bosnia and Herzegovina. The Gothic necropolis in Rakovčani near Prijedor (more than 70 graves) is a testament to the occurrences in this period.

Brooch from the Arian basilica in Globasnitz, Hemmaberg.

That the Alemanni tribe at that time lived in the southern Alpine area is evidenced by the finding of a silver brooch from the early 6th century. The brooch was found in the Arian-Gothic basilica in the Austrian town of Globasnitz, Hemmaberg. These events and their dwelling in this area is evidenced by the Roman senator and writer

Aurelius Cassidorus as well.

Rakovčani near Prijedor is the largest archaeological site associated with the Goths, containing 70 graves. All of them are, typically for the Gothic manner of burial, arranged into rows. This site in Rakovčani represents the first recorded early phenomenon of arranging graves into rows. This phenomenon would remain deep into the Middle Ages and in all necropoleis in which we find stećci arranged into rows, we can say that they are graves of Gothic origin. In Rakovčani, hollowed-out trees into which bodies were lowered (Totenbaum) and protective wooden slabs (Totenbret), which are typical for Goths were found. In the necropolis on Gradina, in the village of Korita near Duvno (lat. Delminum), the graves are encircled with stones, and in some cases with irregularly cut slabs. In them, ornamental or utilitarian parts of clothing (fibulae, clasps, rings, bracelets, earrings) were found. Axes, small knives, and unusual arrowheads were found as well. Among the ornamental objects, necklaces made of differently sized amber pearls and glass paste, flat tibulae, a pair of golden earrings with simple cubes and a large number of clasps of different types, mainly made of bronze, iron, and silver. There are also examples of in the form of bronze and silver styluses with emphasized perforated heads. The valuable jewellery was discovered in Potoci near Mostar. In one grave a golden chain was found, which is a rarity among jewellery of that time across the entire territory of Europe. In another, a pair of gilded silver arched fibulae, a pair of gold earrings, and part of a gold necklace were found. This collection of gold jewellery also belongs to luxurious Ostrogothic jewellery from the beginning of the 6th century.

A significant finding is also the pair of silver and gilded arched fibulae, a pair of silver earrings and a large pearl of chalcedony from Gornje Pećine near Travnik. In Gornje Turbe near Travnik, a gold necklace with eighteen circular medallions was found. Some of them have a depiction of a lamb on them, while others that of an angel. These decorative items are found in all regions where eastern Goths lived, from Ukraine to Italy. They stem from the famous Gothic gold workshops in Crimea, Podunavlje, Srebrenik,

Sirmium, Aquilea, and others.

Gothic tombs on the soil of Bosnia and Herzegovina were found in Bijeljina, Batkovići; Doboj, Žabljak; Prijedor, Rakovčani; Velika Kladuša; Donji Vakuf, Oborci; Bugojno, Čipuljić; Gornje Turbe; Dželilovac; Gornje Pećine; Zenica, Bilimišće; Stranjani; Breza; Višegrad, Mušići; Sarajevo, Debelo brdo; Rajlovac, Mihaljevići; Vrdolje, Lisičići; Duvno, Korita; Han Potoci; Čapljina, Nerezi.

Along with the ones listed, numerous coins from the period of Byzantine emperors (Zeno, Anastasius I, Justinian I and Maurice), but the coins of Gothic rulers have a special value. Silver coins of Athalric, 526–534, were found in Vinica near Duvno, while silver coinage of Theodahad, 534–536, was found in the vicinity of Bihać. All of these findings confirm that Ostrogothic coinage circulated in the territory of Bosnia and Herzegovina during the time of their kingdom.

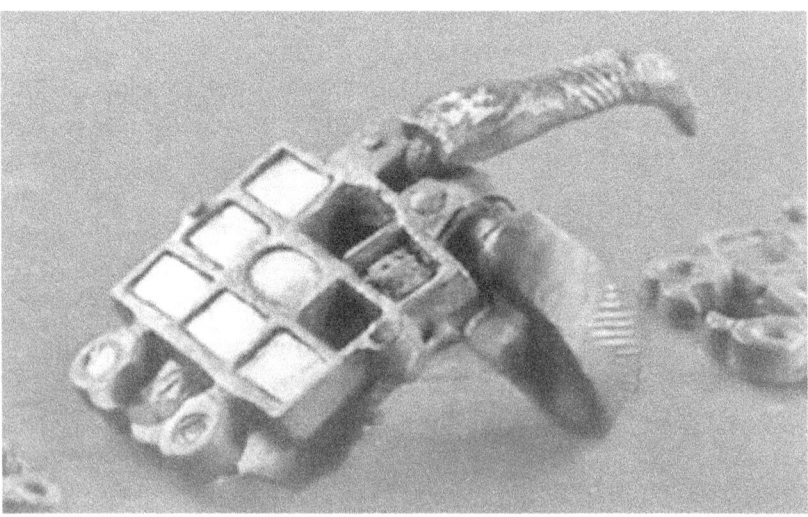

Belt buckle

A buckle from the belt of a Gothic officer was found in a tomb. The buckle has the head of an eagle, which was a favourite symbol for easter Germanic peoples. In heraldry, the eagle is associated with the structure of large empires, and it appears first in the Achaemenid (Persian) Empire, Rome, and Byzantium. Although unsuited to small people, in our region, the symbol of an eagle was adopted by the Serbs during the medieval Nemanjić dynasty, 12th–14th century. The buckle is a unique exemplar with transparent glass pebbles. The underset red leather, which is found on another leather belt, is reflected through it. With its appearance, it evoked the sense as if it were decorated with granite pebbles.

Aside from this, Arian Goths built many Arian basilicas; more than 50 of them have been found until now in the area of Bosnia and Herzegovina. The basilicas differ from others that were found, thus in this case they are called basilicas of the Bosnian, Arian type. Based on their number, it can be concluded that Arianism was accepted by the masses, by the Gothic as well as the native Illyrian population.

Runic script from Breza /Futhark/

In the Arian or Early Christian basilica in Breza, which was discovered in 1930, on one semicircular stone an engraving of Gothic runes was found. In this site, an engraving of the Latin script was found as well. The runic alphabet is a testament to the presence of Goths in this area and the use of multiple languages and scripts in Bosnia, as is part of its centuries-long tradition. Tineke Looijenga places the engraver of these runes into the Langobard tribe, which lived around Breza from 535 to 567, and Helmut Arntz (indogermanist and runologist) dated this inscription to the year 525.

With the appearance of the Gothic bishop Wulfila, 311–383, in Illyria, the Goths accepted Arianism, which had already established itself in the higher strata of Roman society, en masse. They abandoned their old mythology and, already integrated into the ranks of the Roman army, they opened the space for a new era of development of Western society. One fact is extraordinarily important. Before the emergence of Christianity, the entire army of the Roman Empire were followers of Mithraism. (Mithras is a Persian deity of light, embodied in an ox, and often paired with Anahit, the deity of water, who was associated with the river Oxus). Here it should be added that the Goths in their ancestral homeland were followers of the deity of water, and thus engaged in their sacrificial cult in swamps and areas with water. In Latin sources, the Goths were named after the river Göta, which means "morning" in the Gothic language.

With the appearance of Arius' teaching and the movement named after him, Arianism, the military of the Roman Empire adopted this form of Christianity and the Mithraistic dualism was Arianised. As this was the time of the rise and reign of the Goths, the entire Mediterranean was Arian. If we consider the relationship between Arianism and Christianity, we will see that there is a constant struggle for supremacy and power. This relationship resulted in the constant persecution of Arians under the accusation of heresy. The Church managed to convert the coastal areas of Illyria (Dalmatia) while the inland areas remained Arian.

Double-faced Mithraic relief. Rome, 2nd to 3rd century CE.

The vacuum that emerged in the territory of the inland areas of the province of Illyricum was filled by the Arians, of different ethnicities, retreating from the lost battlefields of the Gothic state. With their arrival and the inability of the Emperor to establish full control of the government, the conditions for the creation of the Banate of Bosnia and the inception of the Bosnian Church, which is based on the teaching of Arius, were created. Considering that Arianism was most widely represented among the immigrant Goths and the native population, the traditions from the age of pagan beliefs of the two peoples was passed down, at least in the symbolic sense. In many Bosnian necropoleis of stećci, the syncretism of Gothic Arianism and Illyrian prehistoric symbolism is obvious. Many necropoleis, whose names are of Gothic origin, hold the memories of the first stećci, and those date to after 348 CE when our region was settled by Wulfila's Arian Goths and eastern Arians from the territories of *aš-Šam*/Syria and Lebanon. All necropoleis from the territory of the Kingdom of Bosnia which have in them stećci arranged into rows, oriented in the direction NW–SE or in the other Germanic direction NE– SW are of Arian Gothic origin, and there are many of them.

In a later period (with the emergence of Islam) stećci in our area transform, in their symbolism, transform into *nišani*, where the symbolism from stećci is transferred to a new form of tombstones. We have the example of the tombstone in the necropolis Modran, Bjelimići, Konjic municipality, which is oriented in the direction NW–SE, which is the typical direction in which Goths would orient their graves.

THE HIDDEN HISTORY OF BOSNIA

Photograph – Emir Medanhodžić / Modran, Bjelimići; Veletin, Konjic municipality.

Another example of the heritage of symbols from stećci is found in Travnik in the cemetery of the Sufi takya where on a nišan tombstone these symbols are engraved.

Photograph by Suad H., Travnik

What was until recently common practice in our country, and is the legacy of a Gothic custom, is the modelling, that is, deforming of children's heads into an elongated shape. The head of the child would be tightened with a scarf or some cloth to get the elongated shape. It is unknown how that custom started.

The pagan custom which was noted in Bosnia and Herzegovina, among Bosniaks, and can be attributed to the Gothic cult of water is that, when someone would pass away, a vessel with water would be left on the window overnight, so that the spirit of the deceased, which for some time still attempts to come home, would be sent to the other side, and would not frighten the inhabitants.

A superstitious, pagan Gothic custom, which is still commonly practiced in the Catholic Church is the celebration of Cvitina, the day of blessing plants. In Bosnia and the northern regions, fir and willow tree branches are traditionally brought to be blessed, in the southern regions those are olive and palm tree bracnhes. In folk belief, a dual power was attributed to the blessed plants: of protection (from thunder, hail, illness) and of fecundity (ensuring good health and an abundant harvest); to that end, the blessed plants would be placed into the yard, inside the house, apartment building, on the graveyard, wells would be decorated with it, young men would gift it to young women, and so on. Olives, cornel trees, bulrush, and palm trees have an important role in folk belief in transferring the vital energy of plants into their home. It is customary to also wash ones face with the water in which the flowers were left overnight.

The Arian-Gothic symbols which are found on stećci are certainly hexagrams and pentagrams; the symbols of the Earth and the skies, the Sun, the Moon, swords, and Arian-Gothic crosses or Greek crosses. On the two oldest Gothic archaeological artefacts, findings of inscriptions (photo) which are found on the combs are engraved with 3 concentric circles. These concentric circles are a phenomenon that was noted on the Bosnian stećak as well, as the heritage of prehistoric Illyrian symbolism.

Aside from these, a favourite symbol of the eastern Goths is the eagle. With this symbolism which is characteristic of the Goths on the one hand, and the symbolism characteristic of the Illyrians on the other, the conclusion is that Illyrian-Gothic symbolism is represented on stećci. We can conclude that the world-view which was present in the time of Late Antiquity or the early Bosnian Church, through the Middle Ages, and up until today, subconsciously remained and in part still is expressed in our communication.

Finally, the question arises: If the deities and symbols of the old Goths and Illyrians are similar or the same, is their source from which they emerged in prehistory the same?

The combs with FUTHARK inscriptions and 3 symbols of concentric circles

Necropolis Ravanjska Vrata, Kupres

Contacts between Arianism and Islam in Illyria

How and in which manner could Islam have influenced the early Krstjani and all those who did not concur with the dogmatic understanding of the Church in the area of Dalmatia and Illyria, who, in the period of Early Christianity, were often of Arian provenance. In our previous texts, on the basis of archaeological findings we shoved what has been in modern times confirmed by genealogy, that in Bosnia and Herzegovina there is Scandinavian genetic heritage, we realised the strong presence of Arianism and Arian Goths, who, throughout the Mediterranean area, wherever they would settle, spread this teaching among other peoples. After the Gothic Kingdom was lost, a large portion of Arians of different ethnicities, most of which Goths, found sanctuary in the area of the Roman province Dalmatia (Illyria) which includes the area of modern-day Bosnia and Herzegovina. The most on this topic was written by Christian writers: *The Chronicle of the Priest of Duklja*, the Byzantine writer Porphyrogenitus: *De Administrando Imperio*, then the scholar Cassidor, a high officer in the Gothic Kingdom in the time of King Theudoric, whose documents about the history of the Goths were adapted by the Roman historian Jordanes in the VI century. So, we have the history of Bosnia in Late Antiquity or Early Christianity only from one perspective and it, out of political and religious reasons, is eager to orient itself in the direction of appropriating and distorting the Illyrian, Arian-Gothic heritage of Bosnian history.

Some Croatian historians attempt to croatise this transitional period from Late Antiquity to the Early Middle Ages, so they call early Illyrian Banates Croatian (Slavic) Banates, thus also place the Neretvan Banate and the Bosnian Banate into the framework of Croatian Banates, which is of course absurd. The area of modern-day Croatia was at this time divided into Illyrian Banates, which later fell under the rule of the Ugric crown. Here it should be highlighted that the historian Nada Klaić, who uses exclusively scientific methods, dates Bosnia as the oldest state in the period of Late Antiquity or the Early Middle Ages.

In historic documents there is no mention of Croatian or Slavic banates from this period, but exclusively of Illyrian banates, which is confirmed by Arabic sources as well.

In the I century, two Roman historians wrote about Slavs, but under different names. Pliny the Elder calls the newly arrived inhabitants (Slavs) around the Visla river the Venedi, and Tacitus (in his work *De situ, moribus et populis Germaniae*) calls the same Venedi people Germanic, and mentions that they live in the lower reachers of the Visla river. Ptolemy, the geographer from Alexandria, also mentions the Veneti in the II century, calling them "giant people". More is written about the Slavs towards the end of the 7th century, when they, in an alliance with the Avars, emerged on the stage of history, marking the beginning of their time in history. From that point on, many travel writers and historians wrote about them. Since 558–563, they had a military alliance with the Avars, which was mostly plundering, and mostly encompassed the western group of South Slavs.

The historian Jordanes, in his book *Historia Gothorum*, mentions that in the beginning of the VI century, the Slavs settled the entirety of the lower reaches of the Danube. He indicated that Slavic peoples are of one blood and are usually divided by three names:

VENEDI – settled the northern coast of the Baltic and the lands in the Vistula River valley in the 6th century

ANTES – the area between the Dnieper and Dniester rivers

SKLAVINI – the lands between the Tisza, Dniester and Danube in Dacia of Antiquity.

About the contact between Arabs and Slavs (Arabic Saqlabi), we will find some data in the documents by Arabic historians who wrote about those events in the Early Middle Ages, after Tariq b. Ziyad stepped onto the area of Andalusia in the year 711 and captured the Iberian Peninsula (Spain, parts of Italy). Arabic sources tell exclusively of Saqlabi (Slavs) who joined the Islamic army and became their advisors, rulers (emirs), military leaders, and mercenaries.

They came into contact with the Saqlabi through the mediation of Byzantine slave traders. All things considered, the Arabs gave the Illyrians the designation for the name Slavs. The origin of the word "Saqaliba" itself (from which the word Slav developed) is of Arabic origin, and was originally "Sqalibi", denoting a group of people who are enslavers, conquerors, pillagers, those who take into slavery. This stems from the Avarian-Sklabenoi raiding alliance. The Saqaliba are mentioned in the writings of Arab writer Al-Akhtal around the year 670, although these contacts could have occurred earlier. The earliest contact between Arabs and Slavs can be traced to the 500s, and it occurred on the territory of the Eastern Roman Empire (Byzantium) or near it. A confirmed case of Slavs meeting Arabs is mentioned by the Byzantine historian Theophanes; according to him, in 664, a group of 5,000 Slavic (Sklabenoi) mercenaries in service of Byzantium joined the victorious army of the Umayyad Caliph Mu'awiya I (ruled 661–680) who was returning from a campaign in Asia Minor. The Caliph settled those Slavs in the area near the city of Apamea in the north of Syria, where to this day, "Sqalibi" remains a derogatory term. There's a theory according to which the Arabs named the Slavs after a certain type of plant of Arabic red beans, which would be nice and peace-loving, but, of course, cannot be true. What the Saqaliba (Sqalibi, Slavs) excelled at and were recognised for in this historical period was pillaging, enslaved people, and conquest.

Procopius of Caesarea, from the VI century, in his historical writings, says that the land which he calls BALAHIA (Wallachia) is already in its entirety settled by Slavs and that the name SCLAVINIA is already being used for it. The oldest mention of the Slavic ethnonym from the 6th century comes from the Byzantine historian Procopius, who wrote in the Byzantine Greek language, using various forms such as Sklabinoi (Σκλαβῖνοι), Sklaboi (Σκλάβοι), Sklabēnoi (Σκλαβηνοί), Sklauenoi (Σκλαβῖνοι). In contrast, his contemporary, the historian Jordanes, used the name Sclaveni in Latin.

In 567, some mixed Antes (Proto-Slavs) and Slavic tribes broke into the area of Illyria with the incursion of Avars. They did pillage, raze and devastate Illyria, so this name in the beginning, probably, referred only to them, and was only later applied to the native population as well. However, although the Illyrians were named after the Slavs, and the Illyrian land was called Slavic land, the Saqalibs (Slavs) could in no case have been dominant in our region during the time of Avar rule, which lasted almost 200 years, in the years 567–796.

According to Einhard's "Frankish Annals", the tribe of Serbs did not arrive in our area with the first emergence of Antes, Slavs (whom Fra Andrija Kačić Miošić calls Goths; *Razgovor ugodni naroda slovinskoga*) and Avars in 582, but are mentioned only in the year 789 on the opposite shore of the Danube under the name Suurbi. At the same time, there is no mention at all about modern-day Croats, and they do not exist as a relevant factor. Based on the "Frankish Annals", it may be concluded that they could not participate in the formation of Illyrian Banates during the time of the collapse of the Roman Empire, Late Antiquity, or Early Christianity.

Frankish Annals (Einhard), 789:

"In the year 789, Wilz went through parts of Sclavaniae, with the help of God, together with his advisors, the Franks and the Saxons, he crossed through Saxony to the Elbe river in Cologne. There he built two bridges, of which one had to be of wood from the property of the village chief. Then he was promoted to the commander of said Slavs through his plan of control. When they were in the same army, the French, Saxons, and Frisians arrived by river in a boat, with the Franks on the Habol river (Elbe), which converged with them. With them were Slavs called Suurbi and people from their military camp called Abotriti, who were led by Prince Wizan. There he was when he once took the hostages and sacraments of Conplura, the God that leads France, they achieved their goal."[13]

---

[13] Ajnhardovi franački anali po godini 798. https://la.wikisource.org/wiki/Annales_regni_Francorum

This theory is supplemented by the fact that genetics identifies over 50% of the native (*more than 30,000 years old*) "I2" haplogroup in the area of the province of Illyria, that is the Bosnian basin or Dalmatia. Therefore, the theory of a great migration of Slavs in Illyria and their domination loses any sense. It could have emerged only from the political ambition to identify our area with the people neighbouring us. The same is the case with the attempts through history to equate Arianism, which was to a large extent present in Illyria (mostly in modern-day Dalmatia and its islands, in Bosnia, Herzegovina, and Sandžak), with Catholicism or Orthodoxy. The greatest testament to Arianism in the area of Dalmatia and Bosnia is the Arian basilicas from the 4th, 5th and 6th centuries, which over time evolved, that is, were the foundation for the indigenous Bosnian Church.

Because of their light skin colour and similarity to Slavs, the Arabs included the Saxons, Germans, and Hungarians into the category of Saqaliba. Yaqub from the 10th century, Masudi Murūj al-Tanhib, Qazwini, Habib the Saqlabi, Ibn Hayyan of Cordoba, Ibn Khordadbeh, and others are Arab scholars who give us a closer look at some names of military leaders from our area, which are interesting to us. The well-known army leader of the Fatimid Caliphate in Kairouan, Abdullah al-Jawhar al-Saqlabi conquered Egypt in 969, he founded the city of Cairo, and the Al-Azhar University. He is thought to have been born in Cavtat near Ragusa. The name al-Jawhar is of Arabic origin and denotes a "gemstone". He had his Illyrian name, which is unfortunately unknown. Jawhar likely changed his name when he accepted Islam. Another name from our Dalmatian-Illyrian area is Zuhayr Saqlabi (Saqaliba), ruler of the Andalusian coast of Almeria, Kairouan at the beginning of the 11th century. This closeness with the Arabs could have occurred due to the Dalmatian, old Illyrian Liburnia and Neretva Banate had strong navies and were constantly sailing the Mediterranean. A part of the seaside coast of Liburnia, from Optaija to Trogir, and the Neretva Banate, from the river Cetina, from Duvno and Livanjsko Polje, crossing Rama, to the river Neretva and Hum and Travunia, were traditionally very experienced in seamanship. The closeness of Arabs to Slavs is seen in joint military campaigns and the attempt to destroy the Byzantine Empire, the joint military blockade of Constantinople in the year 677 and the generous help that the Arabs gave to the Slavs from the Peloponnese during their uprising against Byzantium, in the years 802–811.

The Islamic army had in its ranks many Islamised Illyrian and Spanish Visigoth soldiers who, thanks to their skill, held leadership positions in the military. It can be concluded that these soldiers could have joined the Islamic army only voluntarily, that they would change their name and accept the faith, based on some closeness and interest. The only possible closeness between the Illyrians and the Arabs is in the Arian-Islamic approach to religion. Islam, as the last religion to have emerged on the soil of Byzantium in the time of religious upheavals within Christianity, through its acceptance of the Old Testament, and, for the Arians, acceptable approach to the nature of Jesus from Nazareth, could offer the required answers. A striking example is the advisor of the Caliph, an Islamic law (Sharia) expert, Al-Saqlabi ibn Zeyd al-Amarna = Noble Slav of the Amarna Castle, towards the end of the 8th century.

The Arabic Emirate of Sicily and the Emirate of Bari

Arabic reports of these contacts are more common and precise after the conquest of Sicily and southern Italy by Arabs. From that time on, the Sicilian city of Palermo was important for trade between Dalmatia and Spain. While the Saracens (Muslims, Arabs) ruled over Sicily, in Palermo, the capital of the Emirate, there existed a city quarter which was called the Slavic quarter (Harat as-Saqalib), located close to the city port. However, the Muslims did not remain only in Sicily. The Apulian Emirate of Bari was an Islamic state in the 9th century, outside of Moorish Spain on the Apulian peninsula in southeastern Italy, with the capital city of Bari as the seat of the Emir in the years 840–871. At the time of its largest extent, in the middle of the 9th century, the Emirate ranged from southwestern Calabria to the eastern cape of Gargano. At that time, Dalmatia was ruled by the Illyrian Ban Vladislav, 821–835. The last Emir of Bari, Sawdan, expanded and built up the capital of Bari, the palace of the Emir, mosques, and developed trade. In the well-known Chronicle of the Priest of Duklja (840–841), among other things, it is noted that at that time, numerous Saracene (Arabic) boats left the port of Sicily. That the Muslim conquerors in the Early Middle Ages achieved a strong expansion towards the coast of the Balkans is confirmed by the writer Constantine Porphyrogenitus, who, among other things, recorded that "36 boats reached Dalmatia". Already in the 9th century, the Arabs had conquered some coastal cities such as the island of Lošinj, Budva, Kotor, Bar, and Ulcinj. Some Arab traders then settled in those regions to maintain the Arabic trade connection with this area. Porphyrogenitus also recorded the presence of other Muslim groups in the Balkans, which came from the north, specifically the region of Hungary.

Early Middle Ages: The map shows the Banate of Bosnia, Liburnia, Neretva Banate (Pagania), Zachumlia, Travunia, and Duklja.

Thus, in this period, the southern part of Italy was Islamised, which promoted the advancement of cultural, religious, and material trade, not only in southern Italy but in all areas to which traders would come. The Arab traders often came to coastal cities where lively trade was conducted, which is evidenced by many findings of Arabic coinage in those regions.

They brought with them Islam and Islamic culture, so that influence was felt daily in those regions. A testament to the Dalmatian–Illyrian relations with the Arabs is the name Saracen (Saracenus) and similar derivations of this name which appear in Dalmatian documents of the 11th century, and in Bosnia two stećci with epitaphs which contain the word "Saracene", and one which is written in Old Arabic script in Kalesija, were recorded. About that, Muslim traders had an influence on Dalmatian and Bosnian Arians, especially during their trade expeditions and migrations in Bosnia.

Stećak with an epitaph in Arabic, in the necropolis Brkića groblje and Zolje, Kalesija; photograph; Emir Medanhodžić: we managed to decipher and read "During the time of the ruler!"

When talking about the arrival of Muslims in our areas, the paths across Hungary and the Adriatic Sea are most often mentioned. A document that evidences Muslim traders being in the Banate of Bosnia is the "Hysmaelite Vel Bissem" from the year 1196 in Osijek, where it is stated that traders paid tariffs to the monastery of Čikador. The oldest Arabic document about the Kalisi (Kalizi) in Hungary is the work by the travel writer Abu Hamid al-Gharnati (1080–1169) titled "Tuḥfat al-albāb wa-nukhbat al-aʻjāb". Abu Hamid lived in Hungary from 1150 to 1154, where he found Maghreb mercenaries – muslims – fighting on the side of Hungary against the Byzantine army. The Muslim-Khazar tribe of Khalis–Ismaelites settled in Slavonia, in Srem, and the Bosnian regions of Usore and Soli. In these battles against Byzantium (115–1154), the Bosnian Ban Borić participated as well, as an ally of the Hungarians. With Ban Borić, a group of muslim Khalis came to the area of northeastern Bosnia. Khalis in Hungary served in the army of Hungarian kings, which is confirmed in the Golden Bull of 1222, by which, besides Jews, Muslims are fired from state services as well, which is a sufficient indicator that they were present in other spheres of social life in Hungary at that time. The toponym of Kalesija is a testament to that—the Byzantine writers John Cinnamus, Choniates, and Michael. Under attacks and later persecutions, members of the Khalyzians retreated from Hungary deep into Bosnia. John Cinnamus writes that the Khalyzians were settled in Hungary from the XI to the XII century in around thirty settlements, that they were good traders, craftsmen, economists and administrative workers.

In our continental areas, material trade was conducted along old Illyrian roads, which are later mistakenly called Roman roads, which from Ragusa and Split led to the Banate of Bosnia along the river Neretva (Via Narenta, Via Bosne), and toward Solin and Split across Jajce, Bugojno, Rama, and Duvno; caravans with goods travelled in both directions. The majority of Arabs were displaced from Europe only in the XII century, i.e., the emirates of Bari, Sicily, and Crete were destroyed.

Genetics confirm that western Sicily in the region of Troina-Sciocca near Palermo has the largest content of the Illyrian-Dinaric genome, where it reaches 16% of the population, which genetically and physically originates from our mountain-dwelling Dinarides.

The Neretvans (Arentani, Narentani, Pagani, and Mariani) of the Middle Ages were old Illyrians who in the VII century inhabited the area between the rivers Cetina and Neretva, which to the north included Duvanjsko Polje, the Rama River valley, islands and the Pelješac peninsula. The Greeks and Byzantines called their land Orontes or Arenta, after the Neretva River, while the Venetians and the Pope call it Pagania, from the word "pagan," i.e., unbaptised.

The inhabitants of the Neretva Banate, because they considered Christianity a means of coercion, had preserved their pagan belief of Arianism, so that they were called "pagans", and the land "Pagan", in Latin, Pagania. Constantine Porphyrogenitus, in his work *De Administrando Imperio,* used the expression Pagania, drawing attention to the unbaptised Neretvans. Exactly because of this reason, that the inhabitants and the army of Illyrian Dalmatia were followers of Arianism (unbaptiased, pagans, heretics), it was easy for them to accept Islam, the belief in one God, which they already had in the Arian teaching and thus to join the Arabic military and administration. The population mostly engaged in fishing and the cultivation of figs and olives, but the most lucrative business was piracy. Neretvans, using their fast vessels, would intercept all foreign ships, especially Venetian ones, and on several occasions, this caused war to break out.

There are a few hypotheses about the origin of the Neretvans, of course, the Croatian and the Serbian hypotheses from the 19th century, which endeavour to appropriate this territorial, cultural and historic area for themselves. However, the Neretvans are of Illyrian origin, which is indicated by the names of a series of their medieval military leaders from the 12th and 13th centuries: Brenna, Sebenna, Maldukh, Kholman, Tollen, Ossor, etc. This theory is confirmed by the new biochemical genetics of the population, which says that those with the special Dinaric type I1b/ Eu7, i.e., most Neretvans, are descendants of the native Illyrians. Knowing about their closeness to southern Italy (Calabria and Apulia), the area which 1500 years before the current era was settled by the Illyrian tribe of Messapians, which is related to the Illyrian-Dalmatian people, their skill in warfare and Arian-Gothic heritage, it is no surprise that they found their place high in the ranks of the mighty Islamic Caliphate that ruled this area. The first well-known Neretvan who, according to Moorish claims, already in the 8th century arrived in the Emirate of Cordoba, in Spain, as a diplomat of the Abbasid dynasty, was Abd al-Rahman Al-Saqlabi (the Slav) who already in 762 appears at the court of the first Moorish Emir, Abd al-Rahman I, (756–788).

(This connection between the Neretvans and Messapian southern

Italy certainly supports the thesis of Bisera Suljić Boškailo in regards to the Messapian script being related to Bosančica and Wulfila's Gothic script.)

Almost throughout its entire history, the Neretva Banate operated autonomously out of Omiš, as an Illyrian-Dalmatian banate, from the early Ban Višeslav in the year 781, up until the native seafaring dynasty of Kadžiki, whose name was Slavicised into Kačići. According to some authors, the Kačići tribe has its origin in Bosnia, and the Ragusan historian Lukarević mentions the father of two Kačić men as "the son of a Saracen". Bogdan Kačić, as the last Neretvan Ban, was militarily beaten by the Venetians and the Hungarians in the year 1287, and thereby forced to sign the surrender of his territory to the Hungarian Anjou dynasty. Only after the "Pacti Conventi" was signed did the Neretva Banate and the Kačić dynasty enter the group of nobility under Hungarian rule. (see Historia Salonitana Maior; Thomas the Archdeacon from the year 1387)

KAČIĆ

Kačići su bili jedno od dvanaest hrvatskih plemena koja su 1102. potpisali Pacta conventa. Područje njihove vlasti bilo je između Cetine i Neretve sa sjedištem u Omišu. Kao susjedi Bosne a još više kao vatreni pristalice bogumila, upletali su se Kačići u unutrašnje prilike u Bosni. Godine 1222. ometaju križarsku vojnu protiv bogumila u Bosni. Osvajanjem Omiša od strane Mlečana strušena je moć Kačića. Pod kraj XV.. stoljeća došla je njihova krajina (od Cetzine do Neretve) pod tursku vlast. Grb Kačića sa nadgrobne ploče u Drašnici iz XV. Stoljeća, slažem se sa grbom Kačića um ovom (Fojničkom) grvoniku.

The Kačić dynasty, Fojnica Armorial

The Neretvan dynasty of bans from 781 to 1287, as followers of Arianism and fervent supporters of the Bosnian Church, tried to interject themselves into the internal issues in Bosnia, and prevented their friendship in the year 1222 when they hindered the crusade on Bosnia. Aside from the Neretva Banate, in this period, the Banates of Hum and the Banate of Travunia (Trebinje), which were under constant pressure from Bosnia, as the first state of South Slavs, and then from Croatia and Raška, acted in parallel.

The Slovenian philosopher Hermannus Dalmata or Hermannus Sclavus (1110– 1160), around the middle of the 12th century, created the first European translation of the Qur'an into Latin. His translation, completed in the year 1143, was published by Peter the Venerable under the title "Lex Mahumet pseudoprophete" (Law of Muhammad the false prophet).

This translation of the Qur'an, judging by its title, was created because Islam was present in the wider European area, the lack of knowledge about it, and the fight against Muslims, as with all heretical movements that emerged at that time. In the Banate of Raška, Muslims are mentioned officially for the first time in the Zakonopravilo of Sava Nemanjić from the year 1219, as "of Ismaelitian faith", which was common at that time, because Muslims believed in one God, accepted the Old Testament, and to a degree also the New Testament. Because of that, they were considered Christian heretics of some special faith.

Herman the Dalmatian, Herman of Carinthia or Herman Dalmatin, was a medieval philosopher, astronomer, astrologer, mathematician and translator.

However, all "heretics", Arians and Muslims in Raška, experienced horrible persecution, killing, robbery, and thus sought sanctuary under the Bosnian Church in the Banate of Bosnia, during the reign of Bosnian Ban Kulin, and in Hum.

Here we will state as evidence an article by Mr. Mustafa Hilmi, from the Herald of the National Museum of Bosnia and Herzegovina in Sarajevo, to show that Islam had its place in the Kingdom of Bosnia long before the arrival of the Ottomans.

"Describes that besides the Haseći-hatun mosque, he found the türbe of some Haseći Hava, who died in 848 according to the Muslim calendar, ie, in the year 1446 after Christ. From that inscription, it is known that Haseći Hava built that mosque nineteen years before the Ottomans entered Bosnia. That mosque lies in the street leading from Ćemaluša to Čemerlina street."[14]

The above-stated can be accepted as reliable, since there exist confirmed archaeological findings which were researched and are

---

[14] Glasnik Zemaljskog muzeja Sarajevo from 1889., book I p.17

here published in scientific periodicals. It can be concluded that Muslims indeed did inhabit the area of Bosnia even before, out of different motivations, likely as traders.

In the historiography of Bosnia and Herzegovina, dozens of eminent scientists have pointed out numerous memorial and cultural ties between Bosnian stećci and the oldest Bosnian nišani, which developed in continuity from stećci. Among them are Šefik Bešlagić, Mehmed Mujezinović, Muhamed Hadžijahić, Alija Bejtić, Vladimir Ćovorić, Vladislav Skarić, Petar Knol, etc. As the historiographer Ibrahim Pašić said, "Stećci and the oldest Muslim nišani are very often common content in wedding graveyards. Primarily because the oldest Muslim nišani developed from stećci. Many nišani are not oriented towards the Kaaba, but are, like the stećci adjacent to them, oriented in the direction of north–south, or NW–SE, or in the direction of east–west. Beneath some nišani, there are dual graves."[15]

Alija Nametak says the following: "The oldest nišani are among Patarene stećci, because the 'new Muslims' wanted to rest next to their fathers and grandfathers, the 'good Bosniaks'. Such graveyards, where Muslim grave markers or nišani are a continuation of Patarene stećci, are quite frequent in Bosnia and Herzegovina." The first and in the Muslim world unique Bosnian nišani were made by medieval Bosnian carvers who previously carved stećci, from which they transferred onto the nišani numerous decorations of the stećci, animal and human figures, medieval weapons, Bosančica, in which the oldest Muslim epitaphs are written out and which is found on Bosnian nišani until 1930.[16]

The Arabs from the Caliphate of Bari and Arabic Lošinj with its neighbouring islands, where the maritime Saracens ruled for almost an entire century, left their cultural and linguistic (and even biogenetic) heritage on the čakavian dialect speaking Adriatic

---

[15] https://hamdocamo.wordpress.com/2016/10/16/od-stecka-do-nisana/

[16] ALIJA_NAMETAK_Islamski kulturni spomenici turskog perioda u Bosni i Hercegovini 1939, Page 31. https://www.cidom.org/ wp-content/uploads/2018/12/Alija-Nametak-Islamski-kulturni-spomenici-turskoga-perioda-u-Bosni-i- Hercegovini-1939.pdf

islands, but that Arabic heritage in the Adriatic is up to now politically undesirable and publicly hidden. Therefore, despite the Bosniak claims that Arabic loanwords are most common mainly in Bosnia, in reality, there are equally numerous older Arabic loanwords among the islanders speaking the Chakavian dialect in Croatia. Still, those mostly are not religious Arabic loanwords like in Bosnia, but on the contrary, practically every day Arabic loanwords which are mostly not present in Bosnia nor elsewhere in the interior of the Balkans (where Turkish loanwords replace them).

The Arabs left quite visible traces in Croatian history, tradition, and literature. Among older poets, who wrote in Croatian, the following sang about Arabs: Gundulić, Baraković, Kačić and others. Preradović, Šenoa, Palmović and Arnold discuss them under the general name of Arabs, or the names Bedouins and Saracens. In his story about a historic event, a poem about the conflict between Neretvans and Arabic pirates, Šenoa presented a Saracen pirate attack on the Neretva Banate. Franjo Marković composed a quite long epic poem titled *Povratak pod hrvatskog kralja (Return under the Croatian king)*, concerning the Slavic guard in Arabic Spain. Velimir Deželić senior developed similar content to a greater degree in his novels U službi kalifa (*In the Service of Caliphs*) (1908) and Hadžibova kob (*Hadžib's Fate*) (1909).

There exists a legend, about which the journalist and writer Enes Ratkušić writes in his book *Tajna bosanskog štapa (The Secret of the Bosnian Stick)*: "The novel is inspired by a legend which, since ancient times, was retained among the spiritual leaders of Bosnia. The story goes that in the time of the emergence of the last messenger of God, Mohammad a.s., a group of forty Bosnian djeds, who were the tribal-spiritual elders of that time, prompted by their following of a religion which was, in the official circles of the Church in Rome, considered heresy, visited Arabia and familiarised themselves with the teaching foretold in sacred scripts. Before their return, they were gifted a cane for them to keep safe, as a symbol of wisdom and dignity. According to the same legend, the cane of the djeds, which is also represented on medieval stećci as well as grave markers (nišani), was handed to Sultan Mehmed Fatih by the

Bosnian djed as a sign of handing over the spiritual and earthly rule into the hands of the Ottomans. During their retreat from Bosnia, Ottoman leaders returned the cane of the djeds to its spiritual authorities, and it was kept in Gazi Isa-bey's Takya, of the Mevlevi tariqa, located in Bentbaša, Sarajevo, up until it was levelled by the authorities of that time in the year 1957. Since then, the cane is lost without a trace, or rather, the story about it and its fate from that point enters the area of esotericism, or a sacred secret."[17]

Ravanjska Vrata, Kupres

---

[17] Enes Ratkušić Tajna bosanskog štapa Narodna biblioteka, 2014

7. THE THEOLOGICAL APPROACH TO JESUS/ISA A.S. AND THE RELATIONS BETWEEN ARIANISM AND ISLAM

The period of the revelation of the Qur'an began with the prophethood of Mohammad and lasted until near the end of his life, from the year 610 to the year 632. This was a time when Arianism was deeply rooted in the entirety of the Mediterranean, the Balkans, and our Bosnian-Herzegovinian area; it was a time when many Christians "heretical" schools streamed towards the Near East.

It is less known, but the Arian explanation of the nature of Jesus is close to identical to Islamic belief. The reason for that is that it emerged in the sphere of Abrahamic monotheism, because Jesus himself, aside from inspiring and enlightening his followers, did not leave a single written document that could serve as instructions or a basis for understanding his nature. So, Jesus (Isa a.s.) is primarily a human who lived a human life, had friends, ate food, and had all other human needs. He was born in a specific manner, from a pure mother who could have born only a human, not a deity. Isa a.s. is the word of God, a messenger who through God's permission and help was able to do many unusual, supernatural things: He brought a dead person back to life, he made a blind person see, he cured severe illnesses, upon his prayer, he was granted a plentiful supper. Those are events which were witnessed by many followers, and would, some generations later, become a stumbling block in understanding his nature, in the form of the question: Is he the Son or the Messenger of God?

A characteristic of Arian belief in Jesus is that they perceive him as a human. For Arians, God who was not created and has no beginning nor end created Jesus and the Holy Spirit. Only God has eternal Wisdom and Existence. The teaching of Arius and his followers is compiled in a scripture called *Thalia*.

A short passage from Thalia;

"1. ......And thus God himself, as he is, is unspeakable to all. Only he has no

one equal, no one similar, and no one of the same glory.

We call him unborn, in contrast to he who by nature is born. We hail him as without a beginning, in comparison to he who has a beginning.

We worship him as timeless, in contrast to he who has with time disappeared".

Greek text:

Αὐτὸς γοῦν ὁ Θεὸς καθό ἐστιν, ἄῤῥητος ἅπασιν ὑπάρχει. Ἴσον, οὐδὲ ὅμοιον, οὐχ ὁμόδοξον ἔχει μόνος οὗτος.

Ἀγέννητον δὲ αὐτόν φαμεν διὰ τὸν τὴν φύσιν γεννητόν,

τοῦτον ἄναρχον ἀνυμνοῦμεν διὰ τὸν ἀρχὴν ἔχοντα,

ἀΐδιον δὲ αὐτὸν σέβομεν διὰ τὸν ἐν χρόνῳ γεγαότα.[18]

Arian belief was accepted by higher social strata of the Roman Empire, nobles, philosophers, artists, writers, and finally the military, which perhaps played the biggest role in spreading this form of belief in Jesus, and with its presence spread it across the entire Mediterranean. Decisive for the acceptance of Arianism among the Goths and the Gothic component of the military of the Roman Empire was the Gothic bishop Wulfila, who, by adapting the old Messapian Illyrian script to the Gothic language, translated parts of the *Bible* into the Gothic language and the Arian Gothic king Theodoric. On the other side, orthodox Christians who accepted the belief in Jesus as the Son of God were regular people, peasants, and craftsmen. The poor strata of society lived in difficult conditions,

---

[18] Text by William Bright, De Synodis 15, (*Historical Writings of St. Athanasius according to the Benedictine Text*, Oxford: Clarendon, 1881, p. 259–60).

with hard work, and, in their subordinate position, awaited relief and salvation through some miracle, thus easily accepted the teaching about Jesus of a divine nature. Among them, the Nicaean belief found fertile soil. The answer to why that is so lies in the political situation. The Roman Empire was always going through political upheavals and power struggles. Thus, with the emergence of an idea, a counter-idea would be born as an opponent of the former. In this manner, a possibility of political conflict, and therefore of seizing power, was created. Such is the case with Arianism and Christianity, which, for a time, would periodically supplant each other as the state religion in the Roman Empire.

The inception of Arianism occurred in Alexandria, only to spread in a very short time across the entirety of Syria, Armenia, Turkey, Egypt, Ethiopia, and finally the entire Near East. Among Arabs and non-Arabs in the Near East, pure monotheism was not unknown, so anti-Nicaean Christianity was very developed and had a strong connection with Islam during the revelation of the Qur'an, from the year 610 to the year 632. A large portion of the population in the Byzantine Empire, be they "heretics" or those "uncertain in belief," accepted Islam when it emerged, exactly because of the unequivocal stance on the issue of the nature of Isa a.s.

The closeness of Islamic belief to anti-Nicaean schools of Christianity is evidenced in a few authentic examples from the history of Islam.

The first example is the relationship between Mohammed a.s. and the monk Waraqa ibn Naufal.

His full name is Waraqah ibn Nawfal ibn Asad ibn Abd-al-Uzza ibn Qusayr Al–Qurashi (Arabic ورقة بن نوفل بن أسد بن عبد العزّى بن قصي القرشي). According to Islamic tradition, he was a priest who was among the first to recognize and accept the prophecy of Muhammad a.s. He followed the teacher Nestorius, whose understanding of Jesus was called Nestorianism, which, in the issue of the nature of Jesus, was completely identical to Arianism.

Waraqah was the patrilineal nephew of Khadija bint Khuwaylid, the first wife of Mohammad a.s. He was also somewhat more distantly blood related to Mohammad a.s., namely, Waraqah's grandfather, Asad ibn ʿAbd al-ʿUzzā, was the nephew of ʿAbd Manāf ibn Qusaiy, an ancestor of Mohammad a.s.

Regardless of his being a Christian and follower of Nestorian belief, Waraqah has a special place in the biography of Mohammad a.s. He taught Arabic and Hebrew and spent much time by the Kaaba, and was considered a learned man.

When he heard of Mohammad's a.s., the First Revelation, he said: "By the God in whose hand is my soul, you are the Prophet of this people. Jibrīl came to you, as he came to Mūsā a.s. People will call you a liar, ill, they will persecute you and attempt to kill you. If I live to see that day, I will be by your side!"[19]

A young Mohammed is being recognized by the monk Bahira. Miniature illustration on vellum from the book Jami' al-Tawarikh (literally Compendium of Chronicles but often referred to as The Universal History or History of the World), by Rashid al-Din Hamadani, published in

---

[19] https://tanah44.wixsite.com/kuran-hadisi-tefsir/waraqa-bin-nawfal-1 and https://de.wikipedia.org/wiki/Waraqa_ibn_Naufal

Tabriz, Persia, 1307 A.D. Now in the collection of the University Library, Scotland

Different sources mention Waraqah under the following names: Dscherdschis, Georgius, Sergius, Sarjisan, Buairah, Bohaǡra. Bahira. In the Armenian language, Bahîra means "the Outstanding".

Waraqah is mentioned under the name Sergius by Petrus von Cluny in a letter from the year 1141 addressed to Bernhard von Clairvaux related to Mohammad a.s. In this letter, the ignorance and negation of the representatives of the Church towards all faiths and teachings not by classic Christianity can be seen.

The letter:

„ In the meantime, the devil, probably with the approval of that which is called "the frightening in his plans for the son of men" and "who has mercy towards whom he wishes and is stubborn if he wishes", helped the deception to be successful. He sent the monk Sergius /Waraqah/, a follower of the heretical Nestorius, who was exiled from the Church to those areas of Arabia and connected the heretic monk with the prophet of lies. Then Sergius /Waraqah/ taught Mohammad what he was lacking. He interpreted for him the Holy Scripture of the Old and the New Testament – more precisely, according to the understanding of his teacher Nestorius, who denies that our Saviour is God, which he followed by deeds and by his discretion. At the same time, he became entangled in the mythos of apocryphal scripture and finally made him a Nestorian Christian."[20]

---

[20] Bahira und Muhammad herausgabe Georg Dittrich Pleinfeld: https://heilig-land-wein.de/wordpress/wp-content/ uploads/2020/03/ PDF-Bahira-gesch%C3%BCtzt.pdf, retrieved 18/12/2022. Letter from Sergius von Cluny to Bernhard von Clairvaux

Monastery of Bahira, the monk in Busra, source:https://www.islamiclandmarks.com/syria/[21]

The amount of ignorance and hate of the Church fathers Petrus von Cluny and Bernhard von Clairvaux, already in the year 1141, towards Islam and Christian Nestorianism, a teaching which they knew nothing about, is astonishing. The two Church fathers thought that Waraqah made Mohammad. A Nestorian Christian, who finally certainly rejected the divine nature of Christ and made him only a messenger of God and a servant of God.

Nestorian Christianity, about Jesus, is completely identical to Arian Christianity. The main sequences of all heresies about the divine nature of Jesus are the same:

Because he was created and has his beginning, Jesus, for some heresies, cannot have a divine nature, while for others the nature of Jesus is dualistic, which means that he has both a human and a divine nature.

---

[21] Abu Huzaifa Monastery of Bahira the monk, https://www.islamiclandmarks.com/syria/monastery-of-bahira-the- monk, retrieved 13/12/2022.

The American Zionist, Richard Gottheil, wrote *A Christian Bahira legend* in 1989. In this legend, it is said that Mohammad a.s. Came to power through the help of the Hebrews, and decided to kill Bahira/Waraqah. When Bahira had understood the power of Mohammad, he went to him to remind him that he was his teacher. However, Mohammad denied that and claimed that an angel was teaching him; he reacted aggressively and secretly killed Bahira. These claims that Muhammad killed Waraqa and that he was in close contact with the Hebrews are arbitrary insinuations, thought up to create biases and hate towards the heretic monk Bahira/Waraqa and to present Muhammad a.s. as a false prophet.

Although said Catholic historians are negatively biased towards Arianism and Islam, they still offer us valuable information that sheds light on the theological closeness of those two faiths. The basic connection should be contained in the following:

Jesus is a human, and the Holy Trinity does not exist, at least not in the sense that the traditional doctrine preaches it.

We will list a few authors who wrote about the relationship between Arianism and Islam. They indicate a strong connection between these two religious worldviews from the very beginning.

Antun Vramec, in the book *Kronika vezda znovich zpravliena Kratka Szlouenzkim iezikom* (1578:27) writes that "Mahomet with the friar Sergius" started his religion.[22]

> 630. Mahomet zSergiufem fratrom vArabie Sara=
> czenzku i Turfzko vero i blud i nechiztochu za=
> chexta. I pozta vezda Sarzczenzkomu ladaniu
> zachetek, i bludu Turzkomu.
> Honorius pozta Papa Rimzki, ouoga Pape vre=
> mena Mahomet Vrafy Prorok iezt bil.

Excerpt from Antun Vramec's book

---

[22] Anton Vramec, 1578, Ljubljana https://upload.wikimedia.org/wikipedia/commons/e/e6/Vramecz_Antol_-_Kronika.pdf, 630.

Pavao Ritter Vitezović, in his work *Kronika aliti spomen vsega svieta vikov* (1696:52), says that "Mahomet, according to instructions by John Antiochen (of Antioch) and Sergius the Italian, or 'Llach monk, began writing the Al-Koran (the expression 'Llach, i.e., 'Wallach monk', refers to an Italian Arian monk). The Chaldeans and the other peoples followed him, and he named them Saracens."[23]

> 623 Heraklius Ceſar genuvsi vojſku na Persiance, Ceſa-
> raſtvo ſvoje i ſina jedinoga ùpregledbu i obrambu Ba-
> nu Abarſkomu preporucsi.
> Bonifacius peti ovoga imena Papom poſta. i odlucsi,
> ki bi Cslovek sto hudo ucsinil, terbi v̄ Cirkev vussel,
> dàga nemore nistor iz Cirkve ſillom vu n vzeti.
> Mahomet po napuchenju Ivanna Antiokena i Sergia
> Taliana aliti Laha Kalugyera Alkoran piſati pocse; i
> zapela krivim naukom Kaldeje i oſtale Narod e Aſian-
> ſke imenuvavsiih Saracene.

Excerpt from Ritter Vitezović's book

Saint John of Damascus (675–749), a great opponent of the Manicheans, Nestorians, in his book *About Heresies* dedicated an entire chapter to Islamic heresy: " This man (Mohammad), after having chanced upon the Old and New Testaments and likewise, it seems, having conversed with an Arian monk, devised his heresy. Then, having insinuated himself into the good graces of the people by a show of seeming piety, he gave out that a certain book had been sent down to him from heaven." He considered Islam and Arianism to be Christian heresies.[24]

Constantine Porphyrogenitus in the 14th chapter of the book *De Administrando Imperio* writes: "He (Mohammed) was believed because a certain Arian, who pretended to be a monk, testified

---

[23] Pavao Titter Vitezovic Kronika Aliti Spomen Vsega Svieta Vikov 1696, page 52, https://pdfslide.net/documents/kronika-aliti- spomen-vsega-svieta-vikov-1696.html, retrieved 09/12/2022.

[24] http://sveci.net/index.php/component/content/article/2-uncategorised/705-sveti-ivan-damascanski

falsely in his support for love of gain."[25]

In another example of the relationship between Islam and Christian representatives is via a person who has a special place in early Islam, the Abyssinian, Christian King Negus. The relationship between Mohammad a.s. and the fair King Negus, who saw no difference between the Islamic and his view of Isa a.s., is commonly known.

Memorial and mosque of the Christian King Negus, Ethiopia; and 15 graves of the as-sahabi (companions) of Mohammed a.s., source: Balkanis.com.

After he offered full support and protection for the Muslims, he drew a line in the ground with his staff, and said: "The difference between 'us' and 'you' is no wider than this line!". After the death of King Negus, Mohammad a.s. and other believers performed a funeral prayer, Salat al-Janazah, for the Christian king, when they find themselves near the memorial of King Negus and his followers (which is located in Ethiopia, Mek'ele, village of Negash), Muslim believers include in their prayers the fair Christian ruler Negus.

Once, as a child, Mohammad a.s. Together with Abu Talib went to

---

[25] https://ia601706.us.archive.org/10/items/cfhb-11.1-nicetae-choniatae-historia/CFHB%2001_Constantine%20VII_De%20 Administrando%20Imperio.pdf, page 77.

Damascus and at that time a Christian priest was preaching in a church, foretelling the arrival of a Prophet from the lineage of Ismail a.s. When he saw Mohammad a.s., he approached the child, looked at him, and said to Abu Talib that this child was possibly the Prophet a.s. and not to tell anyone, and especially not the Hebrews. Another legend about this event says the following: "When Mohammad a.s. was taken by Abu Talib with him on a trade journey to Shaam, they stayed in Basra, a city in which a priest nicknamed Bahira lived. As soon as he saw Mohammad a.s., he recognised him by his features and characteristics which were earlier revealed in the Holy books. He took the child by the hand and said: "This will be the prophet to all the world. Allah will send him as a mercy to all worlds." Abu Talib then asked: "He is the prophet to all the world. How do you know that?" He answered: "When you gazed from Aqaba, no stone, nor plant, nor tree, that did not perform sajdah, and they do not perform sejdah before anyone except the Prophet. I recognise him by the Seal of Prophethood – the birthmark above the upper cartilaginous bone, in the shape of an apple. I heard of him in our revelations." Bahira then asked Abu Talib not to go with him to Shaam, but to take him back home. He was afraid the Hebrews would harm him. And thus, Abu Talib with his men took Mohammad a.s. Back to Makkah.

A young Mohammed being recognized by the monk Bahira, detail; (source: From the book Jami' al-Tawarikh Compendium of Chronicles; Edinburgh University Library, Scotland).

In these examples, the closeness of Islam and Arianism in the time of the emergence of Islam can be seen.

Saint John Damascene (675–749), John of Damascus, inhabitant of the capital of the Caliphate, described the Saracens (Arabs) at the beginning of the 8th century as follows: „In the city there are also people who keep the cult of the Ishmaelites, the forerunner of the Antichrist, which prevails to this day. The people are descended from Ishmael, who was born to Abraham of Agar (their holiness Ibrahim a.s. and Hagar), and for this reason, they are called both Agarenes and Ishmaelites. But, they are also called Saracens, because Sara sent them away with empty hands, as Agar herself said to the angel: "Sara sent me with empty hands" (Genesis XXI, 10, 14). Those people then became worshippers of the morning star (Venus) and Aphrodite, who is in their language called Akbar or Chabar and means "great". They were recalcitrant idolaters to Heraclius, and then among them appeared a false prophet named Mohammed, who learned of the Old and New Testaments and seemingly converted, and then together with an Arian monk, they became heretics. Through flattery and hollow piety, he spread rumours among people that he received Holy scriptures from the sky. He founded some senseless doctrine and wrote it inside a book that became an object of veneration.

John Damascene here mentions Heraclius, the ruler of Byzantium, to whom Mohammed, a.s. sent his messenger with a call to accept monotheism.

In this, it can be seen that strict monotheism was present and known to the highest authority of the mighty empires of Byzantium and Rome the whole time, from Arianism to Islam.

Mohammad a.s. was awaited not only by Christians, but also the Hebrews, although they thought that he will be a man who will lead the Hebrew people into victory. When the Hebrews realised that the Prophet a.s. is calling the entire human race to join the faith, they distanced themselves from him.

Considering that Arianism, as a folk religion, was created under the auspices of monotheistic Judaism, the monotheism which Arianism endeavours to realise with its teaching is found in Islam. Thus, their relationship is natural, and it is unsurprising that many authors, foreign and domestic, pay special attention to the relationship between Islam and Arianism. Authors from our region could have written about this relationship only based on personal experience or experiences passed on to them. The motivation for authors from our region to deal with this theme could have come from Arians or members of the Bosnian Church who lived in the area of the early Illyrian Banates.

There are a few examples that illustrate this thesis, and one is expressed in the relationship between the Arabs and Saqaliba (Slavs) who encounter each other for the first time in the VI century in their joint incursions into the Byzantine Empire. At that time, Caliph Malik ibn Marwan attracted to his side around 20,000 Slavs (Skalampi-Saqaliba) – mercenaries from the Byzantine army, whom he, after they accepted Islam, resettled in the area surrounding modern-day Aleppo. On one occasion, Arabs and portions of South Slavs even besieged Constantinople together.

Staff of the didovi on a stećak; necropolis Radimlja, Stolac

A very interesting topic that is related in Bosnian takyas. Inspired by that legend, the journalist and writer, the late Enes Ratkušić, in his novel "Secret of the Bosnian Staff" relates the same to the attention of a wider readership, where he tells that in the time of the appearance of the prophet of God, Mohammed a.s., a group of forty Bosnian djeds, who were the tribal-spiritual elders of that time, prompted by their following of a religion which was, in the official circles of the Church in Rome, considered heresy, visited Arabia and familiarised themselves with the teaching foretold in the Holy scriptures.

Before their return, they were gifted a cane (staff) for them to safekeep, as a symbol of wisdom and dignity.

According to the same legend, the cane of the djeds, which is also represented on medieval stećci as well as grave markers (nišani), was handed to Sultan Mehmed Fatih by the Bosnian did, as a sign of handing over the spiritual and earthly rule into the hands of the Ottomans. During their retreat from Bosnia, Ottoman leaders returned the cane of the djeds to its spiritual authorities, and it was kept in Gazi Isa-bey's Takya, of the Mevlevi tariqa, located in Bentbaša, Sarajevo, up until it was levelled by the authorities of that time in the year 1957.

Since then, the staff is lost without a trace, or rather, the story about it and its fate from that point enters the area of esotericism, or a sacred secret."

Although we would love to and want to know the fate of the Bosnian staff of the djeds, even if we never discover it, we find its moral in the wise story about Musa a.s.: The wisdom and power lies not within the staff, but in the hand that holds it.

In the laid-out relations between Arianism, Islam, and Christianity, a strong connection between Arians and Muslims can be noticed, which the Church received with rejection, desiring all the time to discredit and destroy these religious movements. They were of the opinion that Islam was just a product of heretical Arianism.

The Catholic Church until up until the year 1500 was of the opinion that Muslims were heretics of Arius...

This connection is obvious in the area that then included the Banate and Kingdom of Bosnia, where the connection between Arianism and Islam is expressed in the transitional form of Arian stećci and Muslim gravestones, the nišani.

The old Bosniaks, former members of the Bosnian Church, by accepting Islam, transformed the stećak, which is part of their culture and tradition, into the nišan.

It is not uncommon for Muslim graveyards to be found in necropoleis of stećci or immediately adjacent to them. In the period of transition from stećci to nišani, a son who would have accepted Islam would have wanted to be interred next to his father, who had been a member of the Bosnian Church. Many early nišani are not oriented towards the Kaaba, but are, like the stećci adjacent to them, oriented in the direction of north–south, or NW–SE, or in the direction of east–west. And beneath some nišani there are dual graves.

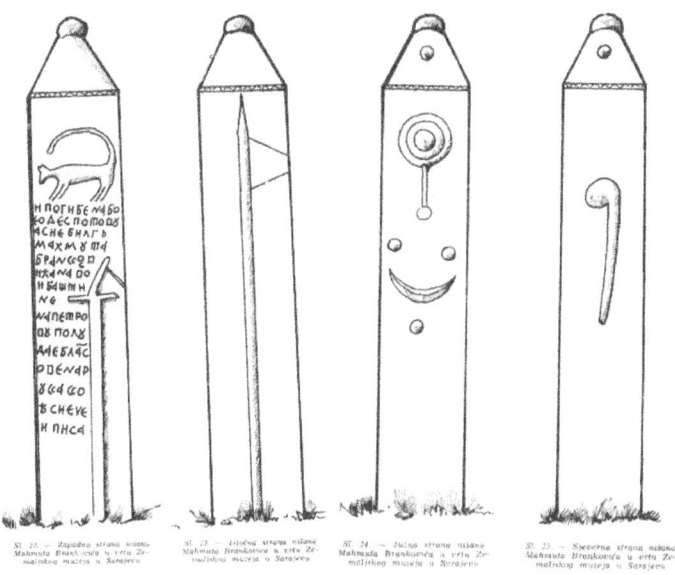

Nišan of Mahmut Branković from Rogatice; today it is located in front of the National Museum of Bosnia and Herzegovina in Sarajevo. Solar symbols, the cane of the djeds, and the apple as a symbol of the Prophet. The apple as a symbol is a phenomenon that is found on stećci as well.

Nišan in the graveyard Uvorići near Visoko. The Arian cross on a Muslim gravestone is another indicator that the cross on the stećak is not of Christian provenance. It is much older than Christianity, adopted as a symbol on stećci and nišani, and it evidences continuity. Photo. Husejn Smajlović

Necropolis Maculje, Novi Travnik

8 AVARS IN BOSNIA

With the fall of the Western Roman Empire in the year 476 under the rule of the eastern Goths, in the area of the modern-day state of Bosnia and Herzegovina, Roman rule disappeared. The sovereign authority over the newly emerged Gothic Empire was taken over by King Theodorich, who supplemented the foundations of the Roman civilisation, because he was a follower of a markedly tolerant variant of Christianity, known in history under the name Arianism, with great freedom and tolerance: freedom of confession for all religions and ethnic tolerance applied in the entire empire. During the middle of the 6th century (in the year 550), Justinian, Emperor of the Eastern Roman Empire (also known in history under the name Byzantine Empire or Byzantium), deposed the Gothic government, but only formally restored his rule over the soil which we nowadays know under the name Bosnia and Herzegovina.

The conflict between Avars and Carolingian Franks in the 9th century

Because of constant internal political upheavals, power struggles, because of wars and continuous pressure from other peoples, that empire did not have the power to really administer these distant, western and northern areas. Simultaneously with the fall of the Gothic Empire in the west, from the east, a people named Avars stepped onto the historic stage (in some sources they are also mentioned as Obri, Abaroi, or Varchonitai).

In that time, the eastern Goths of Arian faith retreat into Bosnia. With their arrival, through the Arian teaching and Arian churches, they achieved significant political influence. Considering that the Byzantine Empire in that area did not manage to attain absolute control, it can be assumed that Arian Goths, unofficially, with the native Illyrian–Roman dignitaries, filled this void and, practically on their own, tended the tasks of administration and organisation of living.

Meaning, with the fall of the Gothic Empire in the west, a people named the Avars stepped onto the scene from the east.

The Avars are a people from modern-day Dagestan and Azerbaijan, who, pressured by Gökturks, after the year 555, retreated towards the west and in the year 558 became allies to the Byzantine Empire. That means that they became citizens of Byzantium, and in the year 560, they defeated the Proto-Bulgarians near the Black Sea. Because of the constant persecution they faced from Gökturks, they continued moving towards the Balkans. In the opinion of many linguists, they spoke an Altaic language. A portion of them said in a Turkmen idiom, and the other in a Mongolian idiom. People called Kutrigurs, Tarniachs, Onogurs, and others, spoke in a Bulgarian-Turkic idiom. In the opinion of the well-known philologist Harald Haarmann, the Avars are of exclusively Turkic heritage. Anthropologically they are a very mixed people, with the Mongoloid and Europoid type being represented. Originally, they were a nomadic people, and later they proved to be excellent cattle farmers and agrarians. Pushed out by Turkmen tribes, sources say that in the year 552, around 20,000 warriors with their families headed west. In this military and civilian march in the year 558, towards a "New World", the Avars were joined by some smaller groups of Antes (who would become Slavs in the future).

The Greek historian Herodotus (around 484 BCE–425 BCE) in his work "Historia" noted, five hundred years before the historian Strabo, that the people called the Medes "settled the areas between the Danube and the Adriatic Sea" long before his time, and that the "Veneti (Venedi) were Illyrians" as well. Herodotus is mistaken here because, as we know today, it is certain that the Venedi were NOT Illyrians. With the incursion of Avars and Slavs across the Sava River, into the area inhabited by Illyrian tribes, mixing could have occurred, and is likely to have happened, as that is the natural course of any contact between different ethnic groups, but today we know – they are NOT Illyrian tribes' predecessors of Proto- Slavic Venedi.

And who, plainly speaking, were the Venedi?

The Byzantine historian of Gothic origin, Jordanes, in his book "Historia Gothorum," mentions that at the beginning of the 6th century, the Slavs settled the entirety of the lower reaches of the Danube. He indicated that Slavic peoples are of one blood and are divided into three names: Venedi, Sklavini, Antes, VI and VII centuries.

VENEDI – who settled the northern coast of the Baltic and the lands in the Visla, ANTES – occupied the area between the Dnieper and Dniester rivers. SKLAVINI – settled the lands between the Dniester, Tisza, and Danube in Dacia of Antiquity.

The Antes lived in a stateless area and a condition of statelessness on the enormous plains north of the Black Sea. Their realm approximately lay on the Don river basin to the east, on the middle and lower reaches of the Dniepr river, including the river mouth to the Black Sea, and to the Dniester river to the west.

The historian Jordanes categorises the Slavs and Antes as Wends. They own, as he writes, the land from the city of Lacus Mursianus on the Mursa river (called Maros), in central Romania, to the

Danaster (Dniester) river, and on the north to Weichsel (Vistula)."[26]

In the year 562, the Avar Khan Bajan managed to occupy the area of the Lower Danube, then on several occasions raided Frankish border regions. In a military alliance with the Langobards (Germanic–Gothic tribe from the area of the Elbe river) during the reign of King Alboin, the Avars managed to supplant the Gepids and take control over the Carpathian Basin.

After the Gothic Langobards moved to the area of modern-day Italy in the year 558, the Avars remained in the Pannonian Basin as the only rulers. A settling of the Wends happened in this area before, which is indicated by archaeological excavations of graves in Hennersdorf near Vienna. The Wends (who are, as we have seen, the predecessors of Slavs) had the obligation of paying taxes–tribute to the Avars. In the final phase of the Avar settling of Pannonia, assimilation with part of the remaining Gothic and Slavic tribes that were on that territory occurred.

In Pannonia, in the year 582, the Avars established a country from which they continued further conquering western Europe and the Balkans – the Avar Khaganate in this period was under the reign of Bayan Khan, the most powerful Avar ruler, most likely the strongest power in Europe as well.

---

[26] Walter Pohl: Die Awaren, C. H. Beck. 11/09/2015, p. 97.

Avar Khaganate, around 582–612

The second Avar siege of Sirmium (Sremska Mitrovica) lasted until the inhabitants had consumed all reserves of food. By conquering this strategically important city on the Sava River, the entirety of Byzantium was within reach for the Avar conquerors. The despair of the citizens of Sirmium is evident from one of the most well-known findings from that time. That is a brick which is kept in the Archaeological Museum in Zagreb, with an inscription reading: "God Christ! Save the city, repel the Avar, save the Roman/Byzantine Empire and the one who wrote this."

The Avar–Slav alliance and the role of Slavs in Avar conquests

As they expanded their empire, realising the benefit of subservience and their plundering, Slavic tribes joined the Avars. Here, the question of the role Slavs played in Avar conquests arises. We know that under Avar rule, the Slavs were a subordinate component, probably, predominantly or mostly, foot soldiers. They ventured into several raiding incursions across the Balkans, Italy, all the way to Thuringia (central part of modern-day Germany), together with the Avars. In those incursions, they set ablaze and levelled everything they encountered, which had importance for the peoples they encountered. Thus, in our region, for example, all Early Christian basilicas which were built by Gothic Arians in the period from the IV to the VI century were razed.

With the support of Slavs, in the year 626, the Avars unsuccessfully besieged Constantinople (modern-day Istanbul). After these campaigns they settled Hungary, Austria, Bajuwaren (Bavaria) – a province that at the time was much larger than today, then Czechia, Slovakia, Slovenia, and parts of Poland, Romania, Croatia, east to the Drina river, the northern part of Bosnia and Herzegovina, and Bulgaria; they settled the basin of the Drava river, north from the Sava river, the Danube river valley and the western Peloponnese.

For over 200 years, the Avars were a strong military factor between the Frankish and the Byzantine Empire. They exerted a strong influence on the development of large swaths of the continent because they settled the conquered pieces of land with loyal Slavs. In the relationship between the Avars and the Slavs, government was in the hands of the Avars, who were organisationally and probably by number the stronger element, while the lower-ranking jobs were given to Slavs, who had no knowledge, organisational skill, or experience in organising and maintaining an efficient administration.

The Avars crossed the Sava River in 602 and invaded the territory of modern-day Bosnia and Herzegovina. It is unlikely that we will ever know what happened during that time, because there are no extensive written reports on the events from this period. Relying on the archaeological material, which provides us with at least some insight into those events, it can be assumed that the incursion of Avars and Slavs into the Bosnian-Herzegovinian area was, to a considerable extent, suppressed by the natives.

The internal crisis in the Byzantine Empire in the first twenty or so years of the VII century made it possible for the Slavs to conduct massive plundering raids in key Byzantine centres in the Balkans. On the Adriatic coast, the Slavs levelled one of the most important Byzantine cities in the Balkans, Salona (modern-day Solin), a metropolis of the Roman province of Dalmatia, in the year 615; it was located near Split and was the religious and administrative centre of the province of Dalmatia.

The year 615 is usually taken to be the definitive end of the period of Antiquity in the Balkans. Seven years later, Slavs and Avars levelled Narona, and only a few coastal and island cities managed to defend themselves. The ruins of antique Narona are found 4 km west of Metkovići, in the village of Vid.

The Byzantines managed to defend the Greek city of Thessaloniki, although it was besieged by Slavs several times from the land and from the sea. The strongest attempt was in the year 617, when the Avars and the Slavs reached Thessaloniki, the Danube River mouth and the Black Sea.

During the reign of Khan Bayan, the Avars were so powerful that they forced the Frankish and the Byzantine Empire to pay taxes – tribute to them. They waged wars against Byzantium up until the year 626, that is, up until they successfully forced the Byzantine government to pay them peace tribute in the amount of 80,000 gold coins, and that amount was later raised to 200,000 gold coins. In this period, the Avars became the sole decisive factor on the northern border of the Byzantine Empire.

On old Illyrian hillforts and some distorted interpretations of historic facts about the relationship between the Avars and the Slavs[27]

Many authors (especially Serb and Croat ones), when writing about these topics, emphasise the Slavic settling of our region. "Our region" includes the area of modern-day Bosnia and Herzegovina and the coastal regions. However, genetic research about the origin of individual peoples has shown that in the territory of Bosnia and Herzegovina, as well as Dalmatia, the emphasized percentage of Slavs is far smaller than what has persistently been claimed in the

---

[27] Text available under the main title Avars in Bosnia, authors Suad Haznadarević, Emir Medanhodžić, on the web page htttps://www. otisci.net/avari-u-bosni/ 20/10/2020, and the same text was retrieved from the portal http://bosanskipogledi. com/2022/10/20/kraljevstvo- barbara-pojava-uspon-i-nestanak-avara/

past 200 years.

It can often be noticed in the literature that the role of the Avars and the Slavs is equated; in an associative manner, without factual evidence, the implied conclusion is that they inhabited en masse the area west of the Drina River and south of the Sava River. While in fact, in the time that is being discussed, the Slavs invaded that area together with the dominant Avars. Meaning, the Proto-Slavic groups of peoples – the Venedi, Antes, Sklavini, north of the Sava river, enter an alliance with the Avars, for plundering (typical for so-called military economies, which are dominant up until the modern era and the industrial revolution), they venture into military campaigns, and thus also cross the Danube, Sava, and Drina rivers, and invade Illyricum; but the Avars remain the dominant force in that alliance and in that area.

In contrast to the Avars, who, after the military campaigns, tend to return to the Pannonian and Carpathian areas, the Slavs show a tendency for settling the conquered Roman (Byzantine) area, where, with time, they gradually entered into interaction (e.g., economic exchange, afterwards also mixing) with the native population. A similar course took place in Greece and the Peloponnese, where the Slavs either assimilated or moved away from that area.

There certainly were also Avar groups that preferred to settle the conquered areas, than return to the Pannonian Basin. We find their traces today in the toponyms of a series of places derived from the name Obri (i.e. Avars), such as: Obre near Kakanj, Obrovac, Oborci near Donji Vakuf, Oboračka river, Obroni Vrat (between Gornji Vakuf and Rama; Šćit), Oborska kosa (Busovača mountain), Obronica near Trnovo.

However, the Illyrian population and their nobles, who did not want to submit to the new Avar rule and Avar persecution, hid in the mountainous and highland areas of modern-day Bosnia and Herzegovina. In the hilly and hard to conquer, one could say impenetrable and almost unconquerable mountains, they come together and erect (build, establish, create) new hillforts as a protection against the invasion of Avars; (from those fortifications they could efficiently resist the invasion and attacks by the Avars, who were not adept at mountain warfare).

Even before that, we know that the Goths established a political centre from which their nobles reigned in the territory of modern-day Bosnia and Herzegovina. A form of state organisation also emerged, under whose rule the native Illyrians and the integrated Goth immigrants participated. The state was divided into banates, and the ruler held the title of king. Bosnia was divided into upper or mountainous Bosnia and lower or flat Bosnia.

Therefore, it could be concluded that from the 7th century up until 1166, Bosnia was independent from Byzantium.

It is well-known that, when travelling through Bosnia and Herzegovina, all over, in almost every city, one can find at least one city from the Middle Ages. However, our hills also hold the ruins of many Illyrian hillforts, which, because of their dilapidation and inaccessibility, almost became forgotten.

Husref Redžić researched medieval cities and published them in the book *Srednjovjekovni gradovi u Bosni i Hercegovini (Medieval Cities in Bosnia and Herzegovina)*, where he documented 149 old towns.

It is important to add to this the very important research which has been and is still being conducted by a co-author of this text, an enthusiast and expert for history, the researcher Emir Medanhodžić, who with each new day informs us about forgotten cities from the period of the Illyrian state and the Early Middle Ages, of which there are a great many who have not been written about in the book by Husref Redžić.

All those hillforts from the Early and High Middle Ages were built on the foundations of old Illyrian hillforts, which in a certain manner evidences the conciousness about the heritage of, now we can already say "Bosniaks", because in the period of the Early Middle Ages under these conditions the Bosniaks had profiled themselves and the oldest early feudal state in the Balkans, the Banate of Bosnia was created.

Avarian Dagh – ancient swastika used by the Avars as well, source – en.wikipedia.org

We find precise descriptions and interpretations of our region in the works by the historian Strabo (57 BCE–25 CE), a Greek from Cappadocia (old Medean Katpatuka). In his work *Geographikon evdomon*, while describing the Illyrian state, he wrote down important data about the indigenousness of the Illyrian population and their very advanced civilisation.[28]

The Illyrian lands, according to his writing, extend between the Alps, the Danube, and the Adriatic Sea, and to the east until the Scordus Mountain (Šar Mountains) (VII, 5,1). All of this area is called Pannonia (VII, 5, 2). Strabo lists the Illyrian tribes which existed in his time: the Breuci, Andizetes, Ditiones, Pirustae, Mazaei, Daesitiates, and to the south of them, the Dalmatae, and the Ardiaei (VII, 5, 3). Those tribes lived in the area of modern-day Bosnia and its surroundings.

When we draw onto the geographic map of modern-day Bosnia, including the surrounding regions, the places where Illyrians lived, we will see that their provinces consisted of the same veležupas as in the time of the Kotromanić dynasty.

A special and very important claim that the historian Strabon makes is as follows: "Despite all advantages provided by the Illyrian coast, up until recently, strangers did not venture there, be it because of ignorance of those regions, be it because of common piracy. The interior of the land is mountainous, cold, and snowy..."[29] From what has been stated, it can be concluded that the area of Illyria, regardless under whose administration it was, of the Roman Empire, the Gothic Empire, the Avars or Byzantium, it managed to maintain its governmental organisational structure and de facto autonomy.

The friar Cacich–Miossich from Brist – friar Andrija Kačić–Miočić, clearly lists Illyrian Banates in his *poskočica* poem, which can be sung in the *kolo* circle dance, contained in his book *Razgovor ugodni naroda slovinskoga* (A Pleasant Conversation of the Slavic People):

---

[28] All cited passages are available in the book Strabo, Geography, Book VII H.C. Hamilton, Esq., W. Falconer, M.A., Ed. on the web address:
http://www.perseus.tufts.edu/hopper/text?doc=Perseus%3Atext%3A1999.01.0239%3Abook%3D7

[29] Strabon, Geographikon evdomon VII, 5, 10

Slidi poskocnicza kojase mozsce u`kollu pjevati;

Slavna Bosna Dalmatia

Iliricka darxavaje (država je)................. Ligonia Alania

Ravna lika i karbava Iosc i lipa Arbanija Iliricka iest darzava

Plodna zemlja Pomeranska i Goria jose suvisce Banovina a i kragnska Slavnogh Puka vazda bisce Vesselise Maiko jaka

Ilirickii vitezova

Dassi punna tii junaka Svitli Bana i knezova;

The poet and historian Fra Andrija Kačić Miošić introduces certain uncertainties in the descriptors of peoples, by also including the Goths, Avars, and Illyrians as Slavic tribes, which is used by frivolous authors and Pan-Slavists to include Illyrian Banates as Slavic ones.

In analysing the remains of the earlier societal structure concerning Bosnian medieval society, the historian Sima Ćirković notes: "Society in Bosnia developed in relative freedom of foreign pressure, and in it the continuity of Slavic societal relations and forms of social organisation can be best seen".[30]

Without the intention to categorise Sima Ćurković as Pan-Slavist, said thought matrix can be seen in this example.

Another quote from the book by the poet and historian Fra Andrija Kačić Miošić:

"Other Slavs named Avars, or Obri, or Abars, to the other side of the Danube into the lands of the Slavs, which they conquered, and grew

---

[30] Sima Ćirković Istorija srednjovjekovne bosanske države; Belgrade, 1964, Chapter one, Obrazovanje Bosanske države, p. 21.

very powerful.[31]

There is still confusion which was introduced by Kačić into the interpretation of the settling of Slavs in the territory of Illyria, and which, during the emergence and strengthening of the nationalist idea among Serbs and Croats, were useful to Croatian and Serbian historiographers (in actuality ideologists of nationalism) to write and convey history to future generations not based on facts, but through an emphasised nationalistic vision. Here are some examples of that:

In the year 584, the Slav Avars destroyed Zemun near Dunav and many other lands. In the year 585, the Slav Avars captured the Edirne.

In the year 591, said Avars attacked Dalmatia and caused many evils. In the year 592, said Avar Slavs caused great evils in the Eastern Lands.

In the year 599, the Slav Avars have destroyed forty cities in Dalmatia.[32]

Based on available archaeological material, the natural conclusion is that the Avar invasion of the Bosnian-Herzegovinian territory was successfully suppressed by the domestic Illyrian, native population. Many historians relinquish the Avar rule, which was established on the conquered area, in an inexplicable manner, so to speak silently, to the Slavs, to justify the theory of Slavicisation and Slavic influence in the formation of the first Banates in Illyria. Thus, instead of Avar rule (which is the historical truth), in literature we find Slavic rule over the territory of Illyricum (which does not correspond to the historical truth). Because, if we know that the Slavs were organisationally and as a civilisation subordinate to the Avars, then it is hard to accept the claim that in the end the Avars entrusted them with ruling. The truth is, and the consensus in objective, non-biased, call it democratic Western science, is: The Avars were key for, so

---

[31] Fra Andrija Kačić Miošić; Razgovor ugodni naroda slovinskoga, from the year 564.

[32] Fra Andrija Kačić Miošić; Razgovor ugodni naroda slovinskoga

to speak, introducing Proto-Slavic tribes on the historical stage, on which they developed and shaped themselves into the Slavic people. Exactly as the Huns caused the movement of Germanic (Gothic) groups and their development into their political forms before, so the Avars were the historic force that caused the movement and development of Proto-Slavic tribal groups into a new ethnic (and political) form of a people, which history today calls the Slavs.

Speaking plainly, we are of the opinion that the term "Slavic lands" emerges in historiography only after the dissolution of the Avar state, the disappearance and assimilation of the Avars (which will be discussed in the following portion of this work). Thus, for example, the Arab travel writer Abu Hamid al-Gharnati al-Andalusi, born near Granada in al-Andalus (Andalusia), modern-day Spain, in 1080, died in 1170 in Damascus in Syria, we find the term "Land of the Slavs". In his travelogue concerning The Land of Saqaliba (Slavs), on his boat journey over the Danube and Sava rivers, he wrote the following: "I entered the land of the Saqalibs from Bulgaria. I came by boat, down the stream of a large river, which is called the Slavic river, whose water is as black as the Atlantic Ocean (Bahru'dh- dhalam), as if the color of ink."

The conflict between Avars and Carolingian Franks in the IX century[33]

Having captured many cities, the Avars were collecting yearly taxes of a hundred thousand golden ducats. The Slavs did not settle the Banates of Hum, Travunia, Bosnia and Konavle, as is sometimes presented, but the domestic rulers under the supervision of Avars, were forced to pay annual taxes. The Avars that settled in Illyria are mentioned for the last time in Dalmatia and 950.

After the Bavarian Duke Tassilo III was dethroned, the rule over the Frankish Empire was taken over by Charlemagne in the year 791,

---

[33] Text available under the main title Avars in Bosnia, authors Suad Haznadarević, Emir Medanhodžić, on the web page https://www. otisci.net/avari-u-bosni/ 20/10/2020, and the same text was retrieved from the portal http://bosanskipogledi. com/2022/10/20/kraljevstvo- barbara-pojava-uspon-i-nestanak-avara/

who after long preparation went to war against the Avars in the year 795. At that point, a conflict about the division of power breaks out among the Avars. In that conflict, the two main leaders, Chagan and Lugurs, were killed, while the (presumed) third son of Bayan, Tudun, takes the power over a large swath of the Avar Empire.

He made a peace offer to the Franks, but they rejecteid his offer, and in the same year, 795, the Frankish army, led by margrave Eric of Friuli and the Italian King Pippin, begins its campaign against the Avars. The decisive attack happened between 795 and 796, when the main Avar centre, on the Balaton Lake (in modern-day Hungary); which was a typical Avar settlement, a so-called "Avar hring", was conquered together with their "treasure". According to some sources, the amount of treasure was huge, and because of that, twelve carts pulled by four oxen each were required to transport it.

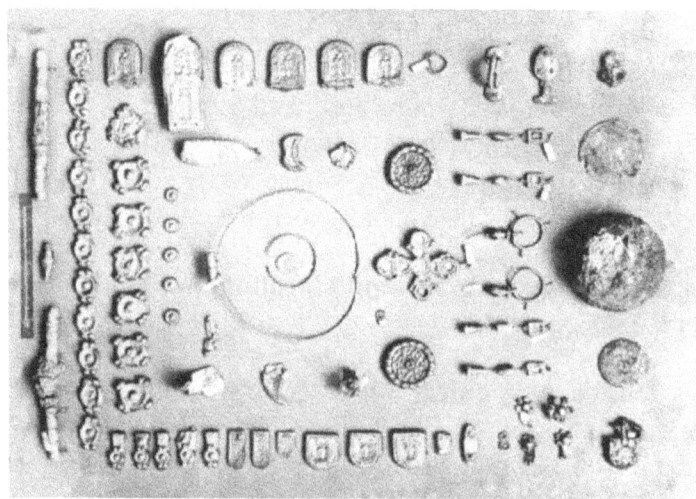

Avar ornamentation; finding from Hungary.

In 796, Tudun was forced to pay taxes to Charlemagne and to sue for peace again, with the addition of this time being ready to accept Christianity to save the state. The following years, from 797 to 799, were marked by war between the Avars and Franks (allied with the Bulgar Khan Krum), and revolt by the portion of Avars who did not accept Tudun as their leader, which in the year 803 struck the final blow against this empire. That year is considered to be the year when the Avars disappeared from the military and political stage of history.

Thus, exactly 200 years after their appearance on the stage of history, the empire of the Avars was destroyed, never to appear again, neither that people nor that empire. A portion of the Avars was baptised and they lived as agrarians in the eastern part of the Frankish Empire, in modern-day Hungary, where they are mentioned up until the year 850.

After the dissolution of their state, the Avars were assimilated by the peoples on whose territory they were settled. This is also supported by the latest human genetic research showing a genetic relatedness of a portion of the population on the island of Hvar with portions of the population of the Caucasus. We find this connection also in language, for example in the case of the surname Badrov, which today can be found in Croatia, Bosnia and Dagestan.

Little is known about the Avar way of life. We know they built their settlements near rivers which they used as sources of fresh water, but also as a natural defensive barrier. They also had fertile land for cattle grazing and farming, as well as forests which they used for hunting wildlife.

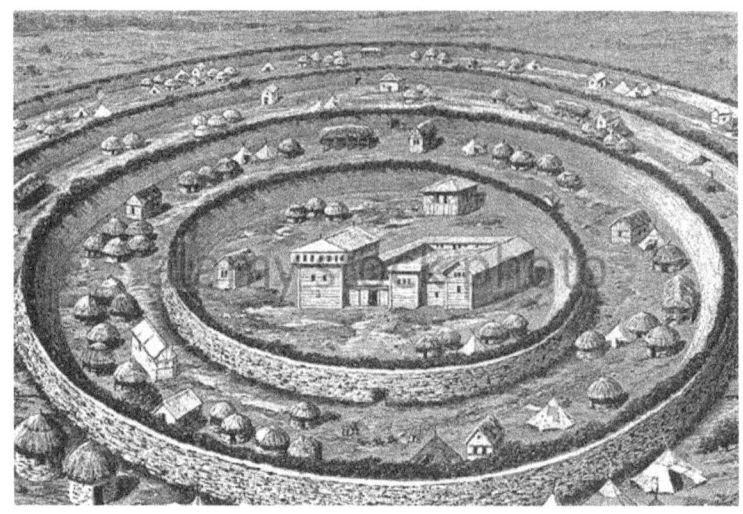

Avar ring-shaped settlement. In the Early Middle Ages, the Avars were a powerful European power whose centre of govrnment was in the Pannonian Basin.

We learn at least somewhat about the Avar culture from discovered Avar gravesites, because they were buried in their regular clothes, and that they would leave the deceased person's weapons with them.

Until now, in the entire territory of the Pannonian Basin, over 80,000 Avar graves were found, of which more than 600 in the territory of Croatia. Many Avar remains, more precisely remains of the Avar-Slavic culture, were found in the valley of the Danube River and in Croatia (Sisak). Well-known sites include Biskupija near Knin, Smrdelj near Skradin, and necropoleis and individual graves in the interfluvial region between Sava and Drava, and one grave was found in 2019 in Šarengrad near Ilok.

The largest Avar graveyard in Croatia is located near Privlaka, and, aside from the already mentioned graveyard in Šarengrad, those in Nuštar, Otok, Stari Jankovci, Brodski Drenovac, and Bijelo Brdo are also well-known. Aside from those larger researched graveyards, some individual findings, such as those in Osijek, Zmajevac, and Bapska, were also found.

Important Avar findings outside Pannonia are found in modern-day Bulgaria (Bononia-Vidin), Slovenia (Ljubljana and Celje), Austria (Zollfeld, Linz, Enns, Melk, St. Pölten in Lower Austria and Burgenland) and in the Czech Republic.

In the period of Avar-Slavic domination in Europe, on the soil of Bosnia and Herzegovina, no archaeological remains of Avars or Slavs were discovered.

The destruction of the Avar Khaganate was followed by a period in which the Byzantine Empire still did not have control over the area of modern-day Bosnia and Herzegovina and Dalmatia. In this period, the previously established Banate of Bosnia develops freely, without foreign influence.

Belt buckle of a high-ranking Avar soldier

Considering that in this area Arian Christianity was already accepted and found fertile soil, presumably, all things considered, the central government of the banates that were formed later, such as Travunia, Hum, Konavle, the Neretvan Banate, and others, could have been located in the Bosnian Banate.

Necropolis Maculje, Novi Travnik

Bosnia And Illyrian Banates Between The Franks And Byzantium

After the Avars entered the Balkans and became allies to the

Byzantine Empire in the year 558, they positioned the centres of their state, in the process of establishing government (from 562 to 568) in the Pannonian Basin, or the Roman Illyrian province of Pannonia; large parts of modern-day Austria and Hungary. The flatlands which were easily arable and were very conductive to the development of herding and agriculture were suited to the habits and skills of the Asian horse riders. Thus, the entire Pannonian Basin, with the main centre of the Avar state by the Hungarian Lake Balaton, was under their influence.

Unfortunately, although it is known where the capital of the Avar Empire could have been located, it has still not been discovered. By the end of the VI century, with the establishing of the Avar Khaganate, the collapse of Roman (Byzantine) rule over the entire Illyrian area began. The central government in Constantinople did not have the power to assert itself because it was constantly waging war in other regions to the east. This is also a time of the local Illyrian communities gaining relative, conditional independence, and creating a political organisation under Avar patronage.

Pannonia Roman province of Illyricum;
*source:https://hr.wikipedia.org/wiki/Dalmacija_(rimska_*
provincija)

Throughout the area of Illyria, from Istra to Bulgaria, territorial units were organised, which were essentially Illyrian tribal organisational structures, adopted from administrative and territorial organisations the of the Roman, Gothic, and Byzantine periods of Late Antiquity. Such units are simultaneously the political core. The representatives of smaller entities within the territorial units were Župans, and the representatives of the most important and likely larger ones – Bans. According to many authors, the names Ban/Bayan/Banate/ Banovina, Kagan, Župan/županija come from the Avar language. The control over finances and collection of yearly taxes lay in the hands of a chosen caste of Avar representatives, while other governmental powers were in the hands of the local nobility. This stems from the reason that the Avars, because of their relatively small population and them being concentrated in the centre of the country, could not control the entire conquered area. As in other empires, the Roman, Ottoman, or Austro-Hungarian empire, the Avar system of government also would return to individual parts of the empire only if there was a need to re-establish rule over them. Following the collapse of the I Avar Khaganate and their retreat into the territory above the Sava River, these units became completely independent, strengthening their political individuality and legal subjectivity, which lead to the formation of separate indigenous units of people. The creation of new territorial units mainly took place according to larger or smaller geographic entities (Bosnia, the Neretvan region, Konavle, Travunia, Usora, Dalmatia, etc.).

The Greek historian Strabo (57 BCE–25 CE) in his work *Geographikon evdomon* gave the most precise and exhaustive descriptions of the area in which Bosnia is located today. Strabo worked as an advisor and notary of Roman rulers, and he was very well acquainted with the situation within and outside the Roman Empire. He recorded important data about Illyria and the indigenousness of the Illyrian population and their superior civilisation.

Greek geographer, philosopher, and historian Strabo; en.wikipedia, original scan from the book André Thevet Les vrais pourtraits et vies des hommes illustres, chap 35, page 76. (Portraits from the Dibner Library of the History of Science and Technology.)

The land of the Illyrians, according to Strabo, extends between the Alps, the Danube and the Adriatic Sea, and towards the east to the Scardus Mountains (Šar Mountains).[34] The area of Illyria was called Pannonia at that time.[35] He writes that, besides Pannonia in extenso, there exists Pannonia strictu senso. In his description of the central part of Pannonia, Strabon lists the Illyrian tribes that lived there in his time, and those are: the Breuci, Andizetes, Ditiones, Pirustae, Mazaei, Daesitiates, and to the south of them, the Dalmatae, and the Ardiaei (VII, 5, 3). Those tribes lived in the area of modern-day Bosnia and the areas surrounding it. Strabo states that, despite all the benefits of the Illyrian coast, it is unknown to foreigners, who rarely venture there because of piracy. The interior of Illyria is mountainous, cold, and snowy.[36] Strabo says that the great Illyrian military leader Bato was a member of the Daisitihat tribe. The Romans waged war against the Illyrians for almost two hundred years in their attempt to subjugate them. Pannonia stricto sensu, i.e. Bosnia, succesfully resisted Tiberius' legions. The war ended with a non-aggression pact negotiated between Bato and Tiberius in the year 9 CE. Pannonia strictu senso, the area of modern-day Bosnia, was not colonised but was added to the Roman Empire, "socius nomini romani", that did not pay tribute (taxes) which other lands conquered by weapons and force. Here it should be noted that Illyria, although it wanted to join the ranks of Pagan areas, still had a high level of development, which is evidenced by many fortifications and tumuli, the legacy of the ancient Illyrian civilisation which found its place also in the south of modern-day Italy, which was inhabited by the Illyrian Messapian tribe. Many emperors of the Roman Empire came from our Illyrian region; Aurelius, Probus, Diocletian, Constantine, Decius!

---

[34] Strabo, Geographikon evdomon (VII, 5,1)
[35] Strabo; Geographikon evdomon (VII, 5, 2)
[36] Strabo, Geographikon evdomon VII, 5, 10

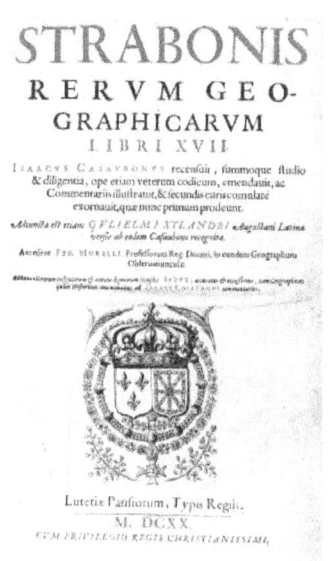

Title page of Isaac Casaubon's 1620 edition of Geographica, (a geographic encyclopaedia of 17 books, written in Greek, which are thought to have been written by Strabo and anonymous educated citizens of the Roman Empire.

We encounter the name "BASSANIA" for Bosnia for the first time in the Roman military manual *"Antonini itinerarium"*[37] from the III century of the current era, in the meaning – region in Lower Pannonia. It is a list of the most important Roman imperial roads and cities. The word "Bassania" can be found in various contexts in other works and inscriptions from Antiquity, with slightly altered pronunciation or orthography. Here we conclude that throughout history, Bosnia was mentioned as a territorial, separate unit. The first ruler of Bosnia that is mentioned in written sources is Ban Stjepan of Bosnia, who ruled from 1084 until 1095. After Stjepan, the names of Bosnian rulers are regularly mentioned in documents. The next known ruler was Ban Borić, who, presumably, was born in the year 1100 and ruled over Bosnia until the year 1163. The second written mention of Bosnia is by the *Greek chronicler Theophanes (Theophanes Homologetes, born around 760 in Constantinople; † 12 March 818 in exile on the island of Samothrace). Although he participated in the II Council of Nicaea in 787, where, in terms of theology, he took a stance as a clear opponent of iconography and the representing of the Divine in human form, which is especially close to the Arian, Paulician, and later Protestant relation with icons; in 815 he was sentenced to two years of exile on the Greek island of Samothrace. Despite all of that, Theophanus is revered as a saint both in Catholicism and in Orthodox*

---

[37] Itinerarium Antonini (full title: Itinerarium provinciarum Antonini Augusti) is a list of the most important Roman imperial roads, which also lists Roman settlements. It was created in its basic form at the beginning of the 3rd century of the current era (Antonin that is mentioned in the title is Emperor Caracalla), the manuscript version was transmitted towards the end of the century under Diocletian. Hans Bauer: Die römischen Fernstraßen zwischen Iller und Salzach nach dem Itinerarium Antonini und der Tabula Peutingeriana. Neue Forschungsergebnisse zu den Routenführungen. Utz, München 2007.

Christianity.

"Theophanis crhonographia", recensuit Carolus de Boor, Lipsiae. In his chronicle, Theophanes recorded that Bosnia bore its name since the 7th century, and that is the record which first mentions Bosnia in written form as a separate state-like community. It acts as a banate within a wider community comprised of seven banates. Based on this record, it is justified to posit the thesis that those banates, and thus Bosnia as well, must have emerged far sooner.

Theophanes Homologetes

Some authors try to place this community of banates under the crown of the Kingdom of Croatia, which is very illogical. In the entire period from the arrival and establishment of the Gothic government, through the time of the Avar Empire, and up until the Franks, these states were directly ruling over these areas. After the fall of the Avar state and the invasion of the Pannonian Basin by the Franks, many parts of modern-day Croatia remained under the influence of the Frankish state and Charlemagne, while Dalmatia,

Bosnia, and the southern banates up to the Drina River are positioned in the interspace between two empires, Byzantium and the Frankish Empire. Exactly because of that, from the northwestern areas, Arians and all those who did not accept Frankish baptism, found sanctuary in Bosnia; in the creation of the first Illyrian banates. According to Theophanes, all Bans act within their banates sovereignly, joined into a single geopolitical or strategic military community. From this document, it can be concluded that the Bosniaks or Bosnians are a native, indigenous people that has been living for millennia on their ancestral land. They used to be Illyrians, and because of the arrival in our area of some peoples, such as the Goths, the Celts, the Slavs, in this period, a symbiosis, melting, unifying and filtration of different cultures and religions happens, and a new specificum in the name Bosnia and its Good Bosniaks emerges! Theophanes called this community the Croatian Kingdom, which cannot be correct. The Croats, as immigrants, emerged and, because of power and political interest, as converted Arians, were infiltrated by the Franks in the interest of the Pope, and under their influence, which does not correspond to the interests of the other Illyrian Arian banates. Thus, interpretations of an early Croatian Kingdom whose rule extends to Raška by Croatian historians cannot be correct. If we examine the number and quality of constructions of old cities, or as is their proper name *gradine*, in Bosnia, and based on the concentration of members of the Arian faith in the banate of Bosnia, in Pagania, Rama, and Zachumlia, we may arrive at the opposite conclusion, that is, that the centre of power of the newly emerging Illyrian banates could have been located only and exclusively in Bosnia. New hillforts were built on top of old Illyrian cities. Here it should be added that historiography, when determining the age of hillforts, starts from the dates which are found on charters and other documents, which gives a false impression of the age of the buildings. Thus, an impression of them being built in the Middle Ages is created, which is not necessarily correct. Aside from that, the cultural and religious indigenousness of the Illyrian population relative to their surrounding, in which the changing rule of different empires changed the structure of the population, created the prerequisite for autonomous governmental organisation. Only a few hundred years later, with the creation and unification of territories under Bosnian administration, was governmental power expressed in the title of Ban, and after King Tvrtko, from the Cetina River to the Drina River, and beyond, from the Sava River to the Adriatic Sea.

Aside from these facts, it is especially important to note the simultaneous development and influence of Arianism, which, since its inception with the exile of Arius to Illyria, after the Council of Nicaea, and the Goths accepting Arianism en masse, found fertile soil among the indigenous Illyrian population. Although the Arian Church in Bosnia was subject to different pressures and worldviews, it persisted and became the cornerstone of the future Bosnian Church or Bosnian Hiža. In the territory of modern-day Bosnia and Herzegovina, until now, over fifty Arian religious buildings which, for different reasons, are called Early Christian basilicas. By unifying all these elements, adding to them a strong economy and trade, all requirements are fulfilled for the creation of a powerful state which, despite many sacrifices and devastations, successfully resisted all misfortunes and enemies.

Theophanes' chronicle in rough translation would be: *"If a ban of any of these seven Slavic provinces – banates – would die without any sons, then his vacant position of ban would be filled by vote of all seven bans, i.e. the Croatian Ban – the first voter, the Bosnian Ban – the second, the Ban of Slavonia – the third, the Ban of Požega – the fourth, the Ban of Podrama – the fifth, the Ban of Arbania – the sixth, and the Ban of Sirmium – the seventh voter."*[38]

So, in this chronicle by Theophanus, the first written mention of Bosnia, where the word Bosnian is used as an adjective, refers to

---

[38] https://bosnjaci.net/prilog.php?pid=66850 pristupljeno 17.februar 2023

the Banate of Bosnia. So, those seven bans are sovereigns in their banates and are joined in a geopolitical community who, and when the need arises, choose one of those seven bans, but also when needed choose the Khan – Ban of all seven banates, as is written in this document.

Theophanes does not mention banates in which the indigenous population has remained to the largest extent, which has not been mixed to that extent with the newly arrived Avars and Slavs, and those are the banates of Zahumlia, Travunia, the Neretvan Banate, Pagania, and Konavle! These banates, together with the Banate of Bosnia, are the main bearers of the political, cultural, and religious (Arian) heritage of the Illyrians and the Goths, who left their ethnic, genetic trace exactly in the areas of Bosnia and Dalmatia. Aside from this fact, in historic records, the trade relations of Bosnia with Dalmatia, Ragusa, and lands across the sea, which at the time were Byzantium and the lands of the Maghreb region, are dominant!! Thus, we can posit the thesis that at that time, a policy of attempted assimilation and crushing of the territories in which Arianism had a staunch presence was implemented, so there is an attempt to link the regions with strong Illyrian heritage to the imposed social castes of Christian Horvats and Suurbs and the banates over which they ruled. As historical facts tell one thing, and the records of historians another, from Theophanes we will take as an important fact his mentioning of Bosnia in his chronicle, which was created in Constantinople between 760 and 818.

The third mention of the Banate of Bosnia is of a later date. It is associated with Emperor Constantine VII Porphyrogenitus, who compiled *"De administrando imperio" (On the Administration of the Empire)* between 948 and 952. The data from chapters 29–36, which concern the history of Southeast Europe up until the time of Constantine Porphyrogenitus. In this work, we find mention of Bosnia (in written form) and its inhabited cities, paraphrased: and in Bosnia, there are two cities, Katera and Desnik. The town of Katera is most likely the place called Kotarac near Butmir/Ilidža/Sarajevo. To this day, in Kotarac, there is a ruin of a hillfort, which evidences the tumultuous history of Bosnia. In the true sense of the word, this is the second mention of Bosnia, which links its existence to the Middle Ages, while Theophanes' mention reaches further back into the past, into Late Antiquity. Strabo's mention of Bassania (Bosnia), which is at the same time the oldest, and based on the next two sources, Theophanes and Porphyrogenitus, as much as archaeologists, historians, and anthropologists question their data, are still unavoidable facts that speak about Bosnia as an independent sociopolitical organisation! Having in mind that the largest percentage of contemporary historians question the validity of Porphyrogenitus's mention of a small land called *"Bosona"*. Most likely, the changes and insertion of modern knowledge in his work *On the Administration of the Empire* emerged in the well-known copies created at the end of the 11th century, which were commissioned by the Byzantine co-regent, Emperor Jovan Duka (1059–1088), and copied by his scribe, Michael. The Byzantine Empire collapsed when it fell to the Turkish Sultanate (May 1453). By some miracle, this literary work was preserved. The next copying of this work was done by a Greek named Antonios Eparhus (1491–1571).

The Council of Duvno

The story about the Council of Duvno takes place when Bosnia and Dalmatia were surrounded by two large empires, Byzantium and the Frankish Empire, which was under the influence of Rome and the Pope. It is absurd to believe that the Franks, although powerful, intended to wage exhausting wars against Byzantium because the Arab conquests of Spain, the Mediterranean and the coastal regions of the Adriatic Sea and southern Italy were in full swing. The Franks were too preoccupied with their war against the Germanic Saxons and the Arabs, who were streaming in from the south of Spain. To the east, the Byzantine Empire was preoccupied with its wars against the Bulgarians and Persia. What could have been in the interest of the Franks and the Pope was a certain degree of influence in the area of Illyria. They could have achieved that only through peaceful means, via the Church and attempts to convert the domestic Arian population. In that sense, much data has been fabricated which has been copied through history, and such is "the Council of Duvno",

"The Croatian Chronicle" and "The Chronicle of the Priest of Duklja".

Tibor Živković sets out from the premise that with medieval historical works, there is always someone commissioning them from the category of high-ranking figures, often rulers, and says: *"History in the Middle Ages is not only a literary work, but, more often, a political tool. In fabricated genealogies, events, and acts, someone can honour one dynasty or noble family, and derogate or unfavourably represent the opposing one. A medieval writer of a history does not question what the truth is, but what he believed to be true, or what the desirable truth for him or for the person that commissioned his work is."*[39]

As Dr. Luka Jelić, in his analysis titled "Duvanjski sabor" (Council of Duvno), indicates and demonstrates the intertwining and relations between the Chronicle of the Priest of Duklja, the Croatian Chronicle, and the Council of Duvno. These writings were created centuries one after another, without either the author or the time of creation of the source, the "Croatian Chronicle", being known. Without delving further into the text itself, it can be assumed that this is a fabricated history, supported to a large extent by fake documents, created because of the need to honour one thing and deny the other. In this case, what has been rejected are the Illyrian banates which emerged during the Avar Empire, and what has been glorified is the Croatian Kingdom, which was attempting to encircle and convert the centre of Illyria and the independent banates which emerged in the territories of modern-day Bosnia, Herzegovina, and Dalmatia. On the other side is the "Chronicle of the Priest of Duklja", with which it was attempted to give importance to the ruling dynasty of Duklja, and to justify the pretensions of the Church of Duklja. All the while, the contents of these copies and additions to the documents reach exactly to the period when the Goths settled in our areas and the dissolution of the Avar Empire.

---

[39] Gesta regum Sclavorum, Volume II, Historical Institute and Monastery Ostroh, Belgrade, 2009, p. 33.

As the historian Muhamed Hadžijahić states in his treatise *O vjerodostojnosti Sabora na Duvanjskom polju (On the Authenticity of the Council of Duvanjsko Polje)*: *"Ferdo Šišić, Milorad Medini, and Vladimir Mošin are the most deserving for the elucidation of the scientific dilemmas which this Chronicle causes. Speaking about the sources which the Priest of Duklja uses, he mentions the falsified bula of Pope Callixtus II (1119–1124) which he copied word-for-word, listing, to the letter, purported suffragan churches of the Archdiocese of Bar at the Council of Duvno."*[40]

As the archiepiscopacy was lost in 1142, everything that could have been done for it to be restored was attempted, and to the benefit of his thesis, for the same clergy of Bar and Ragusa do not hesitate to falsify legal documents against each other. The Papal Bull was falsified and they even brazenly brought to the Pope to prove that the metropolitan diocese of Duklja was founded together with the restored one in Salona-Split already in that ancient age, when the settled Slavs had accepted the holy cross, and thus, as if both metropolitan dioceses were established with the consent of the Pope and the Emperor (from Constantinople). In this process, fake Bulls of Alexander II and Callixtus II, so that the Ragusan bishopric would be attributed to Split, and all the others to Bar. As the falsified Papal Bull was used to achieve political goals, so were these documents of unknown authorship and without a date of creation, as is the document which speaks of the Council of Duvno, can with certainty be treated as forgeries created for the achieving of some goals.

The Council of Duvno (920), through its contents, indirectly defines the borders between the Eastern Roman Empire and the Western Roman Empire, while trying to place on their line of separation the "Kingdom of Croats", which in said Early Middle Ages did not even exist. It is said that by invitation from King Petar Krešimir, representatives from Rome came to the Council of Duvno; Pope Stephen sent the cardinal Honorius and his wise men, and Emperor Michael sent Leo and John with their retinue to the

---

[40] Muhamed Hadžijahić: O vjerodostojnosti Sabora na Duvanjskom polju, ANUBiH No. 8, 1970, p. 201.

Council of Duvno.

The King with the cardinals welcomed them with honour. We will take a moment here to consider the Kingdom of the Croats which is mentioned; Einhard's "Frankish Annals" (*a list of events in the Frankish Empire during the 8th and 9th century*) says that the Suurbi (Serbs) in 789 entered an alliance with the Franks and joined the Frankish attack against the Avars in 791, in the lower reaches of the Danube. *Lat. "Fuerunt etiam Sclavi eum eo, quorum vokabula sunt Suurbi"; Ger. "Es gab auch mit ihm die Slawen, deren Namen Suurbi sind")*. For a legally valid council to be established and held in Duvno, with such political importance, it would be necessary to create political and military power, moreover the agreement of other rulers, bans, to join the Kingdom of the Croats. Therefore we will analyse the emergence and the realistic capabilities of the Croats in that time to achieve such a rise in the militaristic and political sense.

Up to now we have heard many theories about the origin of the Croats, the theory that they came from an area of Iran, from Poland, and that they lived in the entire area of Northern Europe and Eastern Europe. The Austrian historian Walater Pohl expressed a thesis about the role and genesis of the Croats, which cannot be archaeologically proven, yet is convincing to modern historiography. Pohl is of the opinion that the Croats were a social, not an ethnic group, whose toponyms with Croatian names are found on the borders, peripheries of the Avar Khaganate. It is thought that they form as a people in the territory of Croatia only in the IX century and that they did not exist before the IX century. When Charlemagne was conducting military campaigns against the Avars, the "Frankish Annals" mention in the year 796 an exceptional military leader of Slavic origin, Vojnomir, as an ally in the struggle against the Avars and Byzantium. This leader could be from Istria, Slovenia, or Austria. Here it can be said that the Croats, converted Arians as a societal class, form as an ethnicity and enter the historic stage only after receiving some privileges from the Franks. This was the transitional period between the VII and the IX century, in 796, when the Franks, led by Charlemagne, established rule over Istria and the hinterlands of Liburnia (Lika) which was inhabited by a native Illyrian population and Slavs which arrived with the Avar conquests in these regions. With the peace accord signed in Aachen in the year 812, the Frankish state received Istria and continental Liburnia, while the other cities in this area – Zadar, Trogir, Split, Ragusa, and Kotor, as well as the islands Krk, Osor, and Rab. "Having consolidated their rule and organised their administration in this area, the Franks continued the process of conversion and establishing the organisation of the Church. With time, the name Croats was extended to the rest of the population and became the denominator of the land which they settled."[41] Here, the first indications of them being members of the military strata, which gradually imposes its ethnic concept. The first written mention of the ruler of the Croats concerns Duke Borna, who is mentioned as a ruler in the year 818, in the Frankish document "Annales regni Francorum" (Annales Bertiniani). Borna, as a vasal of the Franks, came to Paderborn (Germany; Nordrhein-Westfalen) and pledged loyalty to the Frankish King Louis the Pious.

Although Fra Andrija Kačić Miošić (*a descendant of the royal family Kačić, who were bans of the Neretvan Banate; in some writings he is perceived as a Bosniak*) he lived almost a millenium after the described events, and, based on previous written sources, in his mention of Duke Borna writes the following:

„*In the year 819 lived the Dalmatian King named Borna, who raised an army against Gliutovid (Ljudevit), the Ban of Slavonia, they did battle with him by the river Kuppa (Kupa) and was defeated by Ban Gliutovid (Ljudevit).*[42]

---

[41] Opća i nacionalna enciklopedija (LZMK) – Hrvati, 1991–2009; or on the website https://www.enciklopedija.hr/natuknica. aspx?ID=26386 accessed 17 February 2023.

[42] Fra. Andrija Kačić Miošić "Razgovor ugodni naroda slovinskoga", p. 12. 13. 1756; accessed 17 February 2023.

In the year 820 from three sides the mighty armies of caesar Ludovik struck at Ban Gliutovid, and, not being able to harm him, in shame they retreated, and many were cut by the Ban's men.

In the year 827 the Dalmatian Slovenes rejected the rule of Rome and of Byzantium

In the year 829 Dalmatia and the land of the Croats was ruled by Tomislav."

Razgovor ugodni naroda slovinskoga

Andrija Kačić Miošić, Dominico Lovix edition, Venice, 1759.

The Frankish sources mention Borna as the Duke of the Guduscani (dux Guduscanorum) in 818, dux Dalmatiae in 819, and dux Dalmatiae atque Liburniae in 821. In the year 818, he did not join the movement of Duke Ljudevit, but as a Frankish vassal fought him at the Kupa river. There, Ljudevit's father-in-law Dragomuž joined Borna's side, but he was abandonded by his Guduscani, and he was defeated. Quickly he again gathered an army and brought the Guduscani who had abandoned him. In the beginning of 820, he reported the emperor about his successes and in the same year he went to Aachen, where the approach to the struggle against Duke Ljudevit was discussed. Upon his return he died, according to some, a natural death, and according to others, a violent one. Therefore, Dux Borna is the first Duke in the region of Croatia whose name was written down.

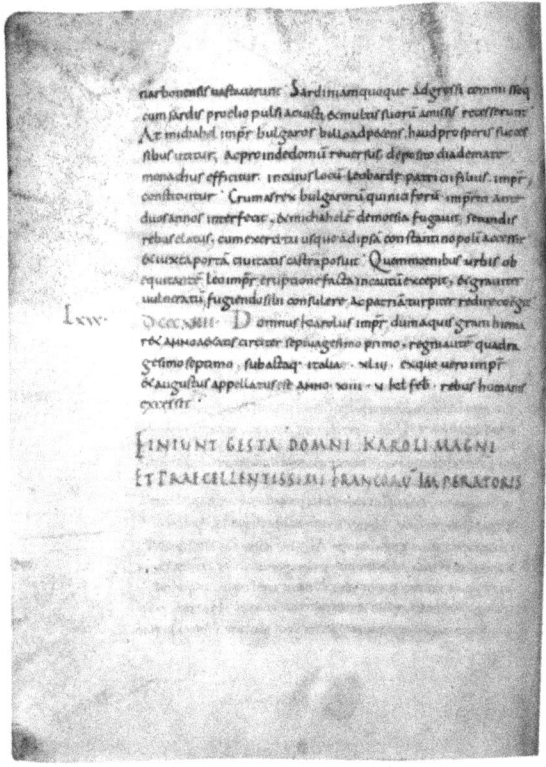

Frankish Annals, source: Wikipedia.

As the issue of the borders between Byzantine Dalmatia and the ducal region of Croatia was not settled by the Treaty of Aachen in 812, Borna accepted the rule of the Franks, which explains, to a degree, his later conflict with Ljudevit, who was supported by Byzantium. However, that the rule of the great powers over duchy was not visible from the data that in the year 827, the Dalmatians rejected Roman and Byzantine rule, and such was the situation also in the Banate of Bosnia. One of the reasons for that is Arianism and the adherence of the population to Arian teaching. This will be visible in the following centuries. Although Rome and the Church endeavoured to convert the Dalmatian population, they had little success in that. Thus, the area in which the Illyrian tribe Dalmatae, later Dalmatia, Liburnia, and Lika, which encompassed the area from Velebit to Cetina, was declared heretical by the Pope, same as the Neretvan Banate, and because of its heresy, given the name Pagania. It is very important to draw a distinction and elucidate the concept of Dalmatia in the process of the destruction of ancient Illyria in the era of new states emerging on European soil, and thus also the emerging of Illyrian banates. As we have seen in the previous text, Duke Borna was the Duke of the Guduscani (dux Guduscanorum) in 818, dux Dalmatiae in 819 and dux Dalmatiae atque Liburniae in 821. In the context of the title Dux Dalmatiae, Dalmatia was the territory of Liburnia and Lika, so, central Dalmatia, in the area between the Krka and Cetina rivers, which are the inheritors of the culture and history of the Illyrian Dalmatae tribe, whose centre was in the city of Delminium in Duvanjsko Polje. To ensure correct interpretation, the fact must not be omitted, that the Neretvan Banate (781–1287) was formed even before the year 781 in southern Dalmatia, which, almost throughout its entire history, acted autonomously out of Omiš, as an Illyrian-Dalmatian banate, from its establishments up to the native maritime dynasty Kadžiki, whose name was Slavicised to Kačići. According to some authors, the Kačići tribe has its origin in Bosnia, and the Ragusan historian Lukarević mentions the father of two Kačić men as "the son of a Saracen". Bogdan Kačić, as the last Neretvan Ban was militarily forced to sign the surrender of his territory to the Hungarian Anjou dynasty in the year 1287. Only after the "Pacta conventa" (which is a non-existent document about the Kingdom of Hungary-Croatia). The Neretvan Banate and the Kačići enter into a vassal relationship, same as the Croatian Banate, which fell under the rule of the Hungarian crown already in 1102.[43] The Neretvans were followers of Arianism and fervent supporters of the Bosnian Church. They tried to interject themselves in the internal issues in Bosnia, and proved their friendship in the year 1222, when they prevented the crusade on Bosnia. Simultaneously with the process of the Illyrian banates gaining independence, in Bosnia, the centre of the great Illyrian Empire, the Banate of Bosnia is formed, which in this later period signed an agreement, entering into alliance with the Hungarian King Bela, under the condition of choosing their ban themselves. Him being confirmed by the Hungarian king afterwards. This happened

---

[43] See Historia Salonitana Maior; Thomas the Archdeacon, from 1387

in the year 1059.

In these events, there is no mention of the Croatian kings, the incorporation of whom is attempted through the Council of Duvno in the area of the banates of Bosnia, Neretva, and Travunia. In the chronicle of Nikola Lašvanin, the differentiation between the Dalmatian and the Croatian banates can be seen.

> du, bi vržen u uzu, i od velike tuge i žalosti umri.
> **1058.** Ižak carig/radski/ cesar posta.
> **1059.** Andre, ung/arski/ kr/alj/; u vojsci od Bele umoren. – U ovo vrime kraljevao je u Dalmaciji i u Hrvatī Krešimir, sin kr/alj: Stipana. – Bošnjaci se pridaše Beli, kr/alju/ ungarskomu; s ovim uvjetom/ da izmedu sebe obiraju bana svoga, koga da kr/alj/ ungars: potvrdi. I tako obraše Ivana Kotromanovića za bana od Bosne.
> **1062.** Bela, 5. kr/alj/ ungarski.

^t Vit.: Volszlova.
^u Vit.: Rumenszke, aliti Drinopolyszke kotare.
¹⁹ sakramenat od oltara. Misli se na pričest odn. euharistiju.

Ljetopis Nikole Lašvanina (Chronicle of Nikola Lašvanin)

Considering that historiography involved itself with the Council of Duvno, because of the non-existence of historical sources and records, except for plagiarised and fabricated records and copies, this issue was never solved, aside from some unfounded claims about the Croatian Kingdom, White Croatia and Red Croatia. White and red have no deeper or more significant meaning, aside from colors being used on maps to demarcate the geographic area that was inhabited by a people. The most famous source and historical monument that tells of Red Croatia is the *Barski rodoslov* (The Genealogy Book of Bar) or the *Ljetopis popa Dukljanina* (The Chronicle of the Priest of Duklja) from the XII century.

In his *Chronicle*, the Priest of Duklja mentions Red Croatia under that name also as a separate autonomous state with defined borders and internal organisation. In that, the Priest of Duklja refers to a few sources he used, but he does not specify those manuscripts, except one under the name "Metodos", which is also non-existent. So, the interlinked political and religious interests were attempted to be solved by the Priest of Duklja, who was a Catholic priest from the state of Duklja, and who, being commissioned by the nobility of Duklja, in his chronicle, states some falsified data which were to be used by the nobility of Duklja to restore the archiepiscopacy they lost. According to his claims, Red Croatia preceded Duklja, which is the antecedent of Zeta, and Zeta is the antecedent of Montenegro.

Kupres necropolis; Rastičevska Mašeta

10 THE RELATIONSHIP BETWEEN BOSNIA AND RAŠKA IN THE EARLY MIDDLE AGES

It is an indisputable fact that the Serbs are mentioned for the first time, in a reliable historical source, in Einhard's Frankish Annals. When the Frankish military forces defeated Saxony, converted the Saxons by force, and joined military forces with them, and with joint forces then began preparations for their final reckoning with the Avar Empire, the centre of which was by the Hungarian Lake Balaton. The Frisians joined the joint Frankish-Saxon military in the year 789, which Charlemagne had already converted to Christianity (a Germanic tribe from the area of modern-day northern Netherlands and Germany).

The Byzantine-Hungarian war, the battle on the Tara River in 1151, in which, according to legend, there happened a duel between the Bosnian Ban Kulin and the Byzantine Emperor Manuel I Komnenos, where Kulin severely injured Komnenos (central detail on the illustration).

With the Frisians, there were also some Slavs named Suurbi, who were given the sacrament (were converted to Christianity), and became part of the Frankish vassal army, which went into battle against the Avars and the Slavs, who were subjugated by them. This battle happened in 795 in the lower reaches of the Danube River, and the Franks routed the Avar forces. It should be noted that the Slavs settled along the Danube and Sava rivers 200 years before the war between the Franks and Avars, and that they were infantry in the service of the Avar conquest and that they performed the dirtiest tasks on the battlefield. Having in mind that the Slavs had already settled this area and that the Bulgars exerted military pressure on the Avars from the south, there is no historical data about some other Serbs, except this small group of warriors already mentioned in Einhard's Annals. As subjects of the Pope and the Franks, they could have been settled in an area where they expected to achieve power and political influence, which was the main goal of Charlemagne – to achieve political influence, conversion to Christianity,

i.e., spreading Christianity to areas which were not Christian, via his vassals. That area was near Duklja, the Illyrian living space, which for thousands of years was inhabited by the Illyrian Diocleati tribe. This is supported in Constantine Porphyrogenitus' document *Concerning the Administration of the Empire* (Chapter 32), where it says that: "The Serbs came to the Balkans from the territory of the Avar Khaganate towards the end of the VII century". Porphyrogenitus says the following: "The Serbs are descendants of unbaptised Serbs who live beyond Hungary, in an area which they call Boiki, where their neighbour is Francia, as is the south of modern-day Poland and Silesia, the unbaptized. In this place, then, these Serbs have dwelt from ancient times."[44]

In recent years, Serb historians have been eager to establish continuity with the Vinča culture, Lepenski Vir, the Triballi,

---

[44] https://sh.wikipedia.org/wiki/Bela_Srbija

Sarmatians, and Dardanians.

- The Triballi – *(Greek: Τριβαλλοί, Romanised: Triballoi)*, an ancient Thracian tribe, whose living space was around the flatlands of modern-day southern Serbia, the northern part of North Macedonia, and western Bulgaria. Celts, Scythians, and Illyrians influenced the tribe.

- Sarmatians – also called Sauromatians– were a tribal confederation of several Iranian equestrian nomadic peoples, first mentioned in ancient written sources in 513 BCE. From the 3rd century onwards, the Sarmatians inhabited areas across the Roman Empire, fought in Roman armies as heavy-armoured cataphracts, and would often receive Roman citizenship. A document of the Roman Empire, *Notitia Dignitatum* (between 425 and 433 CE), names 18 centres of Sarmatian settlement in Gaul and Italy. The Sarmatians also settled in Thuringia. The Sarmatian troops were also deployed in the Lower Rhine region, for example, in the Roman fortification of Gelduba, in the location of modern-day Krefeld. The centre of Sarmatian ceramics was discovered near Budapest.

- The Dardanians – one of the many Illyrian tribes who lived in the region of modern-day Kosovo, Macedonia, Montenegro, and Serbia. The historian J. J. Wilkes thinks that their capital was in Damastion (near Lake Ohrid).

The Dardanians lived in the border regions between the Illyrians and the Thracians and were influenced by them, and, because of the symbiosis that emerged, they are called a Thracian-Illyrian tribe.

Of course, from said interpretations, it is clear that there is no basis on which the Suurbi, which were mentioned, could be linked to the Triballis, the Sarmatians, and the Dardanians. There are no connections and links that could bring into connection the Serbs that arrived towards the end of the VII century with this ancient people.

Raška and Duklja

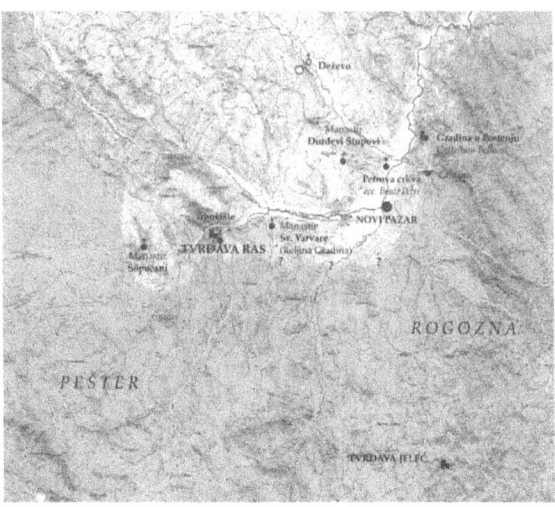

Marko Popović "Tvrđava Ras" (Ras Fortress), Archaeological Institute, Special Editions 34 – image

The region of Raška is first mentioned in the VI century, named for the dominant Illyrian fortification Arsa in the work *De aedificiis* by the Byzantine historian Procopius. The name Raška is derived from the name of a fortification which in historic documents is sometimes mentioned as Arsa, sometimes as Ars, as is the case in *De administrando imperio* by Constantine Porphyrogenitus. Also known is the seal of John, a governor of Ras, used in the period from 971 –976. When this old Illyrian city, Ras, became the seat of the Eastern Eparchy, the eparchy was named after this hillfort, and that name began to be used to denote this entire region, which was under its administration.

Raška is only a geographic concept that is understood to mean the southwestern parts of modern-day Serbia, the northeastern parts of Montenegro, and the easternmost parts of Bosnia and Herzegovina. The core part of Raška today is in Sandžak.

Photo taken from the book by Marko Popović, "Tvrđava Ras" (Ras Fortress)

In the times of Roman administration, this region was named Dardania (municipium Dardanorum) because the Illyrian tribe of the same name, the Dardanians inhabited it. Archaeological research in several sites has shown that this area has been settled for a long in the past. Towards the beginning of the current era, this area fell under the rule of the Roman Empire. In the times of the Roman Empire, the Illyrian Docleatae tribe inhabited the area from Podgorica to Nikšić. After the incursion of the Celts into these regions, in the 4th century BCE, a mixing between the Celts and the Illyrians occurred. From the third to the eleventh century, different peoples settled in these regions. The Goths, Avars, Cumans, Mijaks, Jarusi, Mataruge, Obardi, and Slavs left traces of their living here. What was discovered by archaeologists in the valley of the Raška river, where the hillfort Ras is located as well, are several pre-Roman churches. By their orientation, these churches correspond to Gothic-Arian provenance. Besides the churches, there are also many necropoleis of stećci, as relentless and undeniable witnesses of the development of the Arian teaching, i.e., the teaching of the Bosnian Church, which was present in this area of Raška.

The

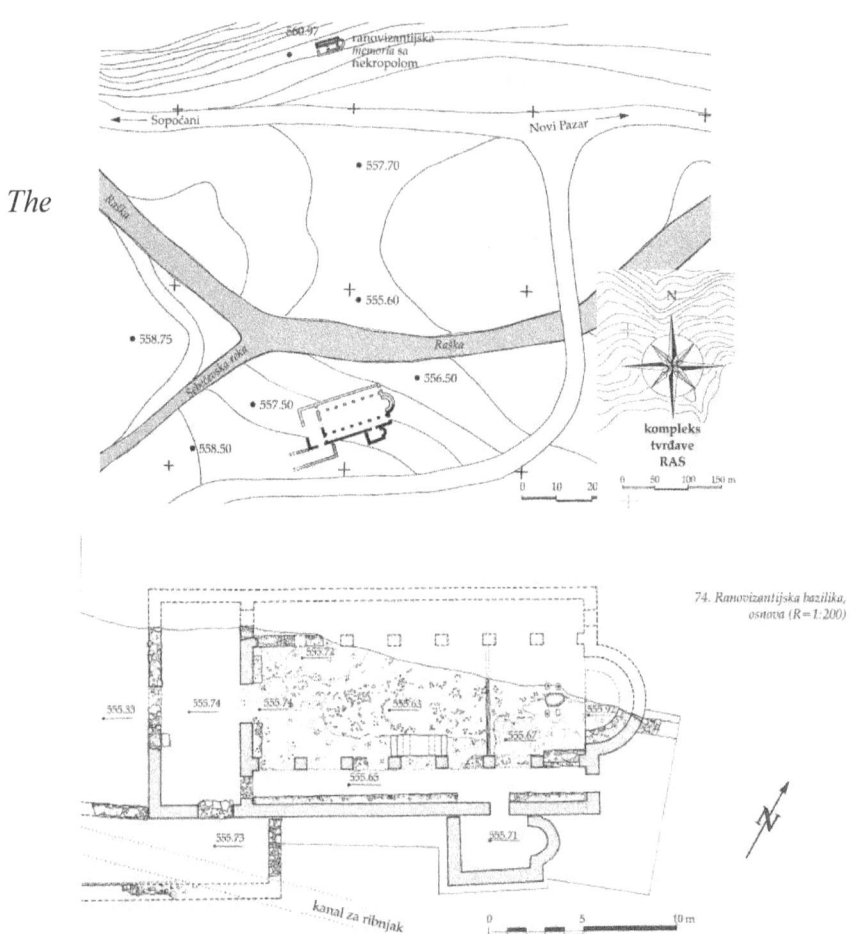

sketch shows two basilicas, which are Arian-Gothic in their orientation. They have been dated to the period before Emperor Justinian, during the time of Theodoric the Great, ruler of the Gothic Empire, when the Arian teaching in Illyria was flourishing.

The following picture has been taken from Google Maps, and is intended to demonstrate the analogy with and remove any doubt in the preceding sketch from the book by Marko Popović.

The flatland along the right-hand shore of the Raška river, near the Sebečevska river mouth, is designated as a site named Bazilika, where a necropolis of stećci is buried atop the late antique architecture. It is interesting to note that the direction in which the basilica is shown in the image is NE-SW, the direction which is characteristic only for the Goths.

The region of Raška from the VI century, with the onslaught of Bulgarians, fell under and was part of the Bulgarian Empire, which ceased to exist in the year 1018, when the last of its territories were surrendered to Byzantium. Recent research shows that the main settlement of Ras was, towards the end of the 9th century, part of the First Bulgarian Empire. Constant wars were waged over this territory. In the year 971, the Byzantine region of Ras was established, but in 976, Bulgarian control was restored. Vasilije II of Duklja conquered it again in the war against the Bulgars, 1016–18. The Byzantine military leader and chronicler Nikephoros Bryennios (Νικηφόρος Βρυέννιος) recorded that, from 1072 to 1075, Constantine Bodin (who would later become the king of Duklja), by order of his father, King Mihailo of Duklja, led an army to assist the rebels in the Balkans. Thus, the region of Raška gradually became part of the state which was ruled by the Vojislavljević dynasty of Duklja. Duklja, also called the Kingdom of Duklja (lat. Doclea, Diocleia), was a medieval state which was located in the area of modern-day Montenegro. It was the first duchy (state) of the Montenegrins. The name Duklja is also etymologically derived from the Indo-European root dhoukl, meaning hidden, dark, black, and is an obvious semantic link between this root and the modern-day name of Montenegro.

King Constantine Bodin of Duklja, illustration from the 19th century; en.wikipedia.org

In Rome, on 8 January 1089, during the reign of King Bodin, a Bull was issued which confirms the archiepiscopacy of the chief prelate of Bar, and the status of the Church of Duklja in its entirety, and thus the Archdiocese of Bar was established. The formal title of the head of the Church of Duklja (which is almost 250 years older than the autocephalous Serb Church) in Papal Bulls was as follows: *Archiepiscopus diocliensis atque antibarensis ecclesiae (in the year 1067) Petro, Doclensis sedis arhiepiscopo (in the year 1089) sancte Dioclitane atque Antibarensis ecclesiae archiepiscopo (in the year 1121)*. By the same Bull, antipope Clement III confirmed Bodin's title of King, inherited from his father Mihailo. The Church of Duklja, the Archdiocese of Duklja, or the Archiepiscopacy of the Church of Duklja was a Roman Catholic archdiocese in Montenegro.

Around the year 1166, another major change occurred in Raška. The rulers of Raška, Desa and Uroš disappeared from the stage, and control was taken over by four brothers (Tihomir, Stracimir, Miroslav, and Stefan, sons of the nobleman Zavida, who is a descendant of the Vukan/Vukanović dynasty of Raška). The old dynasty was replaced by a new one, at the beginning headed by Tihomir Zavid.

From the beginning of Tihomir's reign, the territory of Raška was divided into four županije, which the Zavid brothers ruled over. Tihomir Zavid, the oldest, was the Great Župan, but was soon overthrown by his younger brother Stefan Nemanja Zavid in the year 1168. This new dynasty ruled over Raška until 1371.

Nemanja Zavid, who was later called Stefan Nemanja, was born in Duklja, in what is today the village of Ribnici near Podgorica, 1113 –1200. The Nemanjići are a medieval dynasty that ruled over Raška between the 12th and the 14th century. The dynasty was named after Stefan Nemanja, who had familial ties to the Great Župan Vukan/Vukanović, who was appointed as the head of Raška together with his court župan Marko by King Bodin of Duklja, after Byzantium conquered Raška.

The Vukanovići were the rulers of Raška in the period 1083–1165, and were very active in the struggle against Byzantium. So, Nemanja is patrilineally related to Vukan, and matrilineally to the Vojisavljevići. The Vojisavljevići are a Montenegrin dynasty, rulers of the Kingdom of Duklja from the middle of the 10th century to the end of the 12th century.

Vojisavljevići are yet another dynasty from Duklja.

So, both families have their origin in Duklja and the Illyrian Docleatae tribe. Nemanja is related on the male (his father's) side to the Vukanovići, and on the female (his mother's) side, to the Vojisavljevići. Thus, we will claim, and rightfully so, that Stefan Nemanja is of Illyrian descent from the Diocleatae tribe (modern-day Montenegro). After King Borodin appointed Vukan, the

Vukanovići made Raška into a regular province of Duklja, with the Catholic Church, where Nemanja himself was baptised, being dominant. In *Žitije Svetog Simeona* (The Life of Saint Symeon), Stefan Nemanjić recorded that (the unnamed) father of Nemanja, because of the revolt of his brothers, was forced to flee Raška and hide in his birthplace, Zeta, where, in Ribnici (area around modern-day Podgorica), his son Nemanja was born. Aside from that, he writes that Nemanja was baptised a second time (according to Orthodox customs) when his father returned to the throne in Raška. It is possible that the father of the Nemanjići, Zavida, was the Župan of Raška on two occasions.[45]

Fresque depicting Mihailo I Vojisavljević, Church of St. Michael in Ston; source: en.wikipedia.org

Nemanja's rise to power and forming closer ties with Byzantium later brought him into conflict with his brothers (battle near Pantina in Kosovo, where his brother, Župan Tihomir, was killed). Nemanja took the title of Great Župan of Raška already in the year 1166 and was granted the small geographic areas of Toplica, Ibar, Rasina, and Reka to administrate, as well as the small župa Duboćica

---

[45] T. Živković, Portreti srpskih vladara (IX–XII vek), Belgrade 2006, p. 119, note 361.

near Leskovac, which he received as a gift from the Byzantine Emperor Manuel I Komnenos. While he was making preparations for the war against the Hungarians, in the year 1162, Emperor Komnenos invited Nemanja to Niš, where he granted him the title of "Imperial Vassal".

In the year 1185, Župan Nemanja, with the help of the Hungarians, conquered the Kingdom of Duklja, destroying all cities of Duklja except Kotor. Having in mind that he had his origins in Duklja and that his father Zavid was from Duklja, and was likely an emissary of Duklja in Raška, this act of taking over power and conquering these territories in one's land could in contemporary language be characterised as a coup d'état. The stated theory will be opposed by many who read in historical publications and students' books about Raška, and have the opportunity, in the same lines, to read the dual name for Raška, that being Raška-Serbia. However, up until the coup d'etat by Nemanja, Raška was a župa within the Bulgarian, then the Byzantine, and finally the Empire of Duklja. Similar research was conducted by the Albanian historian Jusuf Budžovi, who presented indications that the Nemanjić dynasty was of Illyrian origin. Budžovi points out: "The Nemanjići are a Christian-Dardanian tribe, of Illyrian origin!" After Nemanja destroyed and occupied Duklja, during the following centuries, Orthodox Christianity would become the dominant faith. Many rulers from the Nemanjić dynasty generously gifted lands and money to the Church. As a result of that, Stefan Nemanja and some of his descendants were canonised as saints. The Church supported the dynasty, depicting Nemanja as the founder of Serbia, and because of that, the preceding history of Raška fell into obscurity.[46]

The question arises: "Why is the Church letting the earlier historical period of Raška fall into obscurity?" We can look for the answer only in the fact that the previous župans of Raška were not suitable for the conception of the future government structure.

---

[46] John V. A. Fine, The Late Medieval Balkans: A Critical Survey from the Late Twelfth Century to the Ottoman Conquest (p. 41), The University of Michigan Press, 2009. (p. 3)

Several answers are possible, for which there are no historic facts by which the efforts of the Church to break with the former župani to be exactly determined.

First, the answer would be that Arianism was widely spread in this area as well (which is evidenced by the Arian basilicas as well as many stećci in this area) and that previous župans were members of the Arian faith, which was in no way acceptable to the Orthodox Church, and that will be expressed in the later persecution and killings of Arians from this area, who also found sanctuary in the Arian Banate of Bosnia.

The second reason could be that the previous župani were of Bulgarian or Bosniak origin. This theory, that the župans of Raška could have been of Bosniak origin, is supported by many stećci written in Bosančica and all the Gothic-Illyrian symbolism found in the entire area under Bosniak rule, which are found in Raška (modern-day Sandžak) as well. In the Ottoman cadastral census from the year 1477, in the area around Prijepolje, the following were registered: Radoje, son of Bosniak, Radonja, son of Bosniak, and Dobrotko, son of Bosniak.

The third reason for the Church to sever its relations with the previous župani is that Catholicism in this region, due to its proximity to Orthodox Christianity, and the split of Christianity into Orthodox Christianity and Catholicism (in the year 1054), was losing its influence, which is reported by the Priest of Duklja as well, who writes about his endeavours to restore the lost regions which were attained at the Council of Duvno, and by the falsified Papal Bull which was supposed to support it.

So, up to Stefan Nemanja, there are several župani of Raška, whom the Orthodox Christian Church is eager to let fall into obscurity. Serb historiographers wanted to insert Nemanja into the royal lineage of Slavic kings, which is fabricated and emerged as a result of an obsolete theory about the Migration period in which the Slavs, i.e., the Serbs and Croats, overwhelmed the Illyrian regions and assimilated into the domestic population, and thus give him Serb legitimacy. In many elements, the Croatian and Serbian list of Slavic kings is intertwined, and it is impossible to justify this with objective historical facts. It reaches the very beginning of the genealogy of Ostrogoth kings, where a conscious falsity is introduced in defining the successors to the Gothic crown, to form the idea of Slavic rulers. Through that, this obsolete historiography wants to categorise our region as territories of Greater Serbia or Greater Croatia, which is, of course, absurd. In the book *Srednjovekovna kneževina i kraljevina Srbija VII-XIII veka* (The Medieval Duchy and Kingdom of Serbia VII–XIII century) by Živojin R. Andrejić, the following is stated: Gothic leaders that invaded Panonia and Illyricum, and afterwards Italy as well, ruled towards the end of the V and during the first half of the VI century: Theodorich (475–526), Atalarich (520–534) and Theodad (534–536)". Goth rulers according to Dukljanin: Svevlad, his sons: Brus, Totilo and Ostroilo, as well as their descendants: Svevlad, Selimir, Vladin, Ratimir, Svetimir... all have Slavic names, rather than Gothic. They reigned towards the end of the VI and in the VII century. "After that, the Goths, with the one called Ostroilo as their leader, conquered the entire province of Illyricum/Dalmatia and coastal cities. Ostroilo's son, called Svevlad, filled the land with many Slavs."[47]

Theodoric the Great – called Ostroilo, according to this already rejected Gothic theory- would be a so-called Slavic king, which, of course, is incorrect because Theodoric did not have a direct successor, as is the case with Ostroilo, who had three sons. Thus, this list makes no sense. Even if some Banates could have a heritage of Gothic rulers, those could be Usora, Soli, Bosnia, the Banate of Vrbas/ Vinac, Rama, the Neretvan Banate, and Travunia. This would be another indicator that Župan Nemanja cannot have any relation to the so-called list of Slavic kings, but is, however, of Illyrian origin, from Duklja. Because we know on the basis of genealogy that the areas of Raška / Sandžak / Bosnia and Herzegovina and Dalmatia were left with the least Slavic genetic influence. This topic

---

[47] Ljetopis popa Dukljanina (The Chronicle of the Priest of Duklja) p. 42. Latin text with a Croatian translation; Matica hrvatska Zagreb 1950.

is written about by Rački as well: "An interesting fact is that many Serb historians, such as Živojin R. Andrejić, admitted they have made a mistake (which he regrets) because they left the Dux (Duke) Borna (dux Dalmatiae atque Liburniae) to be called a Croat and the founder of the Croatian Kingdom (although he is not Croatian)"[48] In the same manner, this entire list of kings is also attributed to the non-existent Croatian Kingdom, because it is the same list of Gothic, or Slavic kings, what is are listed as absurdities (lies), one after the other.

This issue of the Church letting the previous rulers of Raška remains very interesting as we have seen, Nemanja by his family lineage from both parental sides of Illyrian origin, from Duklja, a Montenegrin.

However, to elucidate this a bit: In this contradiction of the Church and the historiographers, the first in the genealogy which they try to let fall into obscurity is the Župan of Raška, Petar Gojnikovic.

What was also discovered is a seal of Duke Peter: "In the name of the Father and Son and Holy Spirit/ Peter arhontos of Dioclia, Amen".[49] The inscription from the seal of Peter indicates the Illyrian Docleatae tribe and Duklja. As the historian Konstantin Jireček writes in his book *Historija Srbije (History of Serbia)*: "Petar was the son of Gojnik, and he was the son of Vlastimir, 830 –851, from the first dynasty of Raška. Gojnik did not have a Slavic name. After his father Peter ruled over Raška from 892 to 917. Petar, in his struggle for dominance against the other members of the family, extended the župa of Raška.

So, this is a narrow period, shortly after the first mention of Suurbs in Einhard's Frankish Annals, that was in the year 795, when they, together with the Franks, waged war against the Avars on the Danube. This fact, in many aspects, narrows down the space and

---

[48] Rački, Franjo, Documenta historiae Chroaticae periodum antiquam illustrantia, Zagreb 1877, p. 325, 334.

[49] Živojin R. Andrejić Centar za mitološke studije Srbije) (Schlumberger, 1884, p. 20)

possibility for linking the later Serbs with this early dynasty of Raška. Based on the provided fact, it is easy to conclude about the actual period of the establishment of Serbia. Having in mind that Raška is mentioned already in the VI century in the work *De aedificiis* by the Byzantine historian Procopius, Serbia cannot be linked to Raška from an earlier period, not even in the XII century to Stefan Nemanja, as it stands, the intentions of the Church.

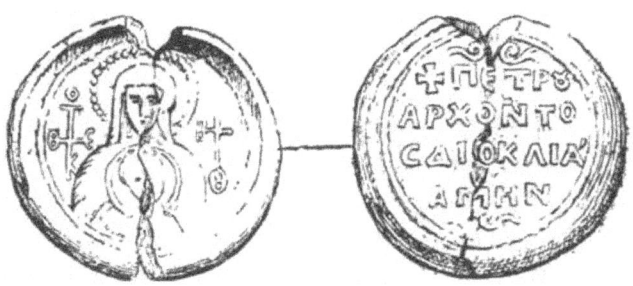

The seal of Peter from the IX century, with a depiction of the Holy Virgin Mary with the Christ Child, on one side and an inscription in Greek: Petro Arhintos Dioklia Amin, on the other side; (source: en.wikipedia.org).

It is clear that before Stefan Nemanja, in the power struggles, the Bulgarians controlled these regions, and after them, the king of Duklja and his župans. In parallel, during this time in which there are attempts to establish the birth of Serbia, west from it, we have the consolidated, well-organised Banate of Bosnia, which is already strong, and has all the elements which characterise all modern states, whose throne and *stanak* (parliament) was headed by the Bosnian Ban Kulin.

In the times of Stefan Nemanja (1166 –1196), the Ras fortress was again restored as the centre of the župa Raška. Knowing that on the west side of Raška, there were strong, in every sense already formed banates (Usora and Soli, Bosnia, Travunia, the Neretvan Banate), Nemanja saw an opportunity to expand his empire in the East and in the surrounding spaces which were already weakened through the ongoing wars against the Bulgarians. Nemanja, as a Byzantine vassal, was loyal to Byzantium in the beginning, only to later still dare to, with the help of Hungary, join the Byzantine-Hungarian war, to organise an uprising in the period 1183–1190 and occupy eastern Raška, Duklja, parts of Bulgaria and Macedonia. On his way, he destroyed and subjugated all cities in Duklja, except Kotor. After the conquest of Duklja by Raška, during the following centuries, Orthodox Christianity became the dominant religion. Only Ragusa managed to resist Nemanja's conquests.

The German Roman King Frederick Barbarossa began his journey in 1189 as part of the Third Crusade, and was met in Niš by Nemanja, who offered him his full support against Byzantium. In that way, Nemanja deepened the conflict with the Byzantine Emperor Isaac II. After signing a peace treaty with Barbarossa, in 1190 Isaac attacked the people of Raška and the Bulgarians. Nemanja was beaten that same year and was forced to return the conquered areas around Sofia, Skopje, Prizren, and Niš. Emperor Isaac continued to tolerate Nemanja which partly meant indulgingly, partly recognising the independence of Raška. After Nemanja was defeated by Byzantium, he had to hand over power to his sons. The government of Raška, by request of Byzantine Emperor Isaac II, he handed to his middle son Stefan Nemanjić Prvovenčani, who became the Great Župan of Raška, while the governing of Duklja he entrusted to his oldest son, Vukan. After all these events, Nemanja secluded himself to Sveta Gora in 1197 as monk Simeon, and there he restored the abandoned Greek monastery Hilandar, with his son Sava, from 1198 to 1199, where he also died in the year 1200. There exists a myth that after his death, his bones were transferred to the monastery Studenica, which during his life he had selected as his final resting place, and he was interred in the southern wall. The Orthodox Church declared him a saint. His son, Saint Sava, the founder of the Serbian Orthodox Church (Rastko Nemanjić 1174 –14 January 1236, the youngest son of Great Župan Nemanja), known as the Enlightener, the first archiepiscopus of the autocephalous Church of Raška, founder of law and diplomacy in Raška. In the year 1219 the patriarchy in Nicaea recognised him as the first Serbian archiepiscopus, and in the same year, he authored the oldest known constitution of Serbia, the Nomocanon or Zakonopravilo, with which he secured full independence; both religious and political. The eparchy of Raška, which existed from the XI century, was located in the župa of Raška, in the area around the old Illyrian city Ras, that is the Church of the Holy Apostles Peter and Paul. Originally, it was part of the Archiepiscopacy of Ohrid, while after the year 1219 it was part of the newly established autocephalous Archiepiscopacy of Žiča in Raška, which would later be called the Archiepiscopacy of Žiča and Peć. "Јоаникије, митрополит рашко-призренски" (*Joanikije, Metropolitan of Rascia–Prizren*)[50]

The abandoning of Catholicism and conversion to Orthodox Christianity among the rulers of Raška was clearly out of pragmatic reasons. The intention was for Raška to adopt the legacy of Byzantium, which lived through many turbulent times in internal wars, power struggles, and constant wars which it led to retain its own territories. In the period of Stefan Nemanja and his sons' reign, the Serbianisation of this region began. Through this process, by applying forceful and brutal methods, to a very small extent the members of the indigenous Illyrian people were Serbianised. This process of Serbianising Raška, modern-day Sandžak, extends throughout history and is still ongoing. In the first Ottoman cadastral census from the year 1477, it is recorded that many parts of the Prijepolje area were settled exclusively Wallachs. The Wallachs were of Orthodox Christian faith, which was the decisive factor for their complete Serbianisation.

---

[50] Радосављевић, Недељко В. (2012)

Church of the Holy Apostles Peter and Paul (source: Wikipedia)

On the "Bogumilism" of the Bosnian Church

Many authors, especially Serb authors, took a strong stance advocating the thesis that the Bosnian Church is based on Bogumilism, which allegedly emerged in Raška, and was mercilessly destroyed and persecuted by Stefan Nemanja. We will present a few facts which are contradictory to the mentioned thesis: "We know that Thomas the Archdeacon states that in 1200 CE, the archbishop of Split, Bernard, persecuted the brothers Matej and Aristodius because they were preaching "ungodly heresy" in his city. He confiscated their property and "throwing them into the manacles of anathema", he exiled them from the land. Further, Toma says that in the end, many who followed the teaching of the brothers were excommunicated, while emphasizing that their heresy truly also was a movement. He also mentions that in the end, the brothers disavowed their heresy, and that Bernard gave them back their property.

Aristodius, Ari-studious – Rastudije, was a skilled goldsmith and artist. He often visited Bosnia and was an expert in Slavic as well as Latin books. He did not disavow his heretical teaching during his time spent in Bosnia, which is also evidenced by the fragment of the Bosnian Gospel, which is kept in the library in Saint Petersburg, where the name of "Mister Rastudije" is found at the top of the column listing allegedly ordained bishops (djeds) of the Bosnian Church. As incorrectly stated by Jean Duvernoy, Rastudije was probably the founder of a new branch of Bosnian Krstjani. [51]However, since the list of Bosnian djedovi, Rastudije is preceded by a series of 16 names of djeds, it is clear that the heresy in Bosnia preceded him as well, so there was no need for restoring the Arian teaching in Bosnia, when it was already constant since the time of Gothic settlement and rule. Some authors took into consideration *Žitije Svetog Simeuna (The Life of Saint Simeon)*.[52] In this document from Raška, according to which this topic would be elucidated, one finds out that as soon as the heresy had spread in his state, Nemanja convened a Church synod, because the heretics did not accept the Byzantine state and Church authority. At the time when the council meeting, suddenly a disturbed young woman appeared, who threw herself before the Župan and started shouting how she, unknowingly, married a nobleman who was a member of a group worshipping Satan. Her appearance and theatrical performance excited and impacted the meeting, so Nemanja demanded an investigation and mobilised the military. He ordered the teacher of the heretics, who was the djed of Raška, tongue cut out, while the rest he burned on a stake, and those who survived he exiled from his state, burning their books and confiscating their property. These exiles found sanctuary in Hum (Herzegovina) and Bosnia, most historians agree with this, because they were the same people, were of the same faith and spoke the same language. The real nature of the heresy is not stated, except that their followers were "Arians" and that they "split apart the Trinity". At this point, historians are eager to erase the traces of Arianism. State: "Naturally, the term "Arians" is only an epithet, considering that Arianism already ceased to exist a few centuries ago!" Also at this point, they do not

---

[51] Jean Duvernoy, L'Histoire des Cathares: Le Catharisme, Toulouse, 1979, p. 72.

[52] "Život Stefana Nemanje", 1166–1196 written by his son Stefan

provide an answer to the question: "Why does Nemanja call the heretics "Arians", if they are Bogomils?" According to Solovjev, these events happened in the period between 1172 and 1180. These are clear examples of the existence of the Bosnian Church even before said Bogomilism (which basically has an identical relation toward the divinity of Jesus as Arianism or the Bosnian Church), and are at the same time examples that disprove the theory that the Bosnian Church originated in Bogomilism. All attempts to date the Bosnian Church to the Middle Ages and to link it with Bogomilism and Raška are always unsuccessful, because its teaching dates back to the period when the teacher Arius was exiled to Illyria at the Council of Nicaea, and naturally the period of Arian Goths, who, having arrived in Illyria, adopted Wulfila's Arian Silver Bible. It should be noted as well that the Goths have spent 250 years in Illyria after their arrival, and for 50 years, led by King Theodoric, they had their Gothic Kingdom, which included the entirety of Illyria. Many historians fall into a trap when they ignore the time the presence of Goths in Illyria, and especially in the area of medieval Bosnia. This is evidenced in the above picture showing two Arian basilicas in the Raška river valley (and about fifty others found in the area of Bosnia and Herzegovina), a few kilometres from the Illyrian hillfort Arsa (Ras), which archaeology dated to Late Antiquity or the Early Middle Ages, so, in the period when Goths were the only real military and political power in our region.

The son of Stefan Nemanja and ruler of Duklja, Vukan, remained Catholic, and in that context wrote a letter to Rome in which, out of his ambition of conquering Bosnia and hoping to weaken it, he complains to Pope Innocent III, the founder of the inquisition, accusing the Bosnian Ban Kulin and his sister, the widow of Duke Miroslav, of being heretics. Vukan warns him that "in the land of Bosnia, a heresy of not small proportions is developing, and to such an extent that Ban Kulin himself, after he was misled with his wife and his sister and with several of his relatives, converted to this heresy more than ten thousand Christians".[53] He explains that their

---

[53] Pismo Vukana Nemanjića rimskom papi, iz 1199. g. (*Vukan Nemanjić's Letter to the Roman Pope, from the year 1199*); https:// de.scribd.com/doc/241979647/Vukanovo-Pismo-Papi#

teaching, which is so widespread in Bosnia, represents a serious threat to the interests of the Roman Church. Therefore, concludes Vukan: "the only solution is that the Pope send the Hungarian king to exterminate this heresy. Therefore, we ask that you advise the king of Hungary to exterminate them as chaff from grain".[54] He notes that the emissaries of the Pope, like the Sun, enlightened his kingdom and that he is glad to have found out that he is related to the Pope. Vukan's actions can be explained by his having some kind of ambitions of taking Bosnia, and that he calculated it would be easiest to weaken and crush the power of Ban Kulin.[55] This letter that Vukan sent to the Pope could have been disastrous for Bosnia, because the Pope sent his legates to Bosnia, which resulted in the council and abjuration that took place in Bilino Polje, near Zenica, in the year 1199.

Map shows Raška, Moravia, Serbia, and Bulgaria, and to the south, there is also Duklja (which is not indicated here); already on first look points towards the myth of the non-existent Slavic kings, which we mentioned at the beginning of the text.

This map, showing Raška, Moravia, Serbia, and Bulgaria, and to the south, there is also Duklja, already on first look, points towards

---

[54] Pismo Vukana Nemanjića rimskom papi, iz 1199. g. (*Vukan Nemanjić's Letter to the Roman Pope, from the year 1199*)

[55] Wikipedia, Željko Fajfrić, "Sveta loza Stefana Nemanje", Šid 1998.

the myth of the non-existent Slavic kings, which we mentioned at the beginning of the text. Namely, based on a non-existent bloodline of Slavic kings, which are sometimes called Croatian and sometimes Serbian, depending which author one is reading, we see that Serbia is drawn in the area of the banates of Travunia and Hum. Serbian authors always mention Serbian lands, as do Croatian authors, who equally lay claim to the same two banates based on the non-existent bloodline of Slavic kings. However, what is at hand here? In our previous text, "Bosnia and Illyrian Banates between the Franks and Byzantium"[56], we have seen that Croatian historians call the Frankish vassal Dux Borna a Croatian župan, even though he holds the title dux Dalmatiae atque Liburniae. That means that Borna, in the terminology, is the Župan of Dalmatia and Liburnia. There is no mention of Croatia in this title, and the named župas, even though Croatian historians speak of Croatian lands and the Croatian Kingdom already in this historical period. The same is true for the župa of Raška, which, as we have seen, is comprised of a few smaller župas. Same as Croatian historians, only substituting "Croatian" for "Serbian", Serbian historians speak of Serbian lands of which there are none in that moment in history, except of the župa of Raška, which is much smaller of the geographic area that denotes Raška itself, and which the Church only in this era is attempting to profile as Serbian. They positioned Serbia into the Banate of Travunia (Trebinje), Hum and Moravia (although no such banate exists), which is absurd, because Hum had its own independent župani, same as Raška did. Aside from these two banates, there are a few more that are the subject of Croatian and Serbian mythomania and appropriation, and those are: Usora and Soli, Bosnia, Zapadne strane, Donji kraji, the Neretvan Banate (Pagania), Konavle, and above the Sava river, there was the Banate of Slavonia. All these župas in the area of modern-day Croatia and Serbia act in conditional independence, as vassal župe of the Franks, the Hungarians, or of Byzantium. Exactly the banates which had the smallest or no influx of Slavic population (which arrived with the Avar and Bulgarian wars) had the greatest degree of independence

---

[56] Article, http://bosanskipogledi.com/2021/03/01/bosna-i-ilirske-banovine-izmedju-franaka-i-bizanta

from the large empires, and that is the area of modern-day Bosnia and Herzegovina and Dalmatia! The Arian Gothic and native Illyrian linguistic, cultural, and historical heritage conditioned the autonomous growth and development of the banates, in which the most successful was Bosnia, whose rise began during the time of Ban Kulin, and reached its apex with Tvrtko I Kotromanić. Here we will draw the conclusion that Serbia and Croatia in the period of the consolidation of future states had very little or, better yet, no influence, neither political nor religious. We can examine the Serbian historiography imposing in its literature the claim that Tvrtko I Kotromanić was crowned the King of Bosnia in the Mileševa monastery near Prijepolje. King Tvrtko is thereby declared to be a Serb, and Bosnia is declared to be Serbian land. These claims are completely false because King Tvrtko was crowned in Mile, near Visoko. The area of Prijepolje, as well as the entire Lim river valley are adorned with many necropoleis of stećci, which unequivocally points towards this area belonged to medieval Bosnia, and that it was inhabited by Bosniaks, the ancestors of modern-day Bosniaks.

Necropolis Maculje, Novi Travnik

11 THE EMERGENCE OF THE BANATE OF BOSNIA AND ITS FIRST BANS

The Illyrian tribes during the time of the Roman and Gothic Empire were more or less compact. They were strongly influenced and transformed during the Gothic Empire, their settling and mixing with the native Illyrian population in a period longer than 200 years, which is how long the Goths were present in the area of Illyria, from the year 350 to the year 553. After the Gothic Empire fell, the Goths did not disappear, many retreated from the area of northern Italy to the territory of modern-day Bosnia and Herzegovina, which is also evidenced by the Gothic graveyard from the area around Prijedor, with about 200 mounds, by numerous toponyms, as well as foundations of Arian basilicas across Bosanska Krajina.

Battle between the Hungarian and Bosnian army, source: J. Thuróczi, Chronica Hungarorum, Theobald Feger, Erhard Ratdolt, Augsburg 1488.

The Goths left a deep and positive impression in our area, and we are living their cultural elements even today without being aware of it. Among the population of Bosnia and Herzegovina, Gothic customs were observed until recently. Above all that is the Arian faith which would develop through the Bosnian Church and be present from the period of Late Antiquity until late into the Late Middle Ages, that is, until the Ottoman conquest of Bosnia, when a majority of the population adopted Islam.

Emperor Justinian with his courtiers, Basilica San Vitale in Ravenna, Italy. Retrieved from Wikimedia Commons © The Yorck Project: 10.000 Meisterwerke der Malerei. DVD-ROM, 2002. ISBN 3936122202. Distribution – Directmedia Publishing GmbH.

After the Byzantine Emperor Justinian, in 553, definitively defeated the Goths and entered Ravenna (modern-day Italy), the rule of the Ostrogoths was over in our region as well. In the following period, under the Avar Khaganate, which began invading the territory of Illyria already from the year 562 and lasted until the year 796, the region of Illyria experienced stratification. The period of Avar-Slavic influence was the most disastrous, the most destructive for the economy and societal development in general of the župas or Sclaviniae, as the territorial and political organisations were called after the collapse of the Avar Khaganate on the territory of Illyria. There are only three hazy historic sources about the military incursions of the Avars onto the soil of modern-day Bosnia and Herzegovina, from which no conclusion of an Avar-Slavic colonisation can be derived, but only of plundering military campaigns.[57] In these military campaigns, 50 Illyrian hillforts and 50 Arian-Gothic Bosnian churches, which is how many were discovered in the area of Bosnia and Herzegovina to this day, suffered damage and were destroyed. Strangely, the Orthodox Christian and Catholic Churches are eager to categorise these Arian basilicas, which are characteristic for their Arian teaching and essentially differ from classical church teachings, as part of their cultural and historic heritage, or at the very least to minimise its influence, not only in Illyria, but in the entirety of Europe.

As Dr. Ibrahim Pašić writes in *O porijeklu vladarske titule "Ban" u srednjovjekovnoj Bosni (On the Origin of the Regal Title of "Ban" in Medieval Bosnia)*: „Having in mind that, on the soil of Bosnia and Herzegovina, before the settling of Avars and Slavs in the VII century, there existed a historical continuity of social and governmental organisation in ten centuries, and that during said period the area of modern-day Herzegovina certainly was part of the Illyrian state, and likely a part of Bosnia, taken together with the fact that 20 Roman emperors were Illyrians, the basic question is: Did the Illyrian-Roman native population of Bosnia wait for a total of ten centuries for the Avar bans to establish their medieval Bosnian state for them?"[58]

Yet, more based on suppositions than on real historical sources, the Croatian historian Nada Klaić opened the discussion about the problem of the two hundred-year-long Avar rule over the Bosnian lands.[59] In the opinion of N. Klaić, the Bosnian lands in the Avar era

---

[57] For more information, see: B. Grafenauer, Proces doseljavanja Slovena na zapadni Balkan i u istočne Alpe, Simpozijum Predslavenski etnički elementi na Balkanu u etnogenezi južnih Slovena, Sarajevo 1969, p. 51; and Manendar and Theophylact Simocatta

[58] Dr. Ibrahim Pašić: *O porijeklu vladarske titule "BAN" u srednjevjekovnoj Bosni*; https://www.bosanskehistorije.com/ historija/35- historija-balkana-svijeta/1034-pasic-porijeklopodrijetlo-vladarske-titule-ban

[59] Dr. Ibrahim Pašić: *O porijeklu vladarske titule "BAN" u srednjevjekovnoj Bosni*; https://www.bosanskehistorije.com/historija/35- historija-balkana-svijeta/1034-pasic-porijeklopodrijetlo-vladarske-titule-ban; B. Grafenauer, *Proces doseljavanja Slovena na zapadni Balkan i u Istočne Alpe*,

had the same governmental organisation as all other Slavs who found themselves part of the Avar Empire. There is almost no historical data about this period, which could offer us a more precise insight into the actual events. Relying on genetics, which has rapidly advanced in recent decades, we see that there is only very little Slavs as an ethnicity in the area of Bosnia and Herzegovina, if we compare the percentage of the Alpine-Dinaric genetic haplogroup (more than 50%) with the later genetic mutations of Goths, Celts and Slavs, and other peoples that settled in Illyria.

Based on this fact, we can offer a logical thesis which, in the absence of written documents, can offer an answer and imply some conclusions. So, after the famous revolt led by Bato was crushed, from 6 to 9 CE, (that war was the toughest conflict Rome had faced after the Punic Wars two hundred years before), the Empire takes a portion of the defeated Illyrians into slavery and sells them. In contrast, a portion is granted the so-called civitates status of being full citizens of the Empire. As they were full citizens of the Empire, the Illyrians would join the Roman army and would often be the rulers of the Empire (it can be said that the Illyrians were even dominant in the power structure of the Roman Empire; it is thought that 16 out of 30 Roman Emperors came from the area of Illyricum, that is, were of Illyrian origin). Meaning, the Illyrians, in the moment of Avar-Slavic incursion into their territory already had a strong cultural heritage, a feeling of exceptionalism in their identity and they also had a tradition of organising government and life in broader and local communities; they were skilled in matters of politics and warfare, and we think that all that influenced their resisting of the Avar-Slavic onslaught. That is exactly the reason why, when consulting the genetic findings of modern-day population, say, of Bosnia and Herzegovina (which is of most interest to us here), the R1a genetic haplogroup (which is considered Slavic) is present as a low percentage. In contrast, the Alpine-Dinaric (which is regarded as Illyrian) I2 haplogroup is most widespread. Political Slavistics until now taught us the contrary.

Still, Bosnia was under Avar influence, but was also freer compared to other parts of Illyria. What is in the interest of all great powers in history, also today, are natural resources, political dominance in a certain area, and taxation of the subjugated people, meaning, material gain, so that the centres of power (in this case, the centre of the Avar Khaganata, the so-called Avar hring in Pannonia) would prosper and further expand their power, was also true in the case of the Avar incursion into the area of modern-day Bosnia and Herzegovina, while the local government was up to the native population.

Avar Khaganate, period 582– – 612, source: William Shepherd R., Wolf Halama (nur der hier überarbeitete Kartenausschnitt) – Ursprung Shepherd, William: Historical Atlas, New York: Henry Holt and Company, 1911

These are the reasons why, in our opinion, the organisation of local government remains the same as in the pre-Avar time throughout this 200-year-long Avar influence exerted on the central portion of Illyricum of the day, and on the Roman province of Dalmatia, i.e., Modern-day Bosnia and Herzegovina and Dalmatia.

About the period of Avar-Slavic dominance, Dr. Enver Imamović states the following:

„*After the tumultuous happenings which followed the collapse of the civilisation of Antiquity and the settling of the Slavs on the Balkan peninsula, Bosnia entered the darkest period of its history. That darkness lasted almost 300 years, that is, from the 7th to the 10th century. Throughout that time, there were absolutely no written reports about Bosnia. What little archaeological monuments are found can in no way substitute for written material. Almost the same is true with the other surrounding lands.*"[60]

The Franks, led by Charlemagne, and certainly his heirs as well, because of the wars against the Spanish Arabs, had no interest nor capacity to conquer our area, and neither did the Byzantine Empire, which could not consolidate its power because of constant wars against the Bulgarians, their eastern neighbours, and because of continuous internal upheavals and power struggles. In this period of Avar rule, the clan and tribe-based society transforms into a feudal one, with its hierarchy of lords, nobility, and petty nobility. Župas and banates were formed as new feudal structures composed of the domestic aristocracy. So, from the VII century and the disappearance of the Avar Empire up to the year 1166, Bosnia was independent from any empire or bordering banate or župa. Istria, Liburnia, Dalmatia, and Slavonia were under direct Frankish patronage; on the other hand, a constant struggle was happening between the Bulgarians and Byzantium, while some coastal cities remained under the influence of Byzantium. Thus, the Banate of Bosnia had its territorial space, culture, tradition, language and script.

Here we point to the research by the professor of German studies, Bisera Suljić Boškailo, who in her book *Goti u Bosni* (Goths in Bosnia) developed a clear thesis and conclusions that the script Bosančica is identical to the Messapian Illyrian script from north-

---

[60] Dr. Enver Imamović PORIJEKLO I PRIPADNOST STANOVNIŠTVA BOSNE I HERCEGOVINE p.14. Sarajevo 1998: Art 7, 1998;
National and University Library of Bosnia and Herzegovina, Sarajevo

eastern Italy and that it was used in Wulfila's translation of the Bible into the Gothic language, and was the foundation of literacy among Goths.[61] All these facts support the presented thesis of the Croatian historian Nada Klaić regarding Bosnia being the oldest state among South Slavs, which she elaborated in her book *Srednjovjekovna Bosna* (Medieval Bosnia).

The Slavs that settled Illyria did so to the least extent in the area of Bosnia and Herzegovina, and the largest extent in the area of modern-day Slovenia, Croatia, and Serbia.

Modern historiography introduced doubt into the data from the *Ljetopis* popa Dukljanina (that is, *Barski rodoslov*) because of the political ambitions Duklja had regarding Bosnia and the Neretvan Banate. Although incorrect, the corrected paragraphs of the *Barski rodoslov* and the falsified Papal Bull should not prevent us from considering the innocuous assessment of the Bosnian rulers, the bans, for whom he says that they are of Gothic origin. Whether we take this fact about the Gothic origin of the Bosnian bans as correct or not, **what is reflected in this statement of the Priest of Duklja is important for Bosnia, because through this, it is highlighted as a specific and separate unit about the surrounding banates and župas settled by Slavs.** *"The period from the VII to the X century is the era of nameless bans."*[62] Many historians who dealt with the history of Bosnia and Herzegovina will gladly say that there are no written traces from this period of 300 years and that everything was destroyed and burned. However, this is only a partial evaluation, from the perspective of potential documents that could have been found in the territory of Bosnia. Now the question arises, what information related to Bosnia in foreign sources from this period, which we certainly do not see. The non-existence of information is still information from which a thesis about the unimportance of the Banate of Bosnia for the great empires can be drawn. As we have stated, the Franks and Byzantium could not consolidate their rule in the territory of Bosnia and Herzegovina and Dalmatia, nor was this

---

[61] Bisera Suljić Boškailo "Goti u Bosni", Bosanska riječ 2016; p.164 and 187.

[62] Dr. Enver Imamović, "Porijeklo i pripadnost stanovništva Bosne i Hercegovine"; p.18 Sarajevo 1998.

area of interest to them, so they did not write down and keep records that would be valuable to us today. This again leads us to the consideration of the relative to widespread political self-government of banates and župas inherited from the Roman and Gothic empires. **Those would be the elements which promoted development, the specificities of the early medieval Banate of Zagora, and finally the Kingdom of Bosnia and banates that are part of it, Pagania (the Neretvan Banate), Hum, Travunia, Konavle and in the cultural sense the župa of Ras (Sandžak).**

Ras has its specificities about the other units in which a symbiosis between the arrived ethnicities and religions was happening (Arianism, Christianity, Islam which in our region was present under the influence of the Illyrian army and the Spanish Saracens, and members of other exiled dualistic schools that found sanctuary in our land). In the župa of Ras, the process of the development of independence was progressing (which is evidenced by numerous stećci and Arian basilicas built from the IV to the VI century).

Although this area was periodically changing hands from Bulgarian to Byzantine rule, the process of the development of new Illyrian autonomy and self assuredness was interrupted by the emergence of the Župan of Raška, Stefan Nemanja (ruled Raška from 1166 to 1196) which, out of personal and political interests, changes sides between the Hungarians, then Rome and the Catholic tradition, and finally Byzantium and Orthodox Christianity tradition.

Old Ras, the main fortification in the župa Ras

The relative compactness of these banates and župas is indirectly attested by the Serbian historian Mihajlo Dinić, a member of SANU (Serbian Academy of Sciences and Arts), writing the following: *"It should be kept in mind that, in Bosnia proper – Hum (Herzegovina) and parts of Raška (Sandžak) are left out – in Tvrtko's time, there were no Orthodox Christians. For us, this issue is solved definitely!"*[63]

So, only during Tvrtko's time (1338–10 March 1391), which is a late period in the context of the age which we are treating, did Orthodox Christianity start to appear. There is much literature and many scientific papers from Croatian and Serbian historians who were eager to categorise our region, through the Church organisation, into the category of Catholicism or of Orthodox Christianity, and to, under that guise, place Bosnia into a politically subordinate position. As in the book *Srednjovekovna kneževina i kraljevina Srbija* by Živojin R. Andrejić, and in the eagerly cited Church Councils of Salona in 530 and 533 (which is considered by many authors to be a fabrication) which mention Andreas episcopus [ecclesiae] Bestoensis[64], Andrija, the bishop of Bestoensis, there is

---

[63] Mihajlo Dinić, Jugoslovenski historijski časopis I godina, p. 151

[64] Ante Škegro, Akti crkvenih sabora održanih 530. i 533. u Saloni, Hrvatski institut za povijest.

an attempt to categorise the banates of Bosnia, Usora and Soli, Hum, and the Neretvan Banate, through the Church organisation, into the category of Orthodox Christianity, that is Catholicism, and so-called Serbian, or Croatian lands. If we examine the fact that an Arian Gothic Basilica, which is likely older than this Council, was found in Salona, then it is clear how great the influence of the Church was in Bosnia and other banates when it had in its centre a completely contrary teaching.

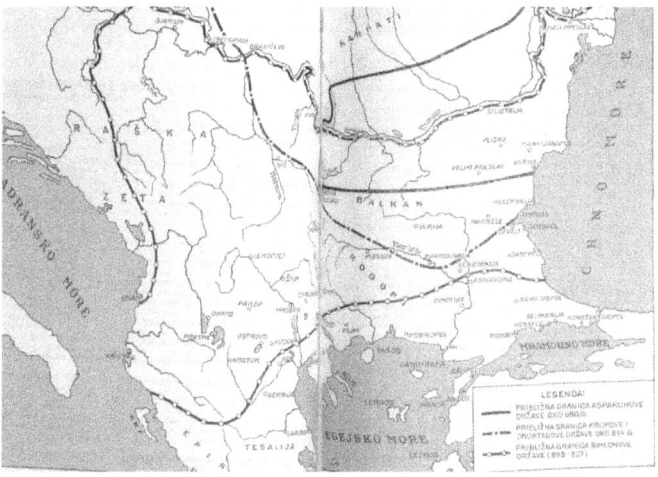

Map of the Bulgarian Empire, source: Wikipedia.

It is a known historic fact that the first Dominicans arrived in Bosnia shortly after the first order was founded in the year 1225, when in Bosnia and other mentioned banates and župas the Bosnian Church was already established, led by its djeds, and where the Arian teaching about Jesus of Nazareth was accepted and consolidated, in this time out of the Banate of Bosnia a university operated in Mile (the university is first mentioned in the year 1175, in which the teaching of the Bosnian Church was studied, a university which was the centre of European heretical movements), modern-day Arnautovići near Visoko.

Therefore, we will not discuss any further the issue of the influence of the Catholic or Orthodox Christian Church in this political, cultural, and religious vacuum that emerged in said banates and župas, because it did not exist or it was declarative only, that is, minimal. After the year 796 and the Frankish military victory against the Avars, in 895, the Hungarians arrived in the area of the Pannonian Plain. They settled Pannonia by the year 900, led by Árpád (Hungarian: Árpádok, Slovak: Arpádovci), where they established the Duchy of Hungary, which was governed by the Árpád dynasty, and, in a short time (from the year 1000), it became a strong early medieval dynasty.[65]

Hungarian ruler Geza, by an anonymous author (P. Magister) – Chronicon Pictum, facsimile, University of Maryland Library.

With their settling of the Pannonian Plain, the further expansion of the Holy Roman Empire to the east of the continent was prevented. They were nomads, pillagers, and pagans. With their settling of the Pannonian Basin, the compactness of the Avar-Slavic ethnicity,

---

[65] History of the Arpad dynasty, https://hr.wikipedia.org/wiki/Arpadovi%C4%87i

which was dominant until then, was shattered. They led constant plundering wars and were the fear of all until their leader Geza (972–997), pressured by the Germans, accepted Christianity in the year 974. What ensued is an en masse conversion of the Hungarian population. In the symbolic sense, the royal crown which Geza received from the Pope, represented the birth of the Kingdom of Hungary (modern-day Hungary) and by that, the borders of Papal influence was extended to the east of the European continent.

In this short description of the Hungarian state we can see that the entire time it was preoccupied with itself. It was not capable of providing and installing its rulers, which would be of Hungarian origin, also in Bosnia. Although some historians wanted to present the blood relatedness or closeness of Ban Borić and the Kotromanić dynasty, that they were of Hungarian or of Croatian descent, there are no reliable historical traces or evidence of that.

The hillfort Esztergom nearby the city of Visegrádi (Višegrad); the residence of early Hungarian rulers

In mentions of Bosnia, in Latin sources, the **phrase "per voluntatem Dei"** (i.e. created by the will of God) is mentioned;

also in the Frankish Annals, which mention in the first half of the IX century the "regio Ratimari ducis" (meaning, Ratimir, the ruler of a land, district, a defined area, which is located between the Frankish and the Bulgarian state, south of the Sava river). This would also be the earliest mention of any Bosnian ruler. In the year 827, the Bulgarians captured a part of Pannonia that today belongs to Croatia, in the year 828, Emperor Ludovik removed from power the margrave of Friuli, Baldric, blaming him for all these losses, and split Friuli into four new administrative parts, called counties. Thus he founded some Bavarian Kingdom, and named Louis the German.[66]

Istria and the Duchy of Dalmatia remained in a close relation to the Kingdom of Italy, while the part of Pannonia across the Drava river (around Lake Balaton) and Carantania (modern-day Carinthia, Carniola, and lower Styria).[67] In these conquests, the Bulgarians removed from power all the Frankish dukes and installed Bulgarian ones, wherein the Bulgarian King Omortag **supported Ratimir, who, all things considered, could be the first mentioned Ban of Bosnia.**

In the Frankish Annals, in the **year 838 the "regio Ratimari ducis"** is mentioned, located between the Frankish and the Bulgarian state, and south of the Sava River. King Louis the German sent a large army led by the margrave of Podunavlje, Ratbod, against Ban Ratimir (he ruled the conquered area 829–838), intending to destroy his military forces. The battle did not happen, because margrave Ratbod had to go to King Louis because of other obligations and problems, and Ban Ratimir retreated from that army into his land south of the Sava River.

Here it is interesting to note that in the year 1150 Ban Borić also owned land along the Drava River, which he allegedly received as a gift from the Hungarian king. The zone without any significant influence of the large empires, the Sclavinia Zagorska or Bosnia, was

---

[66] T. Smićiklas CODEX DIPLOMATICUS diplomatički zbornik Hrvatske, Dalmacije i Slavonije, Volume three, p. 12

[67] Ferdo Šišić, Povijest Hrvata prvi dio 600.–1526., pages 99 and 100

intended by the Franks to be militarily weakened so it would not join an alliance with the Bulgarians and become a threat to their border. *"The name Bosnia was gradually transferred from the area of Visoko onto the neighbouring annexed župas and regions, so that, even before the end of the X century, on the soil of Bosnia a state which the Priest of Duklja mentions in his chronicle as an equal to Raška and Croatia. Furthermore, there is completely founded evidence that Bosnia as a state had been shaped before other neighbouring South Slavic early feudal states. It is believed that Sclavinia (Sclavonia), which is mentioned in the Frankish Annals and other early feudal sources, is Bosnia. The Frankish Annals mention in 838 the Duke Ratimir, who ruled the area of the Sclavinia, i.e., Bosnia.[68] In the opinion of some, the council of Duvanjsko Polje was likely held towards the end of the IX or the beginning of the X century, and in any case sometime between 877 and 917. According to that, "Regnum Sclavorum", which is mentioned in the Chronicle, is Bosnia, and the "blessed King Budimir" is a Bosnian ruler. In any case, in the data of the Chronicle of Duklja, there is "an unbroken series of chronological anchor points related to well-known historical events, which happened in the period from the middle of the X to the end of the XI century".[69]*

Bosnia is presented in the Chronicle of Duklja as a relatively large land, which extends from the Drina river to the upper reaches of the Vrbas river and the Adriatic watershed, with an organised government, which is headed by the ban."

During these happenings, Ban Ratimir provided sanctuary to Duke Pribina, the ruler of Nitra in Slovakia, who was exiled from there by the Moravian Duke Mojmir. It is important to note the period of 300 years, from Ban Ratimir to Ban Borić. Since in the year 1150 Ban Borić owned property along the Drava river, which he received as a gift, it could be an indication that the bans of Bosnia even before Ratimir had "claim", influence, or some rights on the

---

[68] mamović Mustafa; Bošnjačka zajednica kulture "Preporod", 1998; Historija Bošnjaka, page 25.

[69]] Imamović Mustafa; Bošnjačka zajednica kulture "Preporod", 1998; Historija Bošnjaka, page 26.

land that extended above the Sava river, along the Drava river, which is quite far away from the later territorial perimeter.

There is no data about the heir of Ratimir. Whether he had a son who could have inherited his throne, or if it was one of his relatives, there is no data about that.

A testament to an autonomous Bosnia is found in the mention of Bosnia, which waged war against the Župan of Raška, Časlav Klonimirović (reigned 933 –950), who briefly captured and ruled over Bosnia. In this period, he managed to take over Zeta, Pagania, Zachlumia (Zachumlia), Travunia, and Rascia (Raška).

The next Ban of Bosnia is mentioned in the year 968, in a war against the Croatian holder of authority, Michael Krešimir II, and this datum is cited by the author of the family tree of the *Bosnian Kotromanić dynasty*, Bosanska dinastija Kotromanić, prof. Enver Imamović.[70]

During Krešimir's reign over Croatia, 949–969, it is mentioned that Krešimir II broke into Bosnia and, in his campaign, pillaged the župas of Uskoplje, Luka, and Pliva, and in the end, conquered the entire area of Bosnia. The Bosnian ban did not offer resistance but retreated to Hungary in the year 968.[71]

The name of Krešimir II is also associated with some fabrications of the ruler's documents. Nada Klaić has proven that the document by which Krešimir allegedly gifted the monastery of Saint Chrysogonus to the village of Diklo is a fabrication from later centuries.

The next mention of a ban on Bosnia is in the Ljetopis (Chronicle) by Nikola Lašvanin, specifically in the **year 1059.** When Dalmatia and Croatia were ruled by Krešimir, due to political upheavals and the power struggle in Hungary, the Bosniaks took the side of Bela,

---

[70] Dr. Enver Imamović: Porijeklo i pripadnost stanovništva Bosne i Hercegovine, National and University Library of Bosnia and Herzegovina, Sarajevo 1998, p.18.

[71] Rudolf Horvat, Povijest Hrvatske I, 1924.

the future king of Hungary, under the condition that they elect their ban among themselves. **Thus, they elected Ivan Kotromanić as Ban of Bosnia.**

The next documented mention of a Bosnian ban comes twenty-five years later, specifically the **Bosnian Ban Stipan, and the mention is related to a war against Bodin, the King of Duklja, in the year 1084**. There is not enough information about the Bosnian Ban Stipan to know more about him. Considering that the father of King Bodin, Duke Mihailo Vojisavljević, captured Travunia and part of Zachumlia, King Bodin, after ascending to the throne in 1083 and 1084, he did his best to retain the conquered territories, and went a step further, launching campaigns against Raška and Bosnia. Both campaigns were successful. A part of Bosnia and Raška became part of Duklja. In conquered Raška, Bodin installed as his regents two župans from his court, Vukan and Marko, while during this time in Bosnia, Ban Stipan is mentioned. It seems that Stipan was not born in Duklja, but was a Bosnian aristocrat who was to help Bodin in Bosnia.[72] In the Archaeological Lexicon of Bosnia and Herzegovina, Volume 1, on

---

[72] T. Živkovič, Gesta Regnum Sclavorum, Nikšić: Historical Institute, Ostroh Monastery, p.116–117. 2006, Belgrade.

page 45, it is stated that Ban Stipan was under Bodin's protection.

Stećak, Dobrigošće near Jablanica.

The political reasons for this could be of the following character: Duklja, during the reign of Bodin, was at the apex of its power. Aside from the centre of the kingdom, the backbone was composed of Travunia and part of Zachumlia, so that Raška and Bosnia comprised the second economic and military ring supporting King Bodin. The priorities of the king of Duklja were the capturing of Kotor, Budva, and Bar, which were to ensure trade exchange and flourishing of craftsmanship, which are the guarantors of advancement, power, and further development. Most likely, the two-year-long siege of Ragusa, 1092 –1094,by Bosnian Ban Stjepan and King Bodin happened exactly for these economic reasons. Bodin managed to capture Ragusa, remove all his cousins from power, and subsequently erect a castle, which he soon gave over to the Ragusans.

The **following ban of Bosnia, of unknown name, is mentioned in the year 1103, whose daughter was married to King Kočapar of Duklja**. The name of this Bosnian ban has not been written down, but it was recorded that, in the context of years-long power struggles in Duklja, King Kočapar was forced to flee to Bosnia, where he married the daughter of the Bosnian ban. The next to come to power in Bosnia after him is **Ban Borić (1154–1163), about whom we have a little more information**, which we will present in the following content. Ban Borić had two sons: Stjepan and Pavle, and the grandsons Odola, Čelko, Detmar, and Matija. Considering that in the literature, only the title "Ban of Bosnia" is stated, because names were not written down in original documents, therefore this period in which Bosnian rulers are mentioned by title only was called by Prof. Imamović "the age of unknown bans".

Based on the attached information, it can be claimed that Bosnia existed for 300 years before Ban Borić or Ban Kulin. Our historiography mostly treated Bosnia from these two rulers of Bosnia onwards, since here for the first time, broader data about them appear, and the reasons for such historiography are to be sought in the hiding of data about the oldest state in the Balkans, Bosnia, by its neighbours.

Illustration (detail) of the ruler of Duklja, St. Mihailo Vojisavljević, around 1080. This fresco in Ston is laid claim to by both Croatian and Serbian historians.[73]

So, after the fall of the Avar Empire, the following period from the VIII to the XI century, the area of modern-day Bosnia and Herzegovina, Dalmatia, and Raška (modern-day Sandžak) through their ethnic, religious (Arianism) and cultural sameness, belonging, and connectedness, were in a more or less independent position in relation to the large empires. What is specific of the župa Ras (central part of Sandžak) is that it was part of the Bulgarian Empire, where, judging by the Arian basilicas (found in the Raška river valley) and stećci, which are a later cultural phenomenon, the Arian–Illyrian, in this period, Bosnian, identity was developing. Up until the emergence of the Župan Stefan Nemanja, who, out of personal interest and currying favour from Byzantium and Rome, entered into conflict with the members of Arianism in Ras. Because

---

[73] Z. Bjelovučić; Hrvatska kruna u Stonu. Starohrvatska prosvjeta: glasilo Hrvatskoga starinarskog družtva u Kninu, 1928; p. 123.

of that, the Croatian historian Dr. Nada Klaić[74] rightfully defines Bosnia as "the oldest state among South Slavs". That is how independent župas and banates, and after the Avar Empire, Bosna, Usora, Soli, Hum, Travunia, the Neretvan Banate (Pagania), and Konavle remained without foreign influence. According to the records of Constantine Porphyrogenitus[75] around the year 950, Bosnia extended over the territory in which the Illyrian Daesitiates tribe (which would mean from the Lašva river to the Drina river, as the nucleus of the large area of central Bosnia).

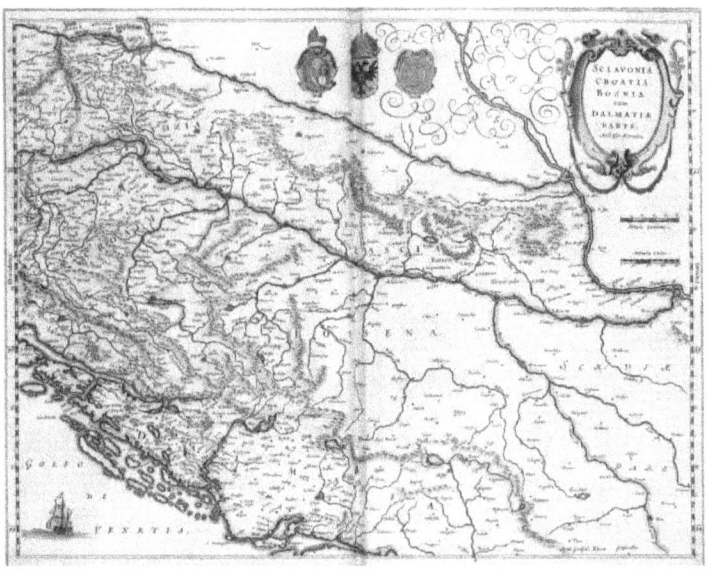

Bosnia – "Bossena" in the IX and X century, source: Scheepvaartmuseum Amsterdam Nederland

Here it must not be omitted, although we do not agree with the Gothic theory of the origin of the Bosnian Kotromanić dynasty, the mentioned Chronicle of the Priest of Duklja, which highlights that the Goths consolidated in the territory of modern-day Bosnia and Herzegovina the political centre from which the Gothic dynasty

---

[74] Dr. Nada Klaić "Srednjovjekovna Bosna", Zagreb 1989, Second Edition, 1994.

[75] Constantine VII Porphyrogenitus „De Administrando Imperio", 945.

ruled. The state was divided into banates, and **the ruler held the title of king**. Bosnia was divided into upper or mountainous Bosnia and lower or flat Bosnia. Therefore, from the VII century up until 1166 Bosnia was independent from Byzantium. In the X century, Bosnia is mentioned as comprising the area of Uskoplje, Luke and Pljevlje to the west, with the Drina county to the east, which was under the rule of one holder of authority – the Ban. If, according to the Priest of Duklja, the ruler of the "Zagorska sclaviniae", banates and župas, held the title of king; And if the Bosnian Kotromanić dynasty is of Gothic origin, as descendants of Theodoric the Great (Theodorich der Grosse), Svetopelek, in that case "The Kingdom of Sclaviniae / Kingdom of Slavs" was in Bosnia and the mentioned župas and banates. This non-existent kingdom cannot be claimed neither by Croatia nor by Serbia, considering that they were vassal župas of the Franks, the Bulgarians, or of Byzantium, and are in their mythological-political approaches to historical facts coming into conflict on this issue. The German anthropologist, lawyer and historian, Theodor Mommsen, who in 1902 received the Nobel prize for his work The History of Rome, considers the Muslims of the north- east Balkans to be direct descendants of the Ostrogoths. Although, according to the latest, empyrical, genetic research, this theory is incorrect as well. Bosnian Muslims are mostly Illyrians, natives in this area, more than all others.

In our opinion, which is certainly subject to criticism because we do not have the historical data, is that the Bosnian aristocracy and the ruling Kotromanić dynasty are of Illyrian, domestic origin. Knowing that the Scandinavian Goths are Illyrians in origin and that some of their surnames end in -ić, many old Gothic words have their Illyrian origin, and so Theodoric is a Germanised name. On his bronze plate with the name of the king written in silver it says Thloderići.

Based on the provided facts we can solve the dilemma on the issue of the origin of the Kotromanić dynasty, whether they are of Illyrian or of Gothic origin. The oldness and origin of the Bosnian Kotromanić dynasty was written and attested to by many contemporaries through the centuries of its reign. A document from the XIII century says that the Kotromanić dynasty are the rulers of Bosnia since old times. In his Charter from the XIV century, the Bosnian King Tvrtko literally emphasises that the Kotromanić dynasty is ruling over Bosnia since its creation.

In parallel to the development and affirmation of the Banate of Bosnia, the Bosnian name was being confirmed as well. Thus, in the imperial title of Manuel Komnenos from the year 1166, the name Bošnjanin or Bosniak. Muhamed Hadžijahić is of the opinion that during the IX and X century, the process of homogenisation of *Zagorska sclavinia*, that is of Bosnia, was progressing, so that Bosnia,

Donji Kraji, Usora, the župas Rama, Drina, Zagorje around the upper reaches of Neretva and Kalinovnik, Podgorje, or, later on, Zachumlia or Hum, are part of it. From that follows that the Bosnian state established its borders early on the rivers Drina and Sava, and to the south towards the Neretva banate all the way to Livno. Many authors are of the opinion that the society and societal organisation of Zagorska sclavinia (Bosnia) was stratified because of the immigration of Slavs. However, it cannot be said that there was a great stratification of the newly-emerged state from today's point of view, because genetic genealogy shows that exactly those sclaviniae (župas and banates) which are listed were under the lowest influence of the immigration of the Slavic population. In Bosnia, half of the population has the indigenous Alpine-Dinaric genetic haplogroup adding the already assimilated Gothic component with a tendency of symbiosis and assimilation of the newly arrived population. The nucleus of Bosnia in those days was the Bosna river valley and the area around Visoko.

Here, Mr. Hakija Zoranić's research into the emergence of Bosniaks should be added.

"Through the analysis of several scientific papers, Zoranić concluded that the Bosniaks emerged during the second half of the VII to the beginning of the IX century, from:

1. *a portion of the indigenous Illyrians, the oldest European people, who lived in this region for several thousand years;*

2. *a portion of the Germanic Goth, who assimilated into the Illyrians during the III and the IV century, and who are also a European people;*

3. *a portion of South Slavs, among whom there were no Serbian nor Croatian tribes;*

4. *a portion of Avars who had invaded together with the South Slavs and whose assimilation into the Slavs was nearing its completion;*

5. *A portion of Romans, and it is also possible that there was an insignificant number of Thracians and Celts, who are also European peoples.*

Through numerous, at first bloody, and later long-lasting peaceful processes of mutual permeation, assimilation, and identification, a characteristic symbiosis emerged, a singular people which named itself Bošnjani, after the land of Bosnia, or after the Bosnia river."

Large nišan in Bakići, Olovo.

12 BAN BORIĆ

Bosnian bans are mentioned 300 years before Ban Borić.[76] The first Bosnian ban about whom there is more information in historical documents is Ban Borić. He reigned from the year 1150 to the year 1163.

> The translation of a Greek text by John Kinnamos is important in the same sense. Describing an event from the Byzantine-Hungarian War in 1150, this writer left a record about the Drina river being the separator between Bosnia and Serbia. The original text reads:
> Ἐπεὶ δὲ ἐγγὺς Σάου ἐγεντό ἐξ ἑτέρου
> ἐκεῖθι ποταμὸν Δρυνᾶν ὄνομα
> ὃς ἄνωθεν τὴν ἐκβολὴν ποιούμενος

Borić certainly ruled over Bosnia even before he was mentioned in the documents, and the period of his reign was likely longer. He was married to the granddaughter of Bosnian Ban Stjepan.[77] With her, he had two sons, who are also mentioned in written sources in the year 1250, those being Stefan and Pavle. There are no documents that could tell us something about the origin of Ban Borić, so all theories about his Hungarian-Croatian origin are senseless because they are based only on the fact that his successors from the XIII to the XV century are mentioned in that area (generatio Borich bani).[78] On one hand, the documents from Venice tell that Ban Borić is originally from Hum, while on the other hand, his origin is placed in the area surrounding Grabarje, near Brod na Savi – in Slavonia, because his family owned land there. The descendants of Ban Borić settled in Slavonia and the lower reaches of the Vrbas river, and one branch of the family also constituted the noble family Babonić, who rose in power in the XII and the XIII century in Slavonia and the Vrbas river valley.[79] The Babonić

---

[76] http://bosanskipogledi.com/2021/07/17/nastanak-banovine-bosne-i-njeni-prvi-banovi/

[77] Ban Stjepan is first mentioned in connection with a war against the king of Duklja, Bodin, in 1084, and she was called the Lioness.

[78] Ferdo Šišić, Povijest Hrvata prvi dio 600.–1526., page 179.

[79] Koszta, László (1994). "Babonić". In Kristó, Gyula; Engel, Pál; Makk, Ferenc (eds.). Korai magyar történeti lexikon (9–14. század) [Encyclopedia of the Early Hungarian History (9th–14th centuries)] (in Hungarian). Akadémiai Kiadó. p. 73.

family can be traced in reliable sources only from the middle of the 13th century. Considering that they reigned to the south of the Sava river and the lower reaches of the Vrbas river, up to Kupa, and the fact that the Bosnian Ban Prijezda, to calm the situation with the constant power struggles with Duke Radoslav, gifted to his brother Stipan Zemljenik (*totam supam Zemlenyk*), through which the Vrbas river flows (*hinc transit Vrbaz*), and considering that those are Bosnian estates, it is possible that the Babonić family is exactly the mentioned descendants of Ban Borić.

After the death of Hungarian King Bela, the Bosnian Ban interjected himself into the happenings related to the struggle for the Hungarian throne. Considering he was underage, he was in opposition to Bela's sons, Geza, Stephen and Ladislaus, being of the opinion that regency should be allotted by skill and seniority, and not by inheritence. Thus, he supported their mother Jelena, and their uncle, Palatine and Ban Bjeloš. Shortly after, the son of King Bela, former Bosnian Duke Ladislaus took over reign in Hungary, only to pass shortly after that and be succeeded by Stephen III. As a sign of gratitude, Stephen III gifted Ban Borić with large estates in Slavonia. He retreated from these estates when Byzantium went to war with the Hungarians.

"Historijska karta srednjovjekovne bosanske države", Marko VEGO, *Naselja bosanske srednjo- vjekovne države, Sarajevo, 1957,* from p. 184.

It was then that parts of modern-day Croatia, Dalmatia, Srem, and Bosnia fell under Byzantine rule. Bosnia is mentioned for the first and last time in the Byzantine Emperor's title, from the year 1166 to the year 1180. Ban Borić maintained good relations with the Hungarian authorities, and it is mentioned in documents that he visited Esztergom.

Photograph description: Esztergom is, aside from the Hungarian city named Visegrád, the hill-fort in which early Hungarian rulers lived.

His independence in relation to Hungary is evidenced in the battle in which he defeated the Hungarian army of King Stephen III, who was trying to bring Bosnia under his rule. That was the first military conflict and first victory of the Bosnian army against the Hungarians.

Ban Borić found mention in the work of Byzantine chronicler, the scribe of Emperor Manuel I Comnenus, John Kinnamos, in the book *Summary of events*. There it is said that he ruled over Bosnia, which extended from the Sava River on the north, to the Drina river in the east, while some sources say he also ruled Hum. Although his main estates were on the Bosnian, and modern-day Croatian side of the Sava River, most likely his administrative centre was a little deeper in the territory of Bosnia, specifically in the hill fort in Srebrenica. Based on sources from the Papal Curia, in the war between Hungary and Byzantium, from 1150 to 1154, at the time of a battle against Byzantium on the Tara River in the year 1150, a certain Župan Banki(u)n, described by John Cinnamos, is mentioned. Considering that the Byzantines adopted this term to their mode of expression, it is possible that this is Ban Kulin, Historical sources state that Ban Kulin was a mountain of a man and very strong, and that he was fearless and very brave on the battlefield.[80]

After being defeated in this battle, he was probably taken to Constantinople and in his place Ban Borić was installed. With that, the possibility is created that Ban Borić ruled over Bosnia on two occasions, and Ban Kulin took for the first time the title "Grand Ban" and rule over the entirety of Bosnia in that time. Because, if in the year 1150 Kulin led the battle on the Tara River, against Byzantium, then he must have been the ruler of Bosnia, because in that time the ruler would lead fighting on the battlefield. Considering that the medieval Bosnian state encompassed the area from modern-day Foča to modern-day Srebrenica, further reaching the Drina river and extending to its river mouth in the Sava River. Along the Sava river valley it extended close to what would later be Bosanski Brod on the north, and to the spring of the Ukrina river, following the line which extended to Banja Luka and the middle reaches of the Sana river. From the Grmeč mountain on the west, the border went south to the župas of Glamoč, Livno and Rama, and following the Rama river valley, emerged in the upper reaches of the Neretva River. Across Jelač the border completed its ring around Bosnia in Foča. The expansiveness of the state territory is stated in a source from 1203, which says that, to cross Bosnia, "it took ten and more days of walking".[81]

In the year 1154, Ban Borić, as an ally of the Hungarian King Stephen III, participated and led the Hungarian-Bosnian army, comprised of Czechs, Saxons, Hungarians, Croats, and the Bosnian army, in laying siege to the village of Braničevo (right-hand shore of the Danube). When Komnenos arrived with his army, the Hungarians went in the direction of Belgrade, while Ban Borić with his army went upstream the Sava River, across the Drina River, into Bosnia. The Byzantine writer John Kinnamos says the following about this event: "When he arrived near Sava, he turned around to another river, named Drina, which springs from somewhere above

---

[80] https://hamdocamo.wordpress.com/2017/04/10/dvoboj-izmedu-bana-kulina-i-bizantskog-cara-manuela-komnena-tokom-bitke- na-tari-1151-godine/
[81] https://bosnae.info/index.php/ban-kulin-1180-1204-doba-mira-prosperiteta-bosne

and divides Bosnia from the rest of Serbia, and Bosnia is not subject to the Arch-župan of the Serbs, but the people in it has a separate manner of living and administration". When he found out that Borić is with the Hungarians as well, Komnenos sent his elite units, led by chartularius, Basil Cinciluk, who was defeated by Ban Borić. If the Byzantine emperor sent his best fighters into battle against the Bosnian ban, then the ban's army was a respectable force, which is evidence of good state and military organisation and military skill. The result of the battle between Byzantium and the Hungarians was such that Byzantium beat the Hungarians, and Ban Borić had to retreat from Bosnia into Slavonia, to his estates which he received as gift to administrate over, from the Hungarian king.

Photograph; Bosnian Kingdom,
Historija srednjovjekovne Bosne

John Cinnamus wrote extensively on these happenings. He named Ban Borić explicitly as an ally of the Hungarian king. A very interesting mention of Ban Borić is found in works of the Templars. When they were looking for estates on which they would build their "houses", and which would serve them in protecting the route taken by European pilgrims on their journey to the Holy Land, Jerusalem, Borić gifted them his estate which is today located on the Drava river in Croatia. This documented deed of donation to the Templars, as a land estate, was located in Esdel (Zdeljica near Most, in Podravina) and the Templars received this gift in the final years of

Ban Borić's life.[82] This is the estate that was gifted to Borić by the Hungarian King Stephen III. In documents from the year 1209, King Andrew II again took under his protection the Templars in Dalmatia and Croatia, and bans anyone from demanding taxes or income from them. Among the Templar estates in this royal document, the village of Esde, owned by Ban Borić (banus Boricius de Bosna) is mentioned as well. There it is stated that the Ban gifted this village to the Templars with the agreement of King Stephen. This deed of donation was confirmed by King Bela III as well. During the reign of Ban Prijezda (1211–1287), it is also mentioned that Borić gifted land to the Templars, which according to Thalloczy (Lajos Thalloczy) indicates the existence of some familial relation between Borić and Prijezda, and even Borić and Ban Matej Ninoslav (1232–1250), who are part of the Bosnian ruling family, Kotromanić. In historical documents, another deed of donation to the Templars was recorded. Namely, a land estate which was gifted by Odola, the grandson of Ban Borić. It is important to note that these land estates were part of Odola's estates and Odola, as it says in the documents, owned them by "inheriting", "jure hereditario".[83][84]

The Ragusan chronicler, Giunio Resti[85] In his work, Cronicha di Ragusina, states that Borić came into conflict with the Ragusans after he previously became lord of Zachumlia, and their conflict began because of a dispute between the Bosnian bishop and the Ragusan archbishop. Mavro Orbini[86] Places the first confrontation precisely in the 11th month of the year 1154, and the second in the following year, which resulted in the Bosnian ban being defeated near Trebinje. On the other hand, according to Resti's writings, the conflict occurred in 1159– 1160. Historiography agrees that Ban

---

[82] Juraj Belaj, Templari I Ivanovci na Zemlji Svetog Martina, 2001. [83] [85] [86]

[83] Maria Karbić, Posjedi plemićkog roda Borića Bana

[84] Helen Nicholson, The Knight Templar, 2002.

[85] Resti, Giunio (Džono), Croatian historian and chronicler, (Ragusa, 1669 or 1671 – Ragusa, 6 IX 1735). He was a member of the Ragusan Senate, Duke of Župa, Mljet, and Ston, emissary to the Bosnian pascha, member of the Lesser Council and twice the Duke of the Republic of Ragusa.

[86] Mavro Orbini, also Mavar Orbin, (* 1563 in Ragusa, Republic of Ragusa; died in 1614) was a Ragusan Benedictine monk, Dalmatian intelectual and historian.

Borić likely also died soon after the mention from 1163.

According to Slavoljub Bošnjak, *Zemljopis i povlestnica Bosne*,[87] Having achieved a truce with Ragusa, Ban Borić gifted the property and the church in Babino Polje on Mljet to the Benedictine order. The pertinent charter of Borić was also preserved, dated to 1158–1159, by which the Benedictines of Lokrum are gifted the estates on Mljet. Subsequently, historiographers brought into question the authenticity of this charter, but not of the event itself.

Byzantine documents state that Borić is the "Exarch of Dalmatian Bosnia", which would mean governor or ruler.

Exarch (Greek ἔξαρχος: duke, excellency, dignitary) is a title which was used in civil and church administration. In the civil administration of the Byzantine Empire, the exarch was the governor or viceroy of a large and important province.

---

[87] Bošnjak, Slavoljub, Zemljopis Poviestnica Bosne, Zagreb 1851; Narodna tiskarnica dr. Ljudevit Gaj, pages 88 and 89.

Charter of Borić dated to 1158–1159, by which the Benedictines of Lokrum are gifted the estates on Mljet.

13 DOMINUS BOSNAE - KULIN, THE GREAT BOSNIAN BAN

After Ban Borić, about whom we find somewhat more data in the sources, and who is, partly for that reason as well, considered the first Bosnian ban (which does not correspond to the truth, because in the source we find mention of Bosnia and its bans up to 300 years before Ban Borić), Ban Kulin is another Bosnian ban about whom we find much more data in historical sources than about his predecessors. Ban Kulin was a person belonging to Bosnian aristocracy and has his roots in earlier generations of the ruling structures of the feudal government.

Ban Kulin, as envisioned by the artist Adis Elias Fejzić.

The basis for this formulation is found in the previous bans, the rulers of Bosnia. Knowing that in earlier periods, ever since the fall of the Avar Empire in the year 791, Bosnia was free of the influence of the two empires which were dominant at the time – the Frankish and the Byzantine – it is possible that in Bosnia there were no dramatic shifts of government, aristocracy, and rulers of land estates, but that ownership was transferred by the implicit civilisational tools: gifting, potential buying, selling, and certainly inheritence.

During the time of Ban Kulin, Bosnia has developed and functioning all components of effective statehood; meaning, it has territory, it has a ruler, an administration, army, implicit state borders, it has a currency, a language, and even its own script, Bosančica, which is widely known today and has a specific cultural heritage and tradition reaching back to the old Illyrian era. Bosnia truly is an entity which, it seems, is the oldest state-building creation in the region of Western Balkans. All stated characteristics are reflected in the well-known historical artefacts such as the Charter of Ban Kulin, issued to Duke Krvaš and the citizens of Ragusa, from 1189, the Confessio Christianorum from 1203, the Humac tablet, the Miroslav Gospel, etc.

Ban Kulin (dominus Bosnae) ruled over Bosnia from the year 1180 to the year 1204. Historiography, considering the availability of historical sources from the period of Kulin's reign, is permeated by the (incorrect) view of Ban Kulin as the founder of Bosnia. In his time, the Bosnian Church's conception of faith was officially the state religion, and to reach that size and power it had to have its inception much earlier in history, as did the Banate of Bosnia; meaning, it had to have some tradition of development, growth, and penetration into the structures of state organisation.

According to a record by the Benedictine Mavro Orbin, in his book Kraljevstvo Slavena,[88] Ban Kulin succeeded Ban Borić and ruled for 36 years. If it is correct that Kulin ruled for 36 years, then he ruled from the year 1168, which would mean that he was actively present during the reign of Ban Borić; therefore, this dating stated by Mavro Orbini could also be correct, because Borić's reign ended in the year 1163. In that period, before the year 1180, sources mention a certain Baculinus, which is likely the Byzantine name for

---

[88] Mavro Orbini, Kraljevstvo Slavena, published in 1601.

Ban Kulin.[89] Still, all these datings should be taken with reservations.

Familial links to his predecessors in power are not certain. Ferdo Šišić endorses the opinion that Kulin is the son of Ban Borić.[90] Nada Klaić also sets out from the thesis that Kulin was a relative of Ban Borić.

Kulin's Banate of Bosnia extended from Drina to Vlašić, with the provinces of Vrhbosna (modern-day Bosnia and parts of eastern Bosnia) and Usora (with Soli). In the year 1164/65, After the exile of Ban Borić to Slavonia, the Byzantine army conquered Bosnia, Usora (with Soli), Dalmatia, Srijem, and parts of Croatia. Considering that he was part of Bosnian aristocracy, under the auspices of Byzantium, he was installed to the throne around the year 1172, during the reign of Emperor Manuel I. Komnenos, and that is the time in which the influence of Byzantium over Bosnia was approching its end.[91] Here it should be elucidated that, if Ban Kulin ascended to power after the death of Ban Borić, then Byzantium could accept the rule of Kulin under certain vassal conditions, and not install him, as is stated in historical literature.

Prof. Mustafa Imamović is of the opinion that Ban Kulin was installed on the throne around the year 1175.[92] After the death of Manuel I Komnenos, Ban Kulin is called the Emperor of Bosnia, which excludes the possibility of a vassal relation towards Hungary. In that time, Bosnia was a strategic and military partner on the side of the Hungarians and Rascians (Stefan Nemanja) in a war against Byzantium in the year 1183. In the Hungarian governmental system, the vassal relationship was not yet known. Thus, all theses of these historians who wish to categorise Ban Kulin into a dependent, vassal relationship towards the Hungarian king are

---

[89] https://dijak.online/ban-kulin-1180-1204/

[90] Nada Klaić, Srednjovjekovna Bosna: politički položaj bosanskih vladara do Tvrtkove krunidbe, 1377, Grafički zavod Hrvatske, 1989.

[91] Pejo Ćošković: Kulin. In: Hrvatski biografski leksikon. Lexikographisches Institut Miroslav Krleža, 2013

[92] Mustafa Imamović, Historija Bošnjaka.

incorrect.[93] Kulin was independent of Hungary, same as his predecessor, Ban Borić.

The rule of Ban Kulin was certainly older than his first mention in historical sources, which happened in the autumn of the year 1180, after the death of Emperor Komnenos. Namely, in a letter of the Papal legate Theobald who writes to "Kulin, Great Ban of Bosnia" (Culin magno bano Bosine), "noble and mighty man, Ban of Bosnia"; in the letter he states: "... the greatness of generosity of your glory, out of benevolence to St. Peter the apostle and the Pope, and for the salvation of your soul, to send two delegates or scholars for a conversation and to send marten hides"[94]

In the manner in which this letter to Kulin is addressed, it can be seen that the Bosnian ban was very well-known and respected in Rome and other lands.[95] Unfortunately, the letter that Pope Alexander III wrote to Kulin was not preserved. Although the letter of the Papal legate does not mention any problems, it can be sensed that the Pope wanted to bring Bosnia and its Church, on which it had little influence, closer to the Roman Church.

As with all aristocracy throughout Europe of the day, the practice of negotiating marital agreements and familial links with other noble families was present in Bosnia as well. Kulin followed the Illyrian line of creating familial ties, because his wife, Vojislava, sister of the Župan of Raška, Stefan Nemanja, his sister was the wife of the Zachumlian (Herzegovina) Duke Miroslav, the brother of Stefan Nemanja, Great Župan of Raška. He was succeeded by his son Stjepan. Kulin had one more son.

One branch of the family, along the female line, from the house of Kulin, was linked to the Hungarian royal family, (middle of the XIV century), that being Elizabeth Kotromanić, the daughter of Stephen II, Hungarian Queen married to the Hungarian King Louis,

---

[93] Malcolm, Noel (1 October 1996) Bosna. Kratka povijest. London: New York University Press. p. 364.

[94] Pejo Ćošković: Kulin. In: Hrvatski biografski leksikon. Lexikographisches Institut Miroslav Krleža, 2013, also Emir O. Filipović Bosansko kraljevstvo, Historija srednjovjekovne Bosne.

[95] Dr Enver Imamović, Kulin Ban i njegova Povelja

then her daughter Hedwig, Polish Queen. Elizabeth's relative, Maria Kotromanić, was married to the German Count Ulrich, from the province of Swabia; there is also the Countess of Cilli (Celje), Catherine Kotromanić.

From the time of Ban Kulin's reign, two stone tablets were found on which Kulin's name is written.

The first was found near Zenica, in a place called Podbrježje, in 1964. On this tablet, the text is engraved from both sides of the plate on which the mention of Ban Kulin is preserved and on which it can be seen that most likely the Church of St. George is erected by Gradješa, "Great Judge", during the reign of Ban Kulin. Draže Ohmućanin constructed the building, and the inscription was written by a person who is, with many reservations, identified as priest Prodan.[96] The great judge was so wealthy that he could construct a graveyard church for himself and his wife. This tablet is very important, because it mentions a "Great Judge" in the time of Kulin; so, it evidences the existence of respected people – judges, and here, among them, the Great Judge Gradješa, it evidences the presence of scribes, and all that confirms the existence of an organisational structure and judiciary within the government of Kulin's Bosnia.

Ktitor's inscription of the Grand Judge Gradiša, end of the 12th century:

V d`ni b(a)na velik(a)go Kulin(a) bješe Gra(d)ješa sudi(ja) veli u njeg(a) i s`zida (crkvu) svetago

Jurija : e se leži u n(e) go : i žena eg(o)va rče položi(t)e me u Nego: a se zida Draže O(h) mučanin' : (to)mu voli B(ož)e

:n(an'). (A)z' pisah' Pro(dan') (po)p

---

[96] Emir O. Filipović, Bosansko kraljevstvo Historija srednjovjekovne Bosne. Mladinska knjiga, 2017; p. 54.

Tablet of the Grand Judge Gradiša, kept in the Museum of the City of Zenica.

In the book of Marko Vego, Postanak srednjovjekovne bosanske države, we find the complete text of this charter, the first and second sides of the tablet.

The inscription on the headstone of the Bosnian great judge Gradeša (Gradiša) from the era of Ban Kulin engraved after 1193-1204. The inscription is engraved on both the front and rear side. Roughly translated it says:

"V' dni b(a)na Kulin(a) bijaše (biše) Gra(d)iša (Gradeša) sudi(ja) (sudija) veli u njeg(a,o) i s'zida /hr'm' = hram'/ svetago Jurija (na kraju jat), i se (ovo) leži u n(e)go (u njemu) i žena jeg/a) Vare (Varvara = Barbara), položi /se/ (s)emo (ovamo) u njego (u njega). A se zida Draže O(h)mučanin' jemu. Voli, b(ož/e nas'! ili vo(z) ljubljeni — voljeni! /A ili i) z'pis/a/h', ili jaz' (ja) pis(a)h' Pro/kopije/, ili Pro(tazije/ ili Pro/kopije) pop'." That is found on the front side.

The text on the rear side is quite damaged and reads:

". . . slava veli/komu/ /gospo/dinu + banu! Az(') pisah' dni maja s (= 6.) aag (theta grčko) (1193.) i (osvješta (treće slovo jat) a/rhi/epi/skop') i pojdo(h') stazama (/b/ana Kulina dobriga (= dobroga) + i pasahu (prolažahu) ki (koji) /iz/ Juroja (na kraju jat) iziti (izići) šta/hu/ = šćahu . . ."

The inscription is written in Bosnian Cyrillic of that era, important for gaining insight into the religious state of the population in Bosnia and the formation of the Bosnian court and feudal administration. It is an obvious example that the feudal system was already established in Bosnia. M. Vego, Zbornik, IV, No. 252.

The second tablet from this period is the Tablet of Ban Kulin. It was found in Biskupići, near Visoko, and is dated to the end of the 12th century. It is kept in the National Museum of Bosnia and Herzegovina in Sarajevo. Our well-known historian, Dr. Ćiro Truhelka, in his text Kulinova ploča[97], describes the discovery of said tablet as follows:

"Travelling through Visoko this spring, I found out that near the town, on the left-hand shore of Bosna, beneath the village of Muhašinović, in the so-called Tuština field owned by Jovo Šarenac, a stone tablet with inscriptions was unearthed while tilling the soil. The inscription on the tablet says:

Siju crkv' ban' Kulin' zida

e g d..... jeni Kučev'sko Zagorie

nade na nu grom(' i) u Podgorie Sljepičišt': i postavi svoj obraz' (za ili nad') pragom'

B(og)' dai banu Kulinu zdravie i banici Vojslavi

In places where the letters are damaged, in the interpretation of the inscription, letters were arbitrarily inserted to give the inscription a possible meaning. So it is given characteristics of "contemporary language", and it would be interpreted as follows:

This church was built by Ban Kulin when he seized Kučevsko zagorje. And it was struck by lightning in Podgorje Slijepčišća.

And his cheek he placed above the threshold

God gives health to Ban Kulin and his wife Vojslava."

So, according to Truhelka, the inscription refers to a church which Ban Kulin constructed in Kučevsko Zagorje, and which was, as the inscription says, struck with lightning, so the Ban rebuilt it and

---

[97] Ćiro Truhelka, Glasnik zemaljskog muzeja u Bosni i Hercegovini, XV, 1903

placed his cheek above the threshold.

Г СНЮ ЧРІСВЪ · ЗЧNЬ
КОЖЛНЬ ЗНАЧ · ЄГА...
ЪNH КОЖУЄВЬСКО
ЗЧГОРНЄ : Н NЧАЄ
NЧ NOЖ ГРОМ...
ОЖ ПОДЬГОРѢ
СЛѢПНЖНЧЬ : Н
ПОСТЧВН СВОН ОБРЧЗЬ...
ПРЧГОМ : БЪ АЧН БЧNОЖ
КОЖЛНОЖ ЗЧРЧВ|Н|Є
Н БЧNНЧН ВОНСЛЧВ|Н

There are two approaches to interpreting this inscription. The first one, held by many historians to be valid, is that Kulin participated as the ally of Hungarian King Bela III and the Župan of Raška, Stefan Nemanja, in the war against Byzantium and, campaigning in Kučevsko Zagorje, built this church from the spoils of war.

On the other hand, Prof. Dr. Emir O. Filipović thinks, which is truly something novel and very interesting for future research, that this insertion of letters (or falsification) to get some explanation of the text is a wrong approach and says that the toponyms "Kučevsko Zagorje" and "Podgorje Slijepčište" should be sought in the area surrounding Visoko, because the tablet of Ban Kulin was found in Biskupići. Finally, there existed a strong religious centre which would be worthy of the builders of the church's attention.

And in documents of the Vatican, Prof. Dr. Enver Imamović and Zoran E. Bibanović[98] Truly did find a datum that during the reign of Ban Borić and Ban Kulin, in the year 1175, there existed a university in Visočko Polje, in Moštre near Visoko, which was among the first universities in Europe, where professors, "magisters", taught the teaching of the Bosnian Church.

This is an additional datum that supports the fact that the Banate of Bosnia was a strong and organised social community not only

---

[98] Prirodno i kulturno naslijeđe Sarajeva. See: https://www.skyscrapercity.com/threads/visoko-%D0%B2%D0%B8%D 1%81%D0%BE%D0%BA%D0%BE-construction-news.1642811/

during the time of Ban Kulin, but also of his predecessor, Ban Borić. It should not be surprising that the Bosnian Church during the time of Kulin was the state religion of the Banate of Bosnia.

Members of heretical movements from across Europe, people who did not accept the Holy Trinity and the crucifixion of Jesus, came to or, fleeing from persecution, hid in Bosnia, as the spiritual centre of their understanding of faith and believing close to their own. There, nobody was attacking them, nobody persecuted them, and they were free to live their belief and learn the specificity of the belief of their hosts, the Good Bosniaks and the Bosnian Church. The Catholic Church later stalked some. So, in discovered documents of the inquisition, the following names are mentioned: Iacopo Bech from Chieri, a town south-east of Turin, Rabellator de Balbis from Chieri, Iohannes Narro, and Granonus Bencius, that they were in Bosnia around the year 1360, and Berardus Rascherius around the year 1380. Thomas the Archdeacon, a writer from Split, states that in the time of archbishop Bernard in Zadar, there lived two brothers, Matheus and Aristodius, from Apulia, who, as good and skilled artists and goldsmiths, knew the Latin and the Slavic language well, and spent much time in Bosnia, spreading heresy "with their vile lips".

Here it should be added that the Neretvan Banate, which extended from the Cetina River to the Neretva river mouth into the sea, with the islands of Brač, Hvar, and Korčula, ruled by the bans of the Kačić family, regardless of the presence of Catholic prelates, was predominantly "heretical" as well, and was called Pagania by the Pope and Catholics. Also, the Bosnian djeds on several occasions travelled through Catalonia and discussed with and taught the Cathars who lived there the teaching of the Bosnian Church, confirming their Cathar teaching as correct. Here we can see that the so-called heresy was not present only in Bosnia, but Bosnia, considering its political independence, was a strong (actually the strongest) centre and thus a problem for the Christian Church.

As we see, the Banate of Bosnia truly was a strong and organised community, in contrast to other Illyrian banates which were partly fighting for their independence or were under the direct influence of foreign powers – Rome, the Franks, Hungary, or Byzantium. Only Bosnia is mentioned as a large banate in historical documents, and that Raška was a župa or a great župa; therefore, the ambition of Stefan Nemanja becomes clear – to destroy Ban Kulin, so he could usurp the position of Great Ban, and thus rule Bosnia.

In the year 1203, the ruler of Duklja, Vukan Nemanjić, the oldest son of Stefan Nemanja, as his father did before (which indicates a continuity in the pressure exerted on Bosnia and the Bosniaks), with the support of the Hungarian (Croatian) King Emeric II, sends to Pope Innocent III a letter in which he accuses Kulin and his wife Vojslava that they, with their relatives and 10,000 others, converted to heresy; in the letter they ask and plead for the Pope to send to Bosnia "...an able man who will investigate the religious situation and amend that which shows need of mending".

"It should be said that Kulin himself, faced with the accusations that he accepted heresy and under threat of military intervention, in the manner of a skilled politician, wrote to the Pope stating that he does not know the difference between the Catholic and the heretical teaching, and is therefore pleading for him, the Pope, to send his emissary to Bosnia so it could be determined if there exists such a difference."[99]

Based on the accusations of heresy, the Pope wrote to the archbishop of Split, Bernard, and the chaplain John of Casamaris, on 21 November 1202, tasking them with investigating the right orthodoxy of the Bosnian population, Ban Kulin and his wife Vojslava, because they are accused of "Catharian heresy". Considering that the archbishop of Split, Bernard, could not set off on a journey to Bosnia, in his place went the Ragusan archdeacon Marin, who understood the Bosnian Church and maybe had a personal relation to it, so he argued to the benefit of Kulin and his djeds. The council happened in spring, on 8 April 1203, on

---

[99] Imamović, M. (2003), Historija države i prava Bosne i Hercegovine, treće dopunjeno i redigirano izdanje, Magistrat, Sarajevo, 67

"Bilinom Poili". "Today, that site is placed in Bilino Polje in Zenica, although some authors think that the styling "near Bosnia" leaves the possibility that it is in the wider area of Visoko, where Kulin's court was as well."[100]

The council (this is explicitly mentioned in the Statement written after the council) was attended by Ban Kulin, his wife, and the djeds of the Bosnian Church, listed by name: Dragič, Ljubin, Dražeta, Pribiša, Ljubin, Radoš and Vladoš. The council was concluded with the Ban and the djeds of the Bosnian Church pledging to adhere to the principles of belief of the Roman Curia. Ban Kulin and the djeds of the Bosnian Church accepted the authority of the Holy See over the Bosnian Church, with the caveat that prayers remained in the folk language, not in Latin.

After signing the Statement and after the Hungarian King Emeric II gave a positive assessment of the conversion, the Papal emissary, John de Casamaris (who, after he finished his mission, took with him two converted Krstjani, Ljubin and Braget, as proof of the return to Christian theological tenets, it is well-known that they were questioned in Rome, but their fate after that is unknown); meaning, after he finished his mission, Casamaris wrote to Pope Innocent III a letter in which he uses the term "former patareni" for the Bosnian Krstjani. He was convinced that he had completed his mission and converted the Krstjani to the "true faith". However, it would turn out that he was wrong. In the following few decades, the "heresy" of the Bosnian Krstjani grows stronger and perseveres despite the crusades against Bosnia, and as such lasts to the middle of the 15th century, when the Ottomans invade Bosnia and it stops existing, that is, its members gradually convert to Islam.

---

[100] Emir O. Filipović, Bosansko kraljevstvo Historija srednjovjekovne Bosne, Mladinska knjiga, 2017.

> XXXV.
>
> Instrumentum, quo Bosniae monachi schismatici constitutiones ecclesiae Romanae servare promittunt. Reg. An. VI. ep. 141
>
> In nomine dei eterni creatoris omnium et humani generis redemptoris. Anno ab ipsius incarnatione M.CC.III. domini vero Innocentii pp. III. anno VI. Nos Priores illorum hominum, qui hactenus singulariter Christiani nominis prerogativa vocati sumus in territorio Bosne, omnium vice constituti, pro omnibus, qui supra de nostra societate fraternitatis in presentia dni I. de Casamaris, Capellani summi pontificis et Romane ecclesie, in Bosna propter hoc delegati, presente patrono Bano Culino domino Besne, promittimus coram deo et sanctis eius stare ordinationi et mandatis sancte Romane ecclesie tam de vita et conversatione nostra, quam ipsius obsecundare obedientie et vivere institutis, obligantes nos pro omnibus, qui sunt de nostra societate, et loca nostra cum possessionibus et rebus omnibus, si aliquo tempore deinceps sectati fuerimus hereticam pravitatem. In primis abrenuntiamus scismati, quo ducimur infamati, et Romanam ecclesiam matrem nostram caput totius ecclesiastice unitatis recognoscimus: et in omnibus locis nostris, ubi fratrum conventus commoratur, oratoria habebimus, in quibus fratres de nocte ad Matutinas, et diebus ad Horas cantandas publice simul conveniemus. In omnibus autem ecclesiis habebimus altaria et cruces: libros vero tam novi quam veteris Testamenti, sicut facit ecclesia Romana, legemus. Per singula loca nostra habebimus sacerdotes, qui dominicis et festivis diebus ad minus missas secundum ordinem ecclesiasticum debeant celebrare, confessiones audire et penitentias tribuere. Cemeteria habebimus iuxta oratoria, in quibus fratres sepeliantur, et adventantes, si casu ibi obierint. Septies in anno ad minus corpus domini de manu sacerdotis accipiemus, scilicet in Natali dni, Pascha, Pentecoste, Natali apostolorum Petri et Pauli, Assumptione Virginis Marie, Nativitate eiusdem et omnium Sanctorum commemoratione, que celebratur in Kalendis Novembris. Ieiunia constituta ab ecclesia observabimus, et ea que maiores nostri provide preceperunt, custodiemus. Femine vero, que de nostra erunt religione, a viris separate erunt, tam in dormitoriis quam refectoriis, et nullus fratrum solus cum sola confabulabitur, unde possit sinistra suspicio suboriri. Neque de cetero recipiemus aliquam vel aliquam coniugatam, nisi mutuo consensu, continentia promissa, ambo pariter convertantur. Festivitates autem Sanctorum a sanctis patribus ordinatas celebrabimus, et nullum deinceps ex certa scientia Manicheum vel album hereticum ad habitandum nobiscum recipiemus. Et sicut separamur ab aliis secularibus vita et conversatione, ita etiam habitu secernemur vestimentorum: que vestimenta erunt clausa, non colorata, usque ad talos mensurata. Nos autem decetero non Christianos, sicut hactenus, sed fratres nos nominabimus, ne singularitate nominis aliis Christianis iniuria inferatur. Mortuo vero Magistro, de hinc usque in perpetuum Priores cum consilio fratrum deum timentium eligent prelatum a Romano tantum pontifice confirmandum: et si quid aliud ecclesia Romana addere vel minuere voluerit, cum devotione recipiemus et observabimus. Quod ut in perpetuum robur obtineat, nostra subscriptione firmamus. Actum apud Bosnam iuxta flumen loco qui vocatur Bolino Poili, sexto Idus Aprilis. Dagrite, Lubin, Brageta, Pribis, Luben, Rados, Bladosius, Banus Culinus, Marinus archidiaconus Ragusii subscripsimus. Deinde nos Lubin et Brageta ex voluntate omnium fratrum nostrorum in Bosna et ipsius Bani Culini, cum eodem domino I. Capellano ad H. Illustrem Ungarie et christianissimum Regem euntes, in presentia ipsius Regis et Venerabilis ... Colocensis Archiepi et Quinqueecclesiensis Episcopi, et aliorum multorum in persona omnium iuravimus hec statuta servare, et si qua alia ecclesia Romana super nos ordinare voluerit, et secundum fidem catholicam constituere.
> Actum in Insula Regia II. Kal. Maii.

https://bs.wikipedia.org/wiki/Bilinopoljska_izjava

The printed copy in Latin of the Abjuration of Ban Kulin and the Bosnian djeds from 1203, with the opening sentence – In nomine dei creatoris omnium et humani generis redemptoris, i.e., translated:

In the name of the eternal God, the creator of everything and redeemer of humankind.

Interestingly, Ban Kulin and the Bosnian Church found themselves exposed to a great danger if they do not accept what is practically dictatorship of Rome (had the agreement not been reached, a military intervention would certainly have ensued), one would expect the accepted text of the Abjuration (Statement of disavowal under oath) to begin as was customary in that time throughout Catholic Europe, with an invocation, i.e. witnessing of the Holy Trinity, meaning – In the name of the Father and the Son and the Holy Spirit, which would mean the acceptance and following of Catholic tradition; however, it is not so. The text begins as follows:

In the name of the eternal God, the creator of everything and redeemer of humankind. In the year of His incarnation 1203, the sixth year (of the pontificate) of Pope Innocent III.

This seems to us as a compromise between the theological tenets of the Curia in Rome and the belief and political circumstances in Bosnia and Herzegovina and its surroundings, considering that this introductory part – In the name of the eternal God the creator of everything and redeemer of humankind – closer to the Arian (therefore, the Bosnian Church's) tradition of the conception of divinity. In contrast, the second part is a de facto acceptance of authority (from the text of the Statement that is unequivocally clear) of Pope Innocent III, meaning, the Catholic Church in Rome.

So, said Abjuration was available to historiographers for over 800 years. The question is: How did no one until now notice this cardinal discrepancy and at least indicate it, if not attempt to decipher it spiritually and in the context of the time? Therefore, this is, we can safely say, a capital contribution to the understanding of the Bosnian Church and its relations towards the dominating Christian dogmas during the time of its existence.

Today, we know that Kulin (who passed shortly after the abjuration), **the Bosnian Church and the Bosniaks after this statement continued with the tradition of belief in their characteristic way, as if the Statement did not exist**; so, this move by Kulin can be understood as one more in the long Bosnian tradition of walking the tightrope, meaning, the skilled adjustment to the objective circumstances and the situation as it is, until it passes. Later we will see how to proceed. Thus, the Bosnian Ban Kulin, with marked diplomatic skill and ability of manoeuvring between the desired and the possible, achieved a successful arrangement and practically prevented a military crusade on Bosnia.

The reign of Ban Kulin was characterised by rapid economic development, conditioned by his economic, diplomatic, and political abilities.

The following adage has been retained in folk legend and can be heard even today in various situations, be they positive or negative: "Since Ban Kulin and the good old days". This expresses the economic prosperity of the Banate of Bosnia and the temporal distance to that period.

Copy of the Charter of Ban Kulin, National Museum of Bosnia and Herzegovina in Sarajevo; two copies are kept in Ragusa, and the original is in Russia, Saint Petersburg.

Another event that gave a strong character and well-known seal to the rule of Ban Kulin is the Charter issued to Ragusa, in which all the forms of Bosnian statehood are manifested. The Charter was issued to Duke Krvaš and the citizens of the Ragusan Republic, on

29 August 1189. This diplomatic act guaranteed free trade for the Ragusan traders in Bosnia. Kulin gives the Ragusans the guarantees of free movement across Bosnia and of freedom to sell and buy goods. Thus, across Bosnia, there existed Ragusan stations where

Ragusan traders lived. Along with many sorts of goods and services from both sides, they also engaged in monetary and crediting business, through which they contributed to the quicker development of all forms of entrepreneurship, mining, mine concessions and tariffs, crafts, etc.

Via the relationship with Ragusa, an influence and connection of Bosnia with Mediterranean countries, such as Italy, Venice, Genoa, Sicily, etc., was realised. Through that, a strong economic base for the future development of Ragusa and certainly of Bosnia was created. Therefore, the popularity of Kulin in Ragusa is understandable. The close relationship with Ragusa, ever since the time of Kulin, was maintained more or less throughout the existence of medieval Bosnia (and later), and it can also be seen as a spiritual heritage to this day.

Charter of Ban Kulin issued to Duke Krvaš and all citizens of Ragusa states the following:

In the name of the Father and the Son and the Holy Spirit. I, Ban Kulin, promise to you, Duke Krvaš, and all citizens, Ragusans, to be a true friend to you now and forever. And maintain justice with you and true trust, as long as I live. All Ragusans who walk where I rule, trading, wherever they want to move, wherever any of them wants to, with true trust and a true heart, without any malice, and whatever I am given as a gift shall be of their free will. They shall suffer no force from my officers, and as long as they stay with me, I will help them as I would myself, as much as possible, without any evil thoughts. So God help me and the Holy Gospel. I, Radoje, the scribe of the Ban, wrote this book of the Ban's Charter, one thousand one hundred and eighty years since the birth of Christ, in August and the twenty-ninth day, on the date of the beheading of John the Baptist.

The Charter was written in the old Bosnian folk language and the Bosnian script, Bosančica, and is considered to be the oldest state document of all South Slavic peoples and states. The Charter of Ban Kulin was written in two languages. Aside from Bosančica and the Bosnian language, there is the Latin script and language. These bilingual charters were created in four exemplars, two for each of the sides, but of the four that were written, only three were preserved to this day. Two are located in the Ragusan archive, and the third exemplar of the Charter of Ban Kulin was stolen in the 19th century and is still located in the Russian Academy of Sciences and Arts in Saint Petersburg.

There is no information about the death of Ban Kulin and the location of his burial site. He was succeeded on the throne by his son Ban Stepan, who ruled until the year 1232. There are some opinions, which, naturally, without any more reliable indicators, suggest that Kulin's life ended in a Constantinople prison. However, this is highly unlikely.

Judging by the epitaph found on the stećak of Bogčin Radinić from the region Bosna Srebrna, where he proclaims that, if he were born again, he would give his life for Kulin and Bosnia, we can sense that the Ban died a natural death, and that his stećak was cut and placed somewhere in his, Kulin's, Bosnia. That epitaph reads:

To Kulin, I was more loyal than Radaci, and I am not ashamed nor do I regret that, and if I were as you are again, I would be the same as I was

You will never be as I am, and I cannot be as I once was

Blessed be he who reads this and thinks about it, and insane he who breaks it in the summer of 1205 year after the Great Ban Kulin was laid into the soil.

Stećak, Konjic

14 ARIAN BASILICAS IN BOSNIA AND HERZEGOVINA FROM THE IV TO THE VI CENTURY

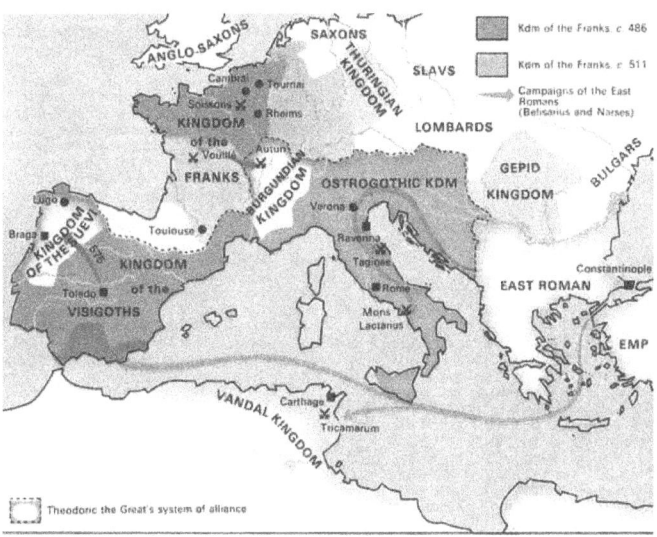

About the first traces of Christianity in Illyria we find the thesis that Saint Paul, sixty years after the death of Jesus, on his journey to Rome, experienced a shipwreck near the island of Mljet in the Adriatic coast, and that the surroundings of this island in the direction of Ragusa was the first in Illyria which Paul missioned. However, those are only suppositions and attempts to explain the question of the first roots of Christianity in our region or the south of the Adriatic. Very bold in this interpretation were Daniele Farlati,[101] Zrinka Žeravica,[102] Marija Buzov[103] and many historians who uncritically accepted and repeated this thesis in their literature.

---

[101] Daniele Farlati. (1751) Illyricumsacrum, Apud Sebastianum Coleti, Venetiis.

[102] In his study dedicated to churches with the titular of St. Paul in the Ragusan area, Z. Žeravica boldly states: "...It can be taken as historic fact that St. Paul on his missionary journey toward Dalmatia and generally Illyricum first sailed into Epidaurus, and consistent with that, spread Christianity in Epidaurus before any Dalmatian cities. He could have visited Ston during his three months long stay on the island of Mljet, after the shipwreck he experienced there when he travelled as a prisoner to Rome in the 60th year after Christ.

[103] Histria antiqua: journal of the International Research Centre for Archaeology (1331–4270) 21 (2012); 491–505.

Narona *(village Vid near Metkovići, on the Norin river)* and Salona *(Solin)*, which is considered to be the first bishopric established in the 4th century, were taken to be important centres for the spreading of Early Christianity. Archaeology still has not found any artefacts or indicators from that period that would confirm the correctness of this thesis. On the other hand, if we examine the Epistles of St. Paul, we will find that in the Epistle to the Romans, written in Corinth in the year 58, he writes:

"Thus from Jerusalem and around, "to" Illyricum, I completely fulfilled my duty of preaching the Good word of Christ..." From this, it can be concluded that Saint Paul came near Illyricum, but was not in it, and thus did not preach there. If one examines the direction of the journey of St. Paul, he sets out from Jerusalem towards Rome. On that maritime journey, he does not encounter the island of Mljet, but the island of Malta, where he could have experienced a shipwreck and there perform his role of missionary.

Eusebius of Caesarea, in his work he mentions Paul's journey to Illyricum: *"In that time, when Paul completed the circular journey, from Jerusalem to Illyricum, Claudius exiled the Jews from Rome."*[104]

The traders and travellers who would come to Narona, Dalmatia, from the 1st to the 3rd century were not enough to establish a new religion in Illyria. Aside from that, the Roman government was strict in punishing and persecuting the Christians and all those who would not offer sacrifices to the Roman deities. The cruelty of Rome was most relevant in the Near East, in contrast to Illyria, where there was no need for it. Aside from two cases, which were written down, Illyria can safely be separated from this context.

Then the question is: Why is that so? In our opinion, because at that

---

[104] After Diocletian's persecution of the Early Christians had ended, Eusebius of Caesarea, Palestinian Caesarea (265–340), was chosen as the bishop of Caesarea around the year 313. In theological discussions with Arius he played an unclear role. At the first Council of Nicaea in the year 325, he defended Arius and his conception of Jesus of Nazareth from the bishop Alexander of Alexandria, and signed the Nicaean symbol and anathema against the Arians with reservations. Origen's pupil, Eusebius, adopted a stance of reconciliation, and he wanted to achieve a compromise between the advocates of Arianism and their opponents. And after the Council of Nicaea, Eusebius was involved in the conflicts regarding Arianism, and fought together with Atanasius of Alexandria (who was later exiled in 335) for the teachings of the true faith. Shortly after Constantine's death, Eusebius passed as well, probably as Caesarea.

time, in the region of Illyricum (Illyria), there was no widespread reception of Christianity.

But, despite knowing of these facts, some historians, having no other explanation, not wanting to search for other answers, stick to this thesis and again and again take the missionary work of Saint Paul as the beginning of Christianity in lower Dalmatia, and date the epistles and Christianity in the time of the apostles. However, the first findings of Christian communities appear only towards the end of the 3rd century.

Simultaneously, on the other end of Illyria, in the time of the settling of Goths in Pannonia, after the Council of Nicaea, in 325, where Arius was declared a heretic together with his followers, and as punishment exiled to Illyricum, and his literature was sought out and was burned by the Roman authorities.

So, in connection with that, the question of the real beginnings of Christianity and the question of its followers in the region of Illyricum or the Roman provinces of Pannonia and Dalmatia arise. We will attempt to give a comprehensive answer to those questions and to realise the connection between Arianism and the medieval Bosnian Church.

Only with this act, the arrival of Arius and Arian bishops, can one speak about the real beginnings of Christianity, or rather Arianism, which emerges in the auspices of monotheistic Judaism and Christianity, in the Roman provinces in Illyria.

Fresco, 38 cm × 27 cm. St. Paul, Rome, latter half of the 13th century, Vatican Museum.

Within Christianity, there existed two great schools that differed in their conception of the nature of Jesus. The first school is Origon, which in the end won the theological struggle, not because it preached the truth, but because it managed to get Constantine, the emperor of the Roman Empire, on its side. The second teaching, which was very widespread in the east of the Roman Empire, was Arianism. Presbyter Arius (Greek presbyteros – senior, elder; Latin presbyter; Church Slavic: презвитерь), name for a member of the Jewish grand council of elders (presbyterium or sanhedrin), the elder of the synagogue in Palestine, and for the person who presides over a Christian community.

After the Resurrection of Jesus, on his advice, the twelve apostles began to spread the word of him, of Jesus, the Messiah, in groups; and Simon went to Egypt, Libya and Armenia. Most likely, the apostle Simon (Apostle James Zebedee), who left his traces in Libya and Egypt, was the base of Arius' positions on the nature of Jesus. Arius (born in Libya) had his experience in monotheism also as a parallel scholar and authority of Judaism and Christianity, and he was also a Hebrew by origin.

Guido Reni – Saint James the Greater – Google Art Project

The relatedness of monotheistic Judaism with Arius' understanding of the nature of Jesus is indisputable. These two main schools or branches within the new religion in the Near East are the Hebrew and the newly emerged Christian aspect, which out for interesting reasons, is eager to differentiate and separate itself from Jewish influence, primarily out of political or other reasons related to power. Because of that, as valid was the telling of Saint Peter, who did not have experience and contact with Jesus, and proclaimed some forbidden things to be allowed: he declared the sacredness of Saturday to be on Sunday. He abolished circumcision as a sign of Abraham's Oath and allowed the consuming of pork, which in Judaism was forbidden.

Following the direction of Simon's travel, so Egypt, Libya, Armenia, we must note that Christianity in these countries is specific from the rest of the Christian world.

The specificity of the apostle's understanding and interpretation was probably retained because these regions were on the periphery of the Roman Empire and the persecution of Christians in the first 3 centuries CE by the Roman emperors. In these regions, the persecution of Christians did not have the same power as it did in the centre of the Near East or the central parts of the Empire.

Francesco Roselli, map of the wider Adriatic coastal areas, Florence, 1476–1484.

The same is true for Illyria, part of the Roman Empire, which was in the 3rd century gradually settled by Goths, who accepted Arius' teaching. Considering that many learned people from the higher social stratus in that time was on the side of Arius (Arius' followers among the clergy – *the bishops: Secundus i Theonas, the presbyters: Achilles, Aeithales, Carpones, Sarmates and two named Arius, as well as the deacons: Euzoïus, Lucius, Julius, Menas, Helladius and Gaius, Arius' friend from school Eusebius, (bishop of Nicomedia) Arianism was widely accepted and spread.*

The Roman emperors Nero and Diocletian committed horrific

crimes against the Christians. Diocletian had several decrees, in 303 and 304, by which he banned Christianity and ordered the persecution and killing of its main figures it.

Modern historiography considers that in this period of persecution, to the 3rd century, between 3,000 and 3,500 Christians were killed.[105] The goal of the Roman authorities was for the Christian clergy and literature to be owned by them. In Illyria (the province of Dalmatia), St. Domnius became a martyr. A contemporary of Arius, St. Dominus was born in modern-day Syria, in the area which was visited by Simon the apostle, and he was ordained in the Dalmatian city of Salona. A basilica was built on his grave, which the Avars and the Slavs leveled in the VII century. An Arian Basilica was discovered in Salona, which could be the original basilica of St. Dominus. With the Edict of Milan in 313, Emperor Constantine gave the Christians the right to preach their faith, only for Emperor Justinian to declare Christianity the state religion.

Some Islamic theologians find evidence of the persecution of followers of the apostles, the Early Christians, recorded in the Qur'an, in the surah Al-Kahf. It tells about a group of believers which, when they asked "How does Allah resurrect the dead?", Allah put in a sleep of around 300 years, and then resurrected again, to simultaneously protect them form the persecution of an evil ruler (possibly Emperor Nero) and show His might in resurrecting the dead, thereby confirming Jesus (Isa a.s.) who was also, through prayer and God's will, received this miracle. (more details in the Qur'an, surah Al-Kahf).

Considering that they were persecuted and under constant danger, followers of the Apostolic faith in the beginning gathered in the catacombs.

Catacombs are the subterranean tombs of the first Christians, which they also used as gathering places for communal prayer. With

---

[105] Frend, Martyrdom and Persecution, Oxford 1965. 393–94; Liebeschuetz, Oxford University Press, 2011. 251–52.

Constantine's rise to power, the persecution of Christians ended, and with the Edict of Milan in the year 313, he granted Christianity equal religious rights.

Interior of the catacombs in Jajce.

At this point, we have to mention the last Roman Emperor who ruled over the entire Roman Empire, that being Flavius Theodosius I The Great (Latin: Flavius Theodosius). He came to power (379 to 395) and solved the issue of the Goths, in that he accepted them as allies into the Roman army. During Theodosius' reign, Christianity was a free religion in the entire empire, which benefited the spread of Arianism amongst the Goths and the native Illyrian population.

There is a thesis stated by the academic Muamer Zukorlić (author of the book Drevna Bosna (Ancient Bosnia)), that Theodosius, when dividing the Empire into its Eastern and Western half, drew the line along the rivers Drina, Sava, and Kupa to the west, and that, because of its cultural and other specificities, he marked the territory which was to serve as a district or buffer zone between the two parts of the empire. Illyrian specificity was reflected for the final time in its "non-acceptance" of slavery in the Roman-Illyrian war from 6 to 9 CE, which was led by the Illyrian military leader Bato (Baton) I the Daesitiate, from central Bosnia.[106]

After the death of Theodosius, his sons took power. Honorius took power in the west, while Arcadius did so in the east. As they were incompetent in ruling, the responsibility of commanding the imperial army lay with Stilicho (military title "Magister militum"). To neutralise the danger from the Goths, he offered to the military leader Alaric and his Goths western Illyricum, on the Western balkans, as a place where they could settle. The peace for which Silicho was hoping however did not happen. In the following years Alaric, King of the Goths, focused on the strengthening of his army.[107]

Thanks to the expansion of the Goths to the west, that is, to northern Dalmatia and Bosnia, rudimentary, undeveloped Gothic cultural achievements which in the area of Illyria developed further: small churches – basilicas, Wulfila's Gothic Bible, the Messapian script, Arian Christianity, art, architecture, to finally in this area, in the cultural sense, surpass other European peoples, aside from the Roman cultural achievements, naturally.

Ivan Mužić, who says the following about the Goths: "It is very difficult to recognise Gothic specificities in all that in the cultural sense originally belonged to the Goths in the areas where they ruled. Goths during their history, especially in the II, III, and IV century, accepted many foreign cultural elements. Thus, the Goths who lived by the Black Sea accepted not only Irano-Armenian (highlighted by D. P.), but also the Hellenic manner of constructing buildings. In historiography it is accepted as indisputable that the Goths quickly

---

[106] „Bato the Daesitiate was a political and military officer of the Daesitiate civitas, an autonomous territorial, governmental, and administrative unit, part of the Roman province Illyricum. The Daesitiates are an Illyrian people which, in the period from the IV century BCE concluding with the II century CE dominated the area of Upper Bosnia and the Lašva river valley. Regardless of the Daesitiate name no longer being used as an ethnic or national descriptor, the ethnic and genetic heritage of the Daesitiates to a large extent is dominant in the modern-day native population on the stretch from Sarajevo to Zenica and Travnik", says Mesihović Selmedin. https:// ilirikon. wordpress.com/2021/12/01/baton-dezitijatski-iz-bosne-vođa-na-koga-je-rimsko-carstvo-poslalo-190-000-vojnika/

[107] Goterina; Ingmar Stenroth, Goterhaus historia, p. 104.

and consistently accepted the achievements of antique culture (Ljubo Karaman).[108]

Since 379 Goths settled this territory, that being the area of modern-day Bosnia and Herzegovina and Dalmatia. The presence of Goths is also evidenced in the genetic research which showed that in Bosnia the genetic haplogroup specific of Gotland in Sweden was retained, and that is the later genetic mutation named the "Dinaric haplogroup" in the science, the oldest haplogroup in Europe. The Goths, whose large tribes were the Ostrogoths, the Burgunds, the Langobards, and the Vandals, were mostly followers of Arianism and their Gothic bishop Wulfila (311– 383). **Even sooner, according to the writings of Thomas the Archdeacon, after the Council of Nicaea (325), Arius was exiled to Illyricum, where he spent a long time with his bishops in Sirmium (Sremska Mitrovica). It is reliably known that with the bishop Cededd, he spent time around the city of Visoko (central Bosnia) and preached his teaching there.[109]**

Although Arianism was banned at the Council of Nicaea, the question arises whether it was really suppressed or outrooted through that.

Eusebius of Nicomedia, the Arian bishop of Libya, sent the monk Wulfila to spread Arianism amongst the Goths, although it was already present thanks to Arius. The mentioned events: the arrival of Arius in Illyria, the appearance of the Gothic bishop Wulfila (Ulfus) and the settlement of the Arian Goths in the area demarcated by "Theodosius' line", conditioned the widespread acceptance of Arian Christianity in Illyria, and the building of the first sacral buildings. Those sacral buildings were built based on pagan buildings. They are called basilicas.

That Arianism was already widespread in Illyricum, before the

---

[108] Damjan Pešut, Goti koji su i slaveni, Zavičajni muzej, Ogulin p. 305. https://hrcak.srce.hr/file/187128

[109] Cededd or Sidid is originally an Arabic word, a noun which denotes a person whose answers to religious questions are undisputed, a religious scholar, an authority in religious matters. The name is most commonly used in Iraq and in Syria. It is possible that the djed of the Bosnian Church, the highest title in the hierarchy of the Bosnian Church, was named after Cededd or Sidid.

official approval of the Roman authorities for the Arian Goths to settle Illyria, is evidenced in the fact that between 347 and 359, four synods were held in Sirmium (Sremska Mitrovica) at which the Arian bishops voted for the so-called Four Sirmian Arian Formulas. Thus, the doctrine of the heretical teaching of the Sirmian bishop Fotin, who denied the characteristic of the Son in the Trinity, was adopted by Bonoz, the bishop of Naisus (Niš), while also claiming that Mary did not remain a virgin.

The biggest danger for Christianity, that is, for the "Nicaean true faith", was Arianism, the "heresy" that denied the core of Christianity.

That Arianism was found in our area in an early period is also shown by Dr. Fra Leon Petrović, a Franciscan from Herzegovina, in his book Krišćani bosanske crkve (The Christians of the Bosnian Church). Fra. Leon writes that at the council in Solin (Salona) held in 530 and 533 (before the appearance of Croats and Serbs in the Balkans), the bishop Andrija is mentioned (Episcopus Bestoensis). What is at hand is an old Bosnian bishopric, which was located in a as-of-yet not definitively determined location in central Bosnia. There are two possible locations of its seat, and those are Zenica and Bugojno.

Ante Škegro places this bishopric in Bilimišće in Zenica, and in Divjaci in Mali Mošunj near Vitez in central Bosnia. In the antique settlement of Čipuljić near Bugojno, an Early Christian oratorium (domus ecclesiae) from the age before Constantine and an Early Christian basilica from the 4th or the 5th century were discovered, and nearby it, also a brickwork fragment with the inscription "Andrija"! These facts could allow the placing of the first bishopric of the Bosnian Church in Bugojno. Considering it was called Ecclesia Bosnesis, i.e. Bosnian Church, there is no doubt that it has its continuity since the Roman era. As the bishopric would be too large, its bishop, Andrija, requested that it be split to be more easily administered. Eight hundred years later, Arianism lives on in our region as the Ecclesia Dalmatia, the Dalmatine Church (which is also called Bosnesis – Bosnian).

Aside from this bishopric, there existed also the *"Kirche des gotischen Gesetzes"*

(ecclesia legis Gothorum), an Arian-Gothic "Church of the Gothic law".

So, Arianism spread to Europe out of Bosnia. As is claimed in one of the writings by the Dominican Anselmo from Alexandria, Italy, who lived in the 13th century: *"The heretics were at first in Bosnia, from whence they spread their teaching to Lombardy, and then further to Francia, from whence it reached Orleans in 1022 and Arras in 1025".*

We find the first data on the conversion of the western parts of Illyria with Charlemagne (748–814), who took as his vassal the Arian convert Duke Borna, *dux Dalmatiae atque Liburniae* (ruled from 810 to 821).

That the heretical, Arian city of Zadar, Liburnia and Dalmatia with their surroundings were not converted overnight, in a short period, is evidenced by the beginning of the Fourth Crusade in 1202, when the crusaders besieged this city for 13 days. After they opened the gates of the town, the inhabitants paid a high price; the crusaders pillaged and devastated Zadar.

Neighbouring these župas was the Neretvan Banate, which was called Pagania by Rome and the Pope, because its inhabitants were unbaptised. The local population (60–75% Alpine-Dinaric or old Illyrian genetic haplogroup) fervently opposed conversion and finally was among the last in the Balkans to accept Christianity. The previous ruler of the Neretvan Banate was Bogdan Kačić, who, pressured by the Republic of Venice, surrendered power to Hungary in the year 1287. Further, the same is true for Travunia, Hum, Konavle, and finally Raška, which in the Early Middle Ages were Arian and had their Arian sacral objects, the basilicas.

Arianism was deeply rooted in all these banates and župas. The

Republic of Poljica positioned itself in a specific manner.[110] After the collapse of the Kačić dynasty of bans and the fall of the Neretvan Banate under Hungarian rule, unbaptised inhabitants of Poljica retained their autonomy under the Hungarian crown. Using the Bosančica script, they wrote the "Charter of Poljice", which was a form of a legal contract between several villages in the hinterlands of Omiš, on the Cetina river. This Charter was written as a decree about the rights and responsibilities of the inhabitants of Poljica, so their specific indigenous cultural heritage would be satisfied and a distance from the Christian influences coming out of the bishopric of Split and its eagerness to gain control over the fertile land of Poljica would be created. It should be noted that they maintained strong ties to the Banate and later the Kingdom of Bosnia. They did not recognise the bishops of Split, and, modelled after the Bosnian Stanak (Parliament), they elected a new Župan each year. The crowning of the Župan was conducted in front of the Arian basilica of Saint George in Gata (hinterlands of Omiš). This basilica was built in the Arian Illyrian-Gothic orientation of NW–SE. Some authors think that Thomas More used the Charter of Poljica in his writing of Utopia.

The Arian basilicas of Saint George in Gata, *in the Illyrian-Gothic orientation of NW–SE.*

Here, a logical question arises: How come that historiography simply attributed the small churches or rather Arian sacral buildings built from the 4th to the 10th century, to Catholicism?

This period is characterised by Arianism and the Bosnian Church, and less so by Mithraism, Zoroastrianism, and Manicheanism. The only answer could be that the period from the 10th century was recorded by writers of history who were mostly clergy, and the order was by Pope Gregory the Great.[111] That the numerous pagan cult sites be given Christian markings.

---

[110] https://www.dugirat.com/kultura/119-tradicija/22196-split-i-poljica-odnosi-kroz-povijest
[111] Gregory the Great was the pope from 590 to 604.

Early Christian basilicas, different ancient Illyrian, pagan customs and beliefs were shrouded in Christianity, so the importance of the cultural and historical heritage of the earlier beliefs, customs, and Arianism in the centre of Illyria, in Bosnia and Dalmatia, would be minimised or christianised.

In those circumstances, in Bosnia, which is the centre of Arianism, Bogumilism, a heretical teaching allegedly from Bulgaria, is placed. However, there is no information or documents about the existence of the priest Bogumil. Nothing is known of his birth, nor is there any authentic record or note of him in any sense. How is it that a teaching can be named after someone about whom there are no historical notes and data?

To remove Arianism from the historical stage, its historical importance was minimised, and to reduce the Illyrians knowledge of themselves, into Illyria the theory of Bogumilism in Bosnia was introduced, as was the incorrect thesis that the Bosnian Church or "Bosnian heresy" forms in the 10th century, while said Ecclesia Bosnesis (Arian Bosnian Church) is indoctrinated in the framework of classical, Nicaean Christianity.

Christian archaeology up to now has been eager to explain the beginnings of Christianity in our region through the prism of Nicaean Christianity, although there is very little basis for that. That Arianism was widespread is also evidenced in the following: in the phases of the formation of Christian counties, there are influences from Asia Minor and Greece, as well as influences from northern Italy, and such ties to the eastern and the western regions exist in the 4th century and continue until the 6th century. The relationship with the province of Dalmatia are evidenced only in the 6th century, while it is unknown what the relations were like before the 6th century, because they are barely researched through sources and archaeology. The ties with the East are conducted through the bishops who were brought in from Asia Minor, and Arianism, which arrived in our region. The relations with Italy are expressed through the activities of Ambrose of Milan, the successor of the

Arian bishop Auxentius, with the Sirmian municipality (Sremska Mitrovica). In the case of Sirmium and its community, there is not much of a doubt because it was the most populous, compared to the municipalities in continental Croatia.[112]

So, there is no dilemma here about this being a historical continuity of Arianism and the Bosnian Church having its roots in the Apostolic belief founded by Arius and his bishops. Arianism didn't appear in our region out of the blue. The Bosnian Church is exclusively Bosnian, of Arian roots, whose religious beginnings are unique and original as much as the Bosnian basilicas of Late Antiquity. The Bosnian folk religion, that is, the Bosnian Church, was given its basic characteristic by the Arian Goths.

We can talk about Arianism in our region in two uninterrupted periods. The first phase was when Arius was exiled to Illyricum, in the time when Arianism had many followers amongst the Church clergy.

The second phase refers to the period of Ostrogothic rule in this region, and so it is to be expected that among the numerous basilicas and hižas built in that period, if not all, then most were Arian. How slowly Nicaean Christianity spread on European soil is also evidenced in the following excerpt from the text by Katharina Winckler, *Die ersten Christen in den Alpen (The First Christians in the Alpine Region)*: "Christianity is first mentioned in the south-east Alpine region in Ptuj, a small Slovenian city. In the year 303, due to Diocletian's persecution of the Christians, the local bishop Victorinus died, leaving certain texts that document that in this city in 342 and 343, a conflict between the Arian and Nicaean Christians occurred. In the context of this misunderstanding, the diocese of Emona, modern-day Ljubljana, is mentioned for the first time. Although many Alpine regions in the 5th century were converted to Christianity, Christianity did not manage to take root because of the constant incursions of the eastern Goths, who were followers of

---

[112] Dominik Kelava. (2018) Early Christian Sites In Eastern Slavonia In Regarding Of New Archaeological Researches, University of Zadar, Archaeology Department, Undergraduate University Studies of Archaeology (single major).

Arian Christianity, and the fact that this was the time of the dissolution of the Roman Empire and its hegemony.

In the region of Mursa and its community, we find no attested known martyrs, but we do see the attested existence of a bishopric with its seat in Mursa, and the only known bishop, Valent. Much was written about him because he was a follower of Arianism, and openly advocated at numerous Church councils for that form of belief, and so in different scientific papers researching the history of Church councils and the struggle against Arianism, it is mentioned that the Pannonian communities and their bishops made the 4th century their own. The development of communities during the 5th and 6th centuries is not well-known, and we find some mentions of bishops. Those sources of evidence the disappearance of the Pannonian community. However, the old Christian findings and the sparse literature show that there still existed communities throughout the 6th century, adapting to this situation.

Although Arian authority did not have much influence on the Alpine structure of Christianity, in everyday relations, there were constant misunderstandings and tension between the Arians and the Catholics. The King of the eastern Goths, Theodoric the Great, in Vita Caesarii Arelatensis, explicitly boasts of being an Arian.

In the region of the Northern Alps in Germany and in Bavaria, there is no indication of the elites of that time supporting the Christian community. The invasion of Slavs and Avars in the 7th century in the Eastern Alps region was disastrous for the Christian community. It was levelled to its foundations. **Various historical documents state that this region was pagan also in the 8th century.**

However, it would be wrong to think that only Goths were followers of Arianism. This was the time of the fall of the Western Roman Empire, and the domination of Arian Goths, which lasted over 200 years, although their Empire lasted only for some 50 years. Thus, in these turbulent times, all those bans of heretical movements, condemnations and persecutions from the Council of Nicaea only existed on paper, and could not be enforced.

Arianism spread, and on several occasions, it was the dominant religion in the entirety of the Roman Empire.

Thus, also the indigenous Illyrians in the area of Bosnia and Herzegovina and Dalmatia accepted this teaching, letting Mithraism and Manicheism, which gradually began to reach our region from the East, fall into obscurity.

After Christianity became the state religion of the Roman Empire, through the presence of Arian Goths in the area of Bosnia and Herzegovina, from the 4th to the 6th century, the construction of basilicas began.[113][114]

We find the ruins of Early Christian basilicas throughout modern-day Bosnia and Herzegovina. To this day, 73 of them were discovered and excavated, and for 56 of them it can be said with certainty that they are the ruins of early buildings of the Krstjani. They were built very simply, in modest dimensions, and the interior features were made of stone with many motifs and symbols.

Out of 56 certain findings of early basilicas of the Krstjani, there are five dual basilicas (basilica gemina), three belong to the type of basilicas with three naves (Otinovci near Kupres, Kumjenovići and Ustikolina near Foča), the remaining 48 are basilicas with one nave.

Considering that these basilicas were built in the time when Goths were dominant in Illyria, the dual basilicas were built in those places where there was a need to satisfy the needs of the followers of Nicaean Christianity. Such examples are found during the reign of the eastern Gothic King Theodoric the Great, who guaranteed the right of preaching for all religions in his empire. As we have stated at the beginning of the text, Arianism is permeated with

---

[113] Alojz Benac, Đuro Basler, Borivoj Ćović, Esad Pašalić, Nada Miletić and Pavao Anđelić, Kulturna istorija Bosne i Hercegovine. Veselin Masleša, Sarajevo, 1966. Accessed 09/03/2022.

[114] Merima Hajdarbegović, Reljefi starokršćanskih bazilika u Bosni i Hercegovini, p. 23 https://www.ff.unsa.ba/files/zavDipl/20_21/ hum/Merima-Hajdarbegovic.pdf

monotheistic Judaism. King Theodoric gave the right of religious expression to the Jews as well, with the note that they may not be forced into Christianity, because there can be no forcing in faith.

From the time of Theodoric, we know that he supported and helped the building of churches of the Nicaean school, and they were often built a few metres away from the Arian ones. We find such an example in the Austrian Hemmaberg (hill of Saint Hemma), where during his reign two basilicas were built; one for the needs of Arians, and the other for the needs of Nicaean Christians.

Dual basilica in Turbe near Travnik

As can be seen, there are also five such examples in Bosnia, one of which is in Turbe near Travnik. The ruins of one of the two basilicas were destroyed during the building of the narrow-gauge rail Travnik–Jajce, and nowadays, a parking lot is located there. The second basilica remained well preserved, it was conserved and is located next to the main road in Turbe.

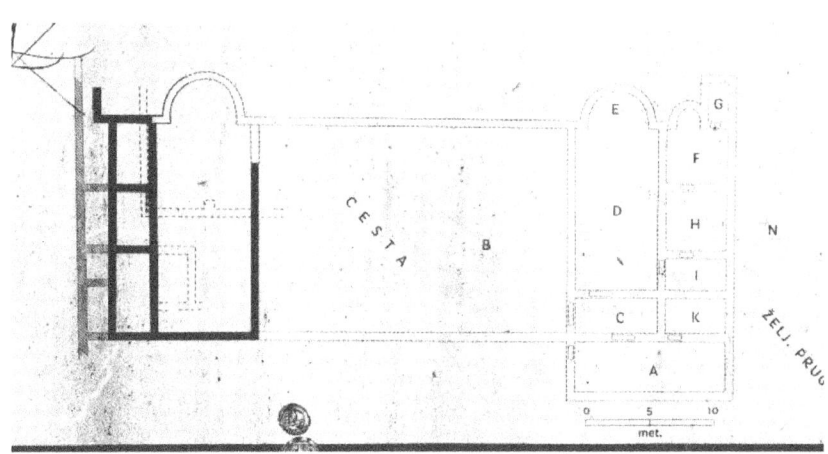

Artefacts: Dual Basilica in Turbe.

The second example of a dual basilica is in Mogorjelo near Čapljina. During investigations of the well-known archaeological site of Mogorjelo, within the ruins of late antiquity architecture, two parallel Early Christian basilicas were found, one of which is from the land of antique Illyricum before and after the Edict of Milan. Aside from the vaulted tombs, there were also found two fragments of Early Christian lanterns. The lantern with a depiction of a menorah indicates that Jews were active in late antique Mogorjelo as well".[115]

Towards the end of the 4th century, the *villa rustica* in Mogorjelo was conquered and partly destroyed by the Visigoths led by Alaric. In the 5th century, the Arian Goths built two Early Christian basilicas using the walls of the original fortification. Besides the dual basilica, there was a residential building and a necropolis with ten stećci.[116] The archaeological material was not preserved, except for one headstone plate, which is now kept in the Museum of Herzegovina in Mostar.

---

[115] https://bs.wikipedia.org/wiki/Ranokr%C5%A1%C4%87anske_bazilike_u_Bosni_i_Hercegovini

[116] Mr. Sc. Radoslav Dodig: Mogorjelo, Copy of the original web-page archived 8 August 2014; published 9 April 2013.

Here, the question of the reason for the destruction of the archaeological material arises. What could it have been that was found, what artefacts were not allowed to be documented and shown to the public?

The third Early Christian dual basilica is in Gradac, it is located in the Briak site, Posušje municipality. It is comprised of a larger church to the north and a smaller one to the south. The larger one was erected towards the beginning of the 5th century, while the smaller one was built at the very beginning of the 6th century.[117] The churches were burned and destroyed in the 6th or towards the beginning of the 7th century in the military onslaught of the Avars and Slavs. The exterior dimensions of the northern church are: 17.40 m in length and 11.20 m in width; and it is comprised of the following rooms: presbyterium, cella, narthex, baptistry, and one more room. The smaller church is abutted against the larger church, and its exterior measurements are: 13.10 m in length and 4.60 m in width; and it is comprised of a presbyterium and a cella.[118]

Within the larger church, there is a vaulted tomb with a sarcophagus made of large marble plates, of which five plates are profiled while two are not. The tomb was plundered before archaeological research was conducted. A silver fibula (buckle) with an iron pin was found, depicting a stylised animal in the act of running, with a hole on its tail, circles on its ankles and eyes, and engraved lines by its hind and fore legs. Similar fibulas with running animals were found in Italy and are attributed to Arian-Langobardic workshops from the 6th or 7th century.

---

[117] Ivo Bojanovski: Bosna i Hercegovina u antičko doba. Academy of Science and Arts of Bosnia and Herzegovina, 1988. Accessed 09/02/2016.

[118] Alojz Benac, Đuro Basler, Borivoj Ćović, Esad Pašalić, Nada Miletić and Pavao Anđelić, Kulturna istorija Bosne i Hercegovine. Veselin Masleša, Sarajevo, 1966.

Dual basilica in Gradac, in the orientation of NW–SE.

Dual basilica in Gradac, in the orientation of NW–SE.

The fourth dual basilica is located in Zenica, in the Bilimišće site. The basilica burned down in a fire. The dating of this old Christian church can be placed with most certainty before the year 530, and therefore was built in the 5th century. Among the numerous findings, a plate with a depiction of the Good Shepherd, defending sheep from hellish forces symbolised in four Biblical beasts: a dragon, a lion, a basilisk, and a snake.

In contrast to other areas of Bosnia and Herzegovina, the region of central Bosnia was never in the focus of interest of the Roman

Empire to such an extent as, e.g., the eastern and northwestern ore-rich portions of this state. However, the larger number of discovered basilicas in this region should not be surprising, when it is known that settlements such as Aqua S in Sarajevo and municipium Bistuensium with an administrative and religious centre existed here, the location of which has been debated in science for the past 120 years. The representative basilica, discovered in Zenica, supports the placement of Bistua Nova in Zenica (Ecclesia Bosnesis).[119]

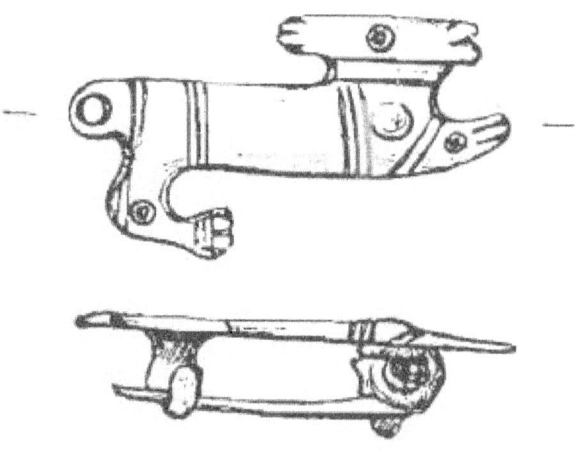

Langobardic silver fibula from the dual basilica in Gradac.

The fifth dual basilica in Žitomislići near Mostar; "Tomislav Anđelić states that the Early Christian Basilica in Žitomislići is a textbook example of a so-called dual basilica (basilica gemina) which has no direct analogues. So, it is comprised of two basilicas, a northern and a southern one, with several rooms and a large fenced-in courtyard. The total length of the dual basilica is 17 m, while its width is somewhat larger, 25.57 m. The layout of the

---

[119] Ivo Bojanovski, Akademija nauka i umjetnosti Bosne i Hercegovine, 1988 - BOSNA I HERCEGOVINA U ANTIČKO DOBA Alojz Benac-Đuro Basler-Borivoj Čović-Esad Pašalić-Nada Miletić-Pavao Anđelić -Sarajevo, 1966- KULTURNA ISTORIJA BOSNE I HERCEGOVINE

basilica was very similar to the basilica in Mokro. Its base is almost square, and the entire interior is comprised of the cella with a semicircular apse, a baptistry which extends along the northern side of the cella, and a narthex which encompasses both the cella and the baptistry.

Around fifteen metres north of the basilica, there was another building located, which was determined to be residential, creating one unit with the basilica. Since the Žitomislići site was situated in a complex comprised of sacral and profane objects, and the site was isolated in the age of Late Antiquity, Anđelić concludes that this was a monastery. The nearby house served as housing for the monastery staff who performed their rituals in the basilicas. For that reason, one of the basilicas could have been reserved for prayer by all believers, while the smaller one was used for the private rituals of the clergy. Anđelić posits the possibility of such a monastery complex also being present in Mogorjelo, Mokro, Turbe near Travnik, Zenica, and Dubravine near Vareš. The wider area of the basilica was adorned with fitting decorations on its stone furnishings and numerous architectural elements."[120]

Dual basilica in Bilimišće, Zenica.

We think that Anđelić's interpretation and understanding of the dual basilica as one for the prayer by all believers and the other for the

---

[120] Merima Hajdarbegović. Reljefi starokršćanskih bazilika u Bosni i Hercegovini, University of Sarajevo, Faculty of Philosophy, Department of History, Chair of History of Art.

private rituals of the clergy only is too rigid, plastic and unilateral, and does not correspond to the realistic situation and relations between Arianism and Nicaean Christianity, nor the social relations themselves.

We think that the dual basilica in Žitomislići, as all other dual basilicas in the area of Bosnia and Herzegovina, and the entire region which the Arian Goths ruled, was built exactly according to the religiously tolerant principles of Arianism.

One basilica served the Arian believers and would be the foundation for the establishment of the Bosnian Church, while the other one was for believers of the Nicaean school of Christianity. Enver Imamović agrees, and writes: "Namely, those are likely buildings of two church organisations, specifically one belonging to the Goths, who were Arians, and the other to the native population, which belonged to the Orthodox Church. More or less, between the present buildings, there are almost no essential differences, neither in the interior arrangement, nor in the furnishings. The only potential indication for their differentiation is that in Arian churches, the baptistries are in most cases outside the church, in a separately erected building adjacent to the church, as we find it in Založje, Skelani, Breza, etc.[121]

---

[121] Enver Imamović, Počeci kršćanstva na tlu Bosne i Hercegovine u svjetlu pisanih izvora i arheoloških spomenika. http://www. infobiro.ba/article/1026385

Ruins of the basilica in Žitomislići near Mostar

It is worth noting that in the basilica in Breza near Sarajevo, aside from the decorative plaster, on one of its pillars, an engraving of Gothic runes (FUTHARK) was found. This finding additionally confirms the presence of Arian Goths and the very likely builders of this basilica.

The symbols or decorations which could be found in this dual basilica in Žitomislići can also be found in other basilicas, as well as stećci in Bosnia and Herzegovina: a grape vine, a grape bushel, a peacock, a lamb, a three-threaded braid in the form of interwoven eights. The lamb as a motif, although used in Early Christianity, is also a votive symbol in the three Abrahamic religions – Judaism, Islam, and Christianity – so, in this sense of early Arianism in our region, it could be interpreted as a Judeo-Christian or Arian motif.

It should be noted, as we wrote before, that the braid, "interlace," is a motif of the Langobards, Arian Goths who found their living space in northern Italy. The artists who made these decorative items continued the continuity of Illyrian decorations and motifs, i.e., the tradition which was present among the Illyrians even before the arrival of the Romans to this region. Simultaneously, this heritage was enriched with new motifs which arrived with the Goths or the religious perspectives from the East. More precise data about the influence of the Langobards on Dalmatia, Bosnia, and Slavonia can be found in the work of the historian Rudolf Kutzli. The impact of the Langobards is also evidenced in the coins found in Slavonia.

Gothic script, runes (German: Futhark) from the basilica in Breza near Sarajevo. Nowadays kept in the National Muesum of Bosnia and Herzegovina in Sarajevo.

It is interesting that in the scientific literature it is noted that most Early Christian basilicas is oriented in the direction east–west. We have inspected several examples and found that a part of the Early Christian Arian basilicas, of which there are 56 in Bosnia and Herzegovina, oriented in the NW–SE direction, which is the direction used by native Illyrians and the newly arrived Goths and other Germanic tribes in Illyria. The other direction in which Arian basilicas are oriented is NE–SW. This direction is Germanic as well.

The basilicas which have the NW–SE orientation: Oborci, Skelani on the Drina river, the basilica of Saint Elijah in Buško Jezero, Doci, the Gradac basilica in Posušje, Breza, Glamoč. The basilicas which have the NE–SW orientation: the crowning basilica in Mile/Arnautovići in Visoko which is the seat of the Bosnian Church, Mokro, Rivine in Stolac, Skelani, Cim, the basilica near Karakaj in Zvornik / eastern Bosnia.

It is well-known that the Ostrogothic King Theodoric the Great built the Arian basilica Sant' Apollinare Nuovo in Ravenna, Italy, the centre of the Gothic Empire. This basilica is oriented in the NE–SW direction, while the palace of Theodoric *(Palazzo di Teodorico)* is in the NW–SE direction.

Langobardic silver coinage found in a tomb in an Early Christian site in Kamenica near Vinkovci (Southern Pannonia), dating this grave to the 7th century.

We find evidence that what is at hand is a continuity and symbiosis of the direction of orientation of Illyrians, Goths, Germanic tribes in our area in the archaeological journal of Boško Marijan: Željezno doba na južnojadranskom području Istočna Hercegovina, Južna Dalmacija – Širi bazen Trebišnice, (The Iron Age in the Southern Adriatic Area of Eastern Herzegovina, Southern Dalmatia – Broader Trebišnica Basin) published in Vijesnik za arheologiju i historiju dalmatinsku. He could not find a publisher for his valuable work. The archaeologist Boško Marjan determined that the skeletons beneath the stećci and in **Illyrian tumuli**, which stem from different periods of time, are oriented in the Illyrian-Gothic NW–SE direction.[122]

Necropolis and tumuli Eraci, Ploče, Croatia. During the construction of the Ploče–Split highway and the toll booth Karamatići, around 5 km from Bosnia and Herzegovina as the crow flies, there is an old village, Eraci, in which Illyrian tumuli were found and excavated to a depth of 9 metres from the skeletons. Aside from the tumulus, ruins of an Early Christian basilica oriented in the NW–SE direction were excavated. It is interesting that the site is called Mavino Guvno, because the local inhabitants were threshing wheat and other grains with the help of horses on the tumulus, not knowing that beneath is an Illyrian grave – a tumulus. In the immediate vicinity there is the necropolis Eraci with 7 stećci and it is interesting that beneath all of them pairs of skeletons were found, a male and a female, and through genetic analysis it was determined that the males had the R1b haplogroup (Celtic immigrants) and the women had the native I2 DNA haplogroup (Alpine-Dinaric or Illyrian) which is evidence of the mixing of the native and the newly-arrived conquering populations.

---

[122] Mate Puljak. (July 2021) Zaboravljeni Dnevnik: dokaz prapovijesnog porijekla dijela stećaka!, p. 28; http://piramidasunca.ba/ images/2021/07/dnevnik3.pdf

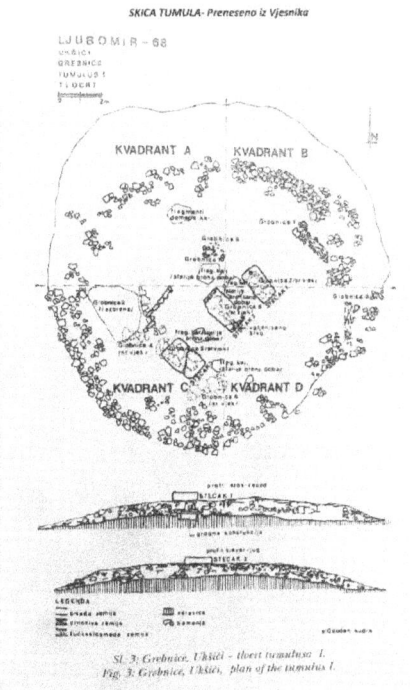

Sl. 3: Grebnice, Ukšići - tlocrt tumulusa 1.
Fig. 3: Grebnice, Ukšići, plan of the tumulus 1.

As we have stated, the ruins of many basilicas with specific features found in Bosnia and Herzegovina are basilicas with one nave built through two centuries, in the time of the Goths, and up to the invasion of the Avars and the Slavs accompanying them, who destroyed them, are of the basilicas found in Golubić, Vrtoče, Blagaj, Čarakovo, Čitluk, Mujdžići, Oborci, Turbe, Šiprage, Mali Mošunj, Zenica, Kakanj, Halajpići, Velika Vrata, Čipuljić, Otinovci, Šuica, Prisoja, Letka, Crkvenice, Dabravine Breza, Lepenica, Lisičići, Vrdolje, Potoci, Cim, Biograci Mokro, Cerin, Klobuk, Borasi, Dolac, Blagaj, Žitomislići, Mogorjelo, Nerezi, Crnići and Skelani, Založje near Bihać.[123]

---

[123] Enver Imamović, Počeci kršćanstva na tlu Bosne i Hercegovine u svjetlu pisanih izvora i arheoloških spomenika. http://www.infobiro.ba/article/1026385

THE HIDDEN HISTORY OF BOSNIA

The Dolac basilica is oriented in the Illyrian-Gothic NW–SE direction, while the one in Mokro is in the NE–SW, Germanic direction of orientation.

We find evidence of the presence of Goths, the builders of the basilica in Potoci near Mostar, in the necropolis in Potoci near Mostar. In one grave, a golden chain was found, which is a rarity among jewellery of that time across the entire territory of Europe. It shows a certain similarity with two findings (one in Hungary, the other in Italy) which belong to the Ostrogoths. In another, a pair of gilded silver arched fibulae, a pair of gold earrings, and part of a gold necklace were found. This collection of gold jewellery also belongs to luxurious Ostrogothic jewellery from the beginning of the 6th century.

Early Christian basilicas on the territory of Bosnia and Herzegovina were built according to the same principle. They were characterised by simplicity, the absence of special ornamentation and construction skill. Bosnian basilicas, in most cases, have a larger width than length, or their sides are almost equal, and they are covered in mortar from the inside.

The study of Early Christian Arian basilicas on the territory of modern-day Bosnia and Herzegovina is an exceptionally complex issue. The first and perhaps most important reason for that is that it became a political issue.

The monopoly in researching the ruins of these buildings is held by the Church, not the university's archaeology and historiography.[124]

This situation precludes the gathering of quality information about the Bosnian Church, as is the case with the Ban's basilica in Crkvine above the village of Vesela near Bugojno. All important archaeological findings were evaluated by Catholic archaeologists and stored in the museum in Livno. The same example of catholicisation of Arian basilicas, a considerable number of them, is found in Liburnia, Dalmatia, and in the Neretva Banate. Thus, the attempt has been made to erase a Judeo-Christian worldview, which was widely accepted in the entire area of the Mediterranean, across Illyria, modern-day Italy, Spain, and France. Arianism in this wide area was the foundation of medieval heretic movements in Europe, from the Black Sea to the Atlantic Ocean.

All these basilicas which were built from the 4th to the 6th century on the territory of modern-day Bosnia and Herzegovina and of Dalmatia, were constructed by Arian Goths and native Illyrians for their needs, and were razed to their foundations by Avar-Slavic barbarian tribes which penetrated into the territory of Bosnia and Herzegovina and Dalmatia in the 6th century, and were not, as is tried to be presented in the Balkans, razed by the Ottomans with their conquest of Bosnia in 1463.

We know that the Ottomans did not raze religious buildings, which is evidenced by the Ahdname, issued to the Bosnian Franciscans, modelled after the Covenant of Muhammad a.s. by which the monks of St. Catherine's Monastery were guaranteed their freedoms and right of confession, Sultan Mehmed Fatih guaranteed to the Bosnian Franciscans and all Catholics that they may freely travel and preach their faith.

---

[124] Edin Veletovac Kasnoantičke bazilike u Bosni i Hercegovini. p. 296. Original scientific paper. https://www.academia.edu/7146163/Kasnoanti%C4%8Dke_bazilike_u_Bosni_i_Hercegovini_Radovi_Filozofskog_fakulteta_u_Sarajevu_Knjiga_XVII_3_Historija_Historija_ umjetnosti_Arheologija_

Addendum to the text:

"Arian basilicas in Bosnia from the IV to the VII century"

Positing the question of the art and symbols of Early Christianity, we conclude that only a few symbols are recognisable as Early Christian motifs. Around 190, Clement of Alexandria, in his work Paedagogus, wrote down a list of symbols which were then adopted as Christian, and those are: a dove, a fish, a boat on the sea, a lyre, an anchor, and a fisherman—afterwards, the symbol of a peacock, and the monogram of Christ.

Why is that so, and why did Early Christianity not use the cross as a symbol?

Having in mind that it emerged from Judaism, Christianity was reserved about images and symbols, which were foreign to Judaism throughout its history. The same rejection of images, symbols, and iconography, as is found in Judaism and Early Christianity, was reaffirmed 600 years after Jesus, in Islam.

The listed symbols in Early Christian Arian basilicas or on stećci were irrelevant, not interesting to their builders, and thus were not a subject of their work. The most deserving in the shaping of this art within Christianity are exactly those who, as "pagans," accepted the new faith. Thus in the early period of the development of Christianity there are basilicas influenced by Nicaean Christianity, and those which, because of their understanding of Jesus, were not pliant to integration and freeing from the monotheistic influence of Judaism, as are the ones in the centre of Arian Illyria, in Bassania (Bosnia).

Unable to spiritually distance themselves from earlier polytheistic beliefs and their heritage, they liberally introduced into their new religion symbols, images and ornaments, and express the desire to present some segments of their belief artistically. Thus, the cultural heritage of previous beliefs was incorporated into Christianity, and that is where it is imbued with new interpretations and new meanings. Many of the symbols that were adopted in Christianity existed in earlier cultures.

Because of this, there are no symbols of Early Christianity in the Arian basilicas in Bosnia, such as the peacock, fish, boat, anchor, etc., except for those which were already present in the culture of the native Illyrian population and the artistic decorations of Arian eastern Goths. These motifs, creative expressions, the Goths potentially accepted from the Illyrians, or they brought with them on their journey from Scandinavia in search of a new area to settle.

Thus, on the stećci and the basilicas, the breath of Arian Illyrian-Gothic cultural heritage is felt: The Moon, a star, the Arian cross, etc. It is very interesting that the subjective and political historians in a conscious approach and minimisation of the role of Arianism in prehistorical Illyrian symbols in Bosnia and Dalmatia were eager to see Christian symbols which emerged under the influence of Nicaean Christianity, wanting to define the geographic area of Bassania (Bosnia) as "some dark, pagan, hilly and nameless area", or at least theoretically place it into a position of inferiority. Such is the case with the book by Ivan Lovrenović, which has a truly enticing title, Bosanski križ (The Bosnian Cross), and which, as it was announced, wants to stir the interest for old Christian tombstone culture. In that way, to categorise the Illyrian, Gothic, and Arian cross into the artistic heritage of Nicaean Christianity.

From the book by Danijel Džino "Becoming Slav, Becoming Croat"

"The term crkvina (church-grounds) was frequently preserved in the Slavic toponyms in the hinterland, which referred to the churches from Late Antiquity which had no continuity of use in medieval times, implying that the population must have been aware of its purpose. In fact, as argued by Grabar, and more recently by Milošević, the stone relief sculpture with ornamental and Christian motifs from the interior of Dalmatia (the churches in Bilimišće near Zenica, Mali Mošunj (Kalvarija) near Travnik and Dabravine-Breza near Visoko) show significant stylistic similarities with 8th century Langobardic sculpture in Italy. In Grabar's opinion they should be dated in the period between the late 7th and 9th century, while Milošević narrows down the dating to mid- to late 8th century.

Grabar 1974; Milošević 2003; 2004. These churches have been dated either in very late Roman, or rather the Ostrogothic period, and accordingly sculptures were dated in the same period (Basler 1972: 78–82, 94–7, 127–34; 1990: 83–116; 1993:

61–2, 79–83; cf. Cambi 2002: 279–80 and Paškvalin 2003: 53–4, 110–25) or as late as the XI/XII century (Nikolajević 1964; J. Maksimović 1971: 41–8). Nikolajević, with somewhat changed positions, argued strongly against the views of Grabar, (Nikolajević 1975: 73–7) but the problem of the dating remains unsolved, and similarities with the Langobardic sculpture striking, as even Basler 1972: 158 notices."

Necropolis Boljuni, Stolac.

The sameness of the figures from the basilica in Dabravine/Breza and the figures engraved into the stećci in the necropolis Boljuni (pictured below) near Stolac. This example, from the basilica in Breza, with a raised open-palm hand as in the well-known necropolis of stećci in Radimlja near Stolac and an aureole or braid around the head of a horseman in Boljuni, is an additional testament to the Arian, Gothic-Illyrian building of Arian basilicas and stećci in the Early Middle Ages in Bosnia. This additionally supplements our thesis about the Arian basilicas built in the time of Ostrogothic domination in the Western Roman Empire and the Gothic tribe of Langobards who were dedicated to architecture, decoration, and ornamentation.

The symbol of a four-leaf clover closely corresponds to the symbol of a three-leaf clover: the realisation, fulfilment, the symbolism of the four-leaf clover – which we all know to represent LUCK! – is achieved through the actualisation, the realisation of the three-leaf clover symbol – faith, hope, and love! Symbols, as can be seen, are concise, compressed messages with profound meanings. One symbol is an entire library by itself!

Stećak with old Illyrian symbols of the Sun and the Moon.

Figure from the pluteus in the basilica in Dabravine – Breza. National Museum of Bosnia and Herzegovina, Sarajevo

15 ARIAN BOSNIAN CHURCHES IV-XIV CENTURY

After the Avars and Slavs razed the Arian churches built in the period of the Gothic Kingdom from the IV century to the VI century, and after, with the fall of the Avar Khaganate, rule was consolidated within the newly emerged Banates and župas of modern-day Bosnia and Herzegovina, Dalmatia, and Sandžak (at that time, župa Raška), the construction of churches according to the same Illyrian-Gothic principles and basic rules, as had been done in the previous period. Historic artefacts and documents prove that wealthy Bosnian nobles, bans, and kings-built churches and hižas. Here are three examples that evidence that:

The first example from the time of Ban Kulin, the stela of "grand judge" Građeša, who built the burial church of Saint George; (this stela is kept at the Museum of the City of Zenica).

Another example and piece of evidence, also from the time of Kulin's reign, is the stela of Ban Kulin discovered in Biskupići near Visoko. The stela reads:

– This church was built by Ban Kulin when he seized Kučevsko zagorje. And thunder struck upon it in Podgorje Slijepčišća; (this stela is kept in the National Museum of Bosnia and Herzegovina in Sarajevo). Unfortunately, the foundations of this church still have not been found.

The third example is the crowning Church of Saint Nicholas near Visoko, where the djeds of the Bosnian Church crowned Bosnian kings, and first of them was King Tvrtko Kotromanić.

Ruins of the crowning church of Bosnian kings in Mile

The churches which we will treatise in this article are always said to be pre-Roman churches. In literature dealing with the architecture, style and symbolism in the construction of medieval churches, we find this term as hazy and vague, and at the same time very broad expression.

The Church of Holy Salvation in Cetina shows the Illyrian-Gothic orientation of NE-SW with a necropolis of stećci, which are, as the church itself, oriented in the Illyrian-Gothic direction.

The Church of Holy Salvation in Cetina was built through the effort and love of King Tvrtko I Kotromanić, who, among others, included Knin as one of his cities (according to Danilo Farlati). During the age of King Tvrtko, the foundations of other churches in Dalmatia were established as well, e.g., the Temple of Saint John the Baptist in Bribir and a church in Klis.

Langobardic interlace; interior of the walls of the Church of Holy Salvation in Cetina.

These are some examples that show that the members of the Bosnian Church built houses of worship and that they cannot, by any measurement of aesthetics and culture generally, be considered "barbarian", but are, on the contrary, a highly sophisticated expression of an authentic culture, and civilisation if you will.

As the Arian faith before the arrival of the Avars and Slavs was widespread in Illyria, during their incursion and occupation, the baptising and Slavicisation of the native population began and progressed even after the fall of the Avar Khaganate. The Arian faith, however, remained; its followers were called Krstjani, and their Church, with time, is associated (attributed) with the adjective Bosnian, hence the Bosnian Church. The Bosnian Church had its internal organisation and hierarchy, and the head of that hierarchy was the djed of the Bosnian Church. That internal cohesion and organisational structure is one of the stronger reasons why Arian belief persevered and did not disappear from the area of medieval Bosnia, Dalmatia, and Raška.

The largest stećak in the region of Dalmatia weighs an unbelievable 17 tons, without any symbolism, in the largest necropolis of stećci near the Church of Holy Salvation at the spring of the Cetina River.

Here is another example of a so-called pre-Roman Arian church found in Dalmatia, in the medieval city of Ston.

The Swiss writer Rudolf Kutzli writes: "Starting from Zmijin Kamen in the Bistrina bay, the way leads to the Pelješac peninsula towards a small church dated to between the 8th and the 9th century; the Church of Saint Michael is located on the top of an elevation near the medieval city of Ston."[125]

---

[125] Rudolf Kutzli, Die Bogumilen, Stuttgart 1977, page 159; https://www.theologe.de/bogumilen.htm

Church of Saint Michael in Ston, Croatia.

At some point, members of the Bosnian Church lived here, and it must be admitted that their living places must be discovered anew. There is little memory of the period of medieval Bosnia in the minds of modern-day inhabitants of Ston. In Europe, such a church, dating to the VIII and IX centuries, would have its place in the cultural and religious life of the population, it would be indicated on way signs and every travel map, the paths leading to it would be marked.

Around the church, there lay several mysteriously decorated stones, as if scattered, and they are gravestones – stećci – which have almost sunk into the ground. On them, we find engravings of decorative Langobardic ornamentation.

Kutzli draws attention to the form of the stećci around this church being reminiscent of the stećci which we know from the necropolis of Radimlja. He stresses: "The place where we are, as nowhere else, illustrates the spiritual relatedness between the Goths, Langobards, and Krstjani. The architecture of the church itself is an illustration of this relatedness. Although it is closed, from the outside it not only appears mighty and primeval, but is also fantastically compact, more like a house than a church".

Kutzli thinks that the Duke of Ston, Miroslav, who had taken over power from Duke Zvonimir, and who is the builder of this church, was a Krstjanin, a member of the Bosnian Church. He also draws a parallel with another Church of St. Michael located on the other side of the Adriatic Sea, that being the church in Monte Gargano, Italy. The exterior impression is diametrically different. In Italy, it is a very popular tourism site, in contrast to the one on the Dalmatian coast, where all is still, as if time had stopped. In Italy, there were the Cathars, known as Patareni, and there were vibrant contacts between them and the Krstjani. Saint Michael symbolises the struggle of the forces of good against the temptations of evil, which was as important to the Cathars and Krstjani as it was to the Gothic Langobard tribe.[126]

The Cathars of southern France are more present than ever in the cultural sense and the sense of phenomena; there are many books about them. Still, after several decades, their existence was violently suppressed and finally ended by the Catholic Church. After that time, the Cathars of Italy and Germany were forgotten, and the inquisition headed by Konrad crushed their spine. In almost the same way, the Krstjani of Bosnia were forgotten, who, so to speak, lasted much longer than the French Cathars; they were active for five hundred years, leaving behind them a unique wealth of visible evidence. When examining the relation between the Langobards and the Bosnian Church, it should be kept in mind that the largest portion of western and eastern Goths, in this case the Germanic Langobard tribe, accepted Arian Christianity, the centre of Langobardic government being in Italian Pavia, which encompassed northern Italy, as well as parts of central and southern Italy. The government was divided into several estates (Italian:

---

[126] Here it should be noted that Kutzli uses incorrect terminology, which is common in literature, when he calls the members of the Bosnian Church Bogumili.) Franjo Rački introduced this incorrect name for Bosnian Krstjani in the year 1869, and through that, without any historical facts and evidence, categorised them as something to which they do not belong, and the teaching of the priest Bogumil for whose existence there is also not a single historical fact.

ducato), administered by dukes.[127]

In the Church of Saint Michael, there is an exceedingly interesting and valuable fresco. It is thought that the fresco depicts a ruler. Croatian and Serbian historiography were eager to attribute it to, and categorise it as Catholic (Croatian historiography) or Orthodox Christian tradition (Serbian).

Some attribute it to the first king of Duklja, Mihailo Vojisavljević, the father of King Constantine Bodin of Duklja, who took over Raška and the surrounding župas and was one of the most important rulers of Duklja. Others attribute it to Mihailo Višević, who was an independent ruler of Zachumlia, in modern-day Herzegovina and southern Dalmatia, who lived in the first half of the 10th century. In Croatian historiography, some were eager to incorporate said Mihailo Višević, ruler of an Illyrian-Dalmatian land, into the, in historical reality non-existent, division into so-called White and Red Croatia, which allegedly constituted the Great Croatian Kingdom. These ideas are completely disconnected from factographic history, and they emerged as an expression of romanticised nationalistic phantasmagorias and pretensions.

---

[127] https://de.wikipedia.org/wiki/Langobarden

THE HIDDEN HISTORY OF BOSNIA

Portrait of Mihailo Vojisavljević or Mihailo Višević from the Church of St. Michael near Ston. [128]

Mihailo ruled as an independent Župan of Zachumlia and later also occupied the Neretvan Banate. He reigned from the year 910 to the year 930. As a Bulgarian ally, he managed to retain autonomous rule throughout most of his reign. Rudolf Kutzli thinks that Mihailo was a Krstjanin, a heretic, an Arian, meaning a member of the Bosnian Church's teaching.

In the work of the Byzantine emperor Constantine Porphyrogenitus, *De administrando imperio, around the year 950, Mihailo, son of Višeta,* is mentioned, who, like many in the Roman province of Dalmatia, is of unbaptised origin. If he was from the unbaptised, and present in this church, then he was a Krstjanin, member of the Bosnian Church, who did not recognise the Holy Trinity; meaning, the same religious situation as was the case with the Neretvan Banate (Dalmatia), the Banate of Bosnia, Rama, and to a large extent, the župa of Raška.

The NW–SE direction in which the Church of Saint Michael is oriented is evidence of Gothic influence, in this case, the Arian Langobard tribe, in this portion of the Dalmatian coast. Other

---

[128] https://hr.wikipedia.org/wiki/Crkva_sv._Mihajla_kod_Stona

churches of the Early and High Middle Ages, near this one, such as: the Church of Saint Mary Magdalene, the Church of Saints Sergius and Bacchus, the Church of Saint Andrew, the Church of Saint John the Baptist, the Church of Saint Martin, the Church of Saint Peter – all of them all oriented in the same, Illyrian-Gothic NW–SE direction or the Germanic NE–SW direction, which is one of the evidences of the widespread nature of the symbiosis of Illyrian and Gothic cultural heritage, the influence of old Christian Arianism and the Bosnian Church, which adopted it and where it was preserved the longest.

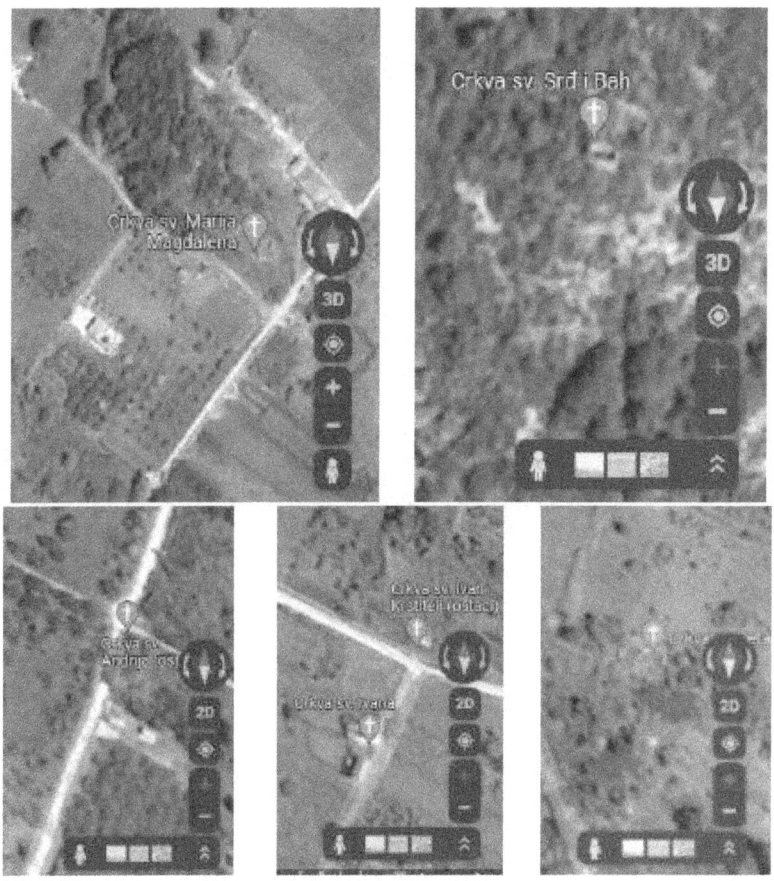

Church of Saint Michael

The decorative interlace (decoration on the window frames of the church) which is a Langobardic form of artistic expression, and the stećci (which are exclusively a characteristic of medieval Bosnia) decorated with Langobardic ornamentation lead us to posit a new way of thinking, that being that it cannot be said that the Church of Saint Michael is the legacy of Mihailo Vojisavljević, nor Mihailo Višević, because in the following text, explaining the ktitor's inscription, provided by historians, mutually negate both of these theses. In this inscription, there is an engraving of an Arian Gothic cross and a decorative interlace, and it can be seen that Mihailo does not mention the building of the church, but his firm control over Roman cities. Rudolf Kutzli thinks that Mihailo was a heretic, an Arian, or an advocate of the Bosnian Church's teaching.

The ktitor's inscription of the church in Ston, King Mihailo, 1080, or Župan Mihailo 910–930, entitles him as:

Michaelvs fortiter super rego pacifico c(i)vitates omnes Romanos. I, Michael, firmly pacify and rule over all Roman cities.

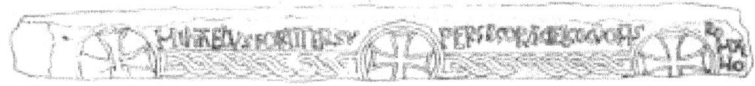

Ktitor's inscription in the church in Ston.

Through these facts and historiographic interpretations, nothing regarding the question of who built the Church of Saint Michael is solved, nor is any relevant answer provided regarding the question of the person from the fresco, holding a castle in his hand, and who that person could be. Therefore, a distancing is necessary from such "interpretations", basically unfounded appropriation by some Serbian and Croatian historians. A new dimension and new outlook on Zachumlia and the Church of Saint Michael is required.

Let's compare the appearance of the church itself with the stećci in Radimlja and other necropoleis. We will see how correct Kutzli is in linking the Langobards and their art with these churches and necropoleis. The historian Dr. **Ibrahim Pašić** arrived at the same conclusion.

Stećci from the Radimlja necropolis.

The following example of the Bosnian Church's architecture comes from the Ragusan coast. The eight-conched church or Rotonda, in the opinion of historians, was built between the VIII and the X century. It is located in the village of Ošlje, near the road, closer to Neum than to Slano, and to the north of Ston. It was given the name Rotonda because of its shape (architectural term for a building of circular layout, vaulted with a dome). It is unknown to whom it was dedicated. Popularly, it is also called "Banovi dvori" (Ban's Courts), "Mirine", or "Grčka crkva" (Greek Church). It should be noted that the adjective "Greek" in naming was used when the precise sources were unknown, or when the dogma of the church differed from the Catholic one. So many necropoleis of stećci were also named "Greek graveyards", although they have no relation to the Greeks, as a link to Byzantium. The same is true for the Rotonda church in Ošlje.

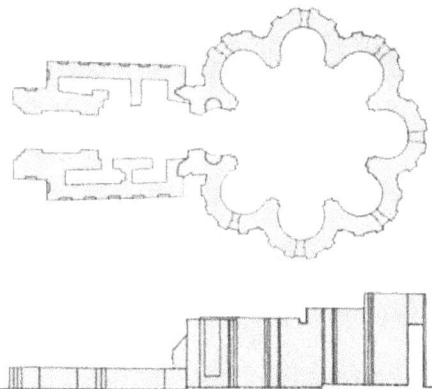

Layout and cross-section of the church in Ošlje. Rotonda church in Ošlje, like all Arian or Bosnian churches, is oriented in the Arian Illyrian-Gothic NW–SE direction.

Constantine Porphyrogenitus, in his work De administrando imperio, mentions Josle (Ošlje) as one of the five inhabited places in Zachumlia. As in the case of the Church of St. Michael near Ston, this church as well is being laid claim to by Croatian and Serbian historians, and so some of them attribute it to Catholic (Croatian) and the others to Orthodox Christian (Serbian) tradition. On these contradictory interpretations of belonging, see (to avoid a lengthy analysis) the official web page of Ošlje.[129]

It is well-known in historiography that this region of Zachumlia was predominantly inhabited by Krstjani, which adds the possibility of it belonging to the Bosnian Church. If we examine the eight arms of the church and compare them to the Illyrian star symbol, which also has eight arms, and because of the stećci (stelae) which are found inside the church itself, we can safely speak of an Arian, Gothic-Illyrian symbiosis.

The specificity of that, nowadays destitute pre-Roman church, is certainly in the form of its layout, which is circular, with eight

---

[129] https://oslje.com/rotonda-2/

radially placed conches, or apses, where the elongated part of the western apse served as the entrance and can be characterised as a vestibule or narthex. The vaults above the conches were not preserved, and neither were parts of the construction that were located above the circular space. [130]There are very few churches of this type in Europe.

Ruins of the old, so-called Rotonda church, Bijela Lokva site, north of the village of Ošlje.

What can be said with certainty is that Bosnia, Zachumlia, the Neretvan Banate, Travunia, and Konavle were lands with deeply rooted Arian belief. In his book Vjera crkve bosanske (Faith of the Bosnian Church), Ivan Mužić concludes: "Members of the Bosnian Church called their Church the Bosnian Church and the Church of God; they called their faith our faith, our law, the true faith, and the true apostolic faith, and they called themselves exclusively Krstjani. If the leaders of the Krstjani call their faith apostolic, then that means that they linked its emergence with the time of ancient Christianity.[131]

Considering that there is not one provable indication that any of the

---

[130] https://www.juzni.hr/uz-zahumsku-damu-s-oslja-legenda-kaze-zakopana-su-zlatna-zvona.
[131] Ivan Mužić, Vjera crkve bosanske, p. 76.

apostles spent time in Illyria, except Arius, whose teaching and interpretation of Jesus "as a man with a beginning", created by God, is linked to original, Early Christianity, in this period we can already speak about an established Bosnian Church.

Zachumlia and the Neretvan Banate were named Pagania by Rome and the Pope, which would mean, or rather, that it can be directly concluded that Rome thought pagans lived there, i.e., heathens and heretics. The Neretvan Banate was located between the rivers Cetina to the west and Neretva to the east, and in the Adriatic Sea, it comprised the islands of Brač, Hvar, Vis, Korčula and Mljet.[132] In the narrower sense, the Neretvans are the inhabitants of the Neretva River valley and river mouth.

---

[132] https://www.juzni.hr/uz-zahumsku-damu-s-oslja-legenda-kaze-zakopana-su-zlatna-zvona.

THE HIDDEN HISTORY OF BOSNIA

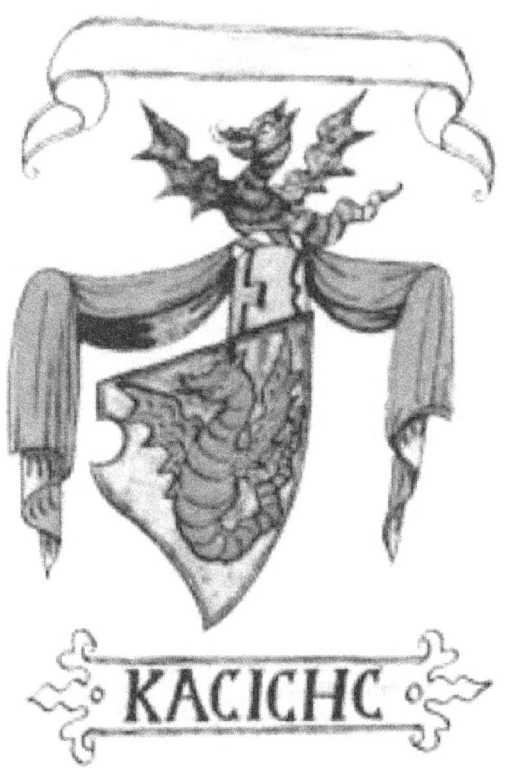

The Kačić dynasty, which autonomously ruled over the Neretvan Banate, was also a follower of the Arian belief, that is, the Bosnian Church's teaching. Exactly for these reasons, they were eager to interject themselves in the circumstances in Bosnia, to exert a certain influence. Thus, it can be stated that they had a certain rivalry with the Banate of Bosnia. The rule of the Kačić family ended when they lost power and were ousted by the Republic of Venice by sea and the Hungarians by land. However, the relation of the Kačić family with Bosnia should be accentuated – when a crusade was being prepared against Bosnia and Ban Kulin, Sebenna Kačić IV (Sebenna Khadzik, 1190 –1208), in an attempt to save Bosnia from the destruction of war, prevented and did not allow the passage of foreign soldiers through his state.

Here we should go back in time to an earlier period, where we have direct accounts regarding Arianism on the Dalmatian islands.

Several Neretvans who achieved great successes, as fleet admirals and military commanders in the service of Spanish Muslims, were born on the islands of Brač and Korčula. They were nobles of the Arian faith, who converted to Islam in Spain, namely: Hajib Badr, general of Abd al-Rahman III, admiral Ghalib, the leader of the Moorish fleet and the army of Caliph al-Hakam II, al-Wahdid al-Amiri, general of Caliph Hisham II, Zuhayr al-Amiri, son of admiral Ghalib and general to 3 Caliphs of the Umayyad dynasty, Khayran al-Amiri, admiral of the Moorish fleet and mayor of the port of Almeria, Mujahid al-Amiri, nephew of the former, admiral and emir of the taifa of Denia- Balearic Islands, Ali al-Amiri, vassal emir of the taifa of Denia.[133]

Let us go several centuries back in history, to the time when the Council in Solin was held, the year 530, 4 years after the death of Theodoric the Great (526), ruler of the Gothic Kingdom centred in Italian Ravenna. Knowing that the Goths had accepted Arian belief, which was closely linked to the power apparatus, which was normal for the time, because government was not separated from religion, the Goths, together with the native Illyrian population, built their places of worship, also in the time of the Councils of Solin being held in 530 and 533. Solin was an important Arian centre, so, unsurprisingly, this council was held there. The foundations of an Arian church were found in Solin as well. Towards the end of the IV and the beginning of the V century (meaning, the reign of the Arian Goths), a dual basilica was built there, of which one is certainly Arian. E. Dyggve considers the other basilica with a baptismal font (anointing), baptistry (discovered in the year 1931) in the centre of the old town, also to be Arian. Gothic presence and rule in Illyria lasted for about 250 years, and ended when the Byzantine Emperor Justinian crushed the last remaining resistance of the Goths in the year 552.

To conclude, we would say: Around 50 churches like those indicated in this text were found in Bosnia. Many basilicas from the Early Middle Ages or the end of Antiquity, in modern-day

---

[133] https://hr.metapedia.org/wiki/Neretvanska_banovina

Dalmatia and Bosnia and Herzegovina, can be attributed to Arian builders, i.e. the Goths, and the native Illyrian population, and in no way to old Croatian architecture and ornamentation, if we know that the Croats, as Arian convertees, emerge in our region with the fall of the Avar Empire in 791, together with the Frankish ruler Charlemagne.

Necropolis of stećci in Radimlja, 3 km west of Stolac, Bosnia and Herzegovina.

The Christian Church in Bosnia is first mentioned under the Latin name of ecclesia bosnensis or bistuensis, boestoensis, in 530 and 533, when on said church councils in Salona, the metropolitans of the Roman province of Dalmatia, its bishop (episcopus) Andrew signs the acts of the church councils, when eastern Goths rule Bosnia and Dalmatia.

Jozo Petrović discovered in the village of Čipuljić near Bugojno, in the location of Crkvina, Grudine, beneath the ancient hillfort Pod, foundations and walls of a solidly built building whose walls were "covered in various vibrant colors", vaulted tombs made of bricks and a channel made of large clay bricks. One of the clay bricks served as a cover of the channel and was stamped BISTVE(s). This stamp leads to the conclusion that in Bistue, there was a local brickwork because of the large quantities needed during the building of this antique complex. The finding of a clay floor brick from the II or III century, with the inscription BISTVES, as well as the documents from the council of the metropolis of Salona in 530 and 533, in which Andrew, bishop of Bistues, is mentioned (ANDREAS EPISCOPVS BESTOENSIS ECLESI(a)E), leads to the supposition that in Bugojno there was a strong civilian and religious centre, MUN(icipium) BISTVES, and in the VI century, also the seat of the bishopric.

It is believed that the seat of this old Christian Church was in Mošunj near Travnik or in Zenica, in the time when eastern Goths ruled over Bosnia.

If the Bosnian Church is mentioned in that time as a fact, then we think that its emergence should be shifted back to the time when Arius arrived in our region, that is – the emergence of the Bosnian Church should be dated even earlier, that being the III–IV century, in the time when Arius was exiled to Illyricum and Arian Goths arrived in our region. That was the time when the entirety of the Roman Empire, from the extreme east to the extreme west, was under a strong influence of Arianism.

That members of the Bosnian Church did live in Zadar is also evidenced in the pillaging and persecution of the population of this city at the outset of the Fourth Crusade to Jerusalem. The town of Zadar was blockaded on 10 November 1202. The blockade lasted for 13 days, until the city surrendered and opened its gates. The crusaders pillaged and burned Arian Zadar to its foundations. From this moment, constant threats and accusations against Bosnia and its population by the Pope began.

In 1216, Pope Honorius sent the Dominicans to Bosnia, a church order that excelled in the persecution of heretics. The first written trace of their presence in Bosnia is the letter by Gregory IX dated 10 October 1233, but the Dominicans certainly were in Bosnia even sooner. In the Ragusan archives, a record by the Dominican Ivan Stojković has been preserved (presided over the Council of the Catholic Church in Basel in 1434) which reads: "Offertur facilis ocasio reductionis regni Bosne quod iam a trecentis annis et ultra infectum heresi arianorum "; translated: "An easy opportunity presents itself, to reduce the Bosnian Kingdom, which for more than three hundred years is infected with the Arian heresy."[134]

If we examine the preserved charter of Ban Borić, dated to the year 1158 or 1159, by which the Benedictines of Lokrum are given the estates on Mljet and if historiography determined that the charter was falsified, by virtue of that, the data contained in this document cannot be reliable. Conclusion: still, the liberty is given to state that Borić's Bosnia, and Bosnia during its earlier and later Bans, via the Bosnian Church, had influence on the coastal cities and the islands. This charter could have been created only on the basis of Ban Borić having estates on and ruling over Mljet.

Based on the mentioned examples, it could be said that actually there existed a strong religious connection which we could call the Union of Bosnia, the Neretvans, Hum, Travunia, Konavle, and Raška. Thus, the small church of Saint Michael, considering all its characteristics, also enters the sphere of influence of the Bosnian Church. If we examine the conquests achieved by King Tvrtko I (1338–10/03/1391), we will see that he captured exactly those areas which, for ages past, were Arian and which, after the invasion of the Avars and Slavs, were not exposed to a strong influence from them. Tvrtko adds them to his name and title – King of Raška, Bosnia, Dalmatia, Croatia, Primorje with the islands of Brač, Hvar, and Korčula.[135]

The Bosnian Church, from its inception in Arianism, built its churches for an entire millennium, meaning, from the arrival of Arian Goths (III century) to Illyria, up until the fall of Bosnia under Ottoman rule in 1463. In this thousand-year-old history, it had influence in all banates and župas, which were not burdened with the settling of individual Slavic tribes. Among them, first of all is Bosnia, as the centre of Arianism and the Bosnian Church, followed by Dalmatia in its entirety, from Zadar to Ragusa, and Raška. As the Krstjani, members of the Bosnian Church, comprised the majority of the population, they supported and had the appropriate

---

[134] Franjo Šanjek, Le christianisme dans les Balkans au temps de Jean de Raguse, 1990; p 293.

[135] Mustafa Imamović, Historija države i prava Bosne i Hercegovine, 1999.

infrastructure. They built their churches and hižas. The churches served the regular public, while the hižas served their spiritual leaders.

The first unsuccessful attempt to influence the population in Bosnia was with the arrival of the Dominican order, and after them, in 1291, two Franciscans, Dalmatian friars, Fra Marin and Fra Ciprijan, arrived in Bosnia. Long after arriving in Bosnia, the Franciscans were not achieving what they wanted, then they managed to move the vicarage to Đakovo. They achieved easy progress only after Sultan Mehmed Fatih signed the well-known Ahdname in 1463, by which the Bosnian Franciscans were granted full freedom of activity. The arrival of the powerful Islamic Ottoman Empire and the increased presence of Catholicism in Bosnia, with time, led to the Bosnian Church ceasing to exist. The course of conversion was evolutionary, so that only in the XVII and XVIII centuries, a clear differentiation of the Bosniak population emerges, who partially accept Islam, partly Catholicism, and partly Orthodox Christianity.

AFTERWORD/REVIEW BY ACADEMIC ABDULAH SIDRAN

Where does the joy from the publishing of this book come from? The joy comes from that people, of whatever level of education they may be, know that through their education, they learned nothing about this subject. We in Bosnia knew nothing about what is most beautiful and most important in Bosnia. If that compatriot of ours and that homeland of ours disappeared into space, it would remain famous and well-known by that. By that, Bosnia is, as was wonderfully written by the writer Miroslav Krleža, dominant in the cultural heritage of all European states. In that way, in whoever's hands this book finds itself, he will be glad and at the same time reminded how neither in primary nor secondary school did he learn about that. In some households with more education or of higher cultural standing, there could be found the book by Šefik Bešlagić concerning stećci. We only learned about the existence of the stećak and the recognition of their powerful messages and meanings with the appearance of Mak Dizdar and his book Kameni spavač, published in 1966. His poem Gorčin quickly spread throughout the world and revealed an entire universe in which our culture, our education, and our cultural policy are simply silent.

For us, the importantyearforstećci was the one in which they, with the commanding power of Krleža, dragged a stećak to the world's fair held in Paris in 1950. Many writers after that understood that a new literary world was opening to them, and began writing novels, and several important novels were created, which are not well-known, the novel Zemlja bogumila – Zemlja heretika, by Zaim Topčić, who is a very important and respected writer. No less important, in some moments even more important than the novel by Zaim, is the trilogy of the writer, whom few remember and have read, and that is Nusret Idrizović. He wrote three novels (Kolo bosanske škole smrti, Kolo tajnih znakova and Kolo svetog broja) with themes of medieval Bosnia and with a philosophical dimension of understanding what stećci were and what they are. So, Nusret Idrizović had the disadvantage of living in Zagreb and not in Sarajevo, and I ascribe to that his insufficient presence in that contemporary narration and outlook, because in Zagreb, this was not interesting to anyone, and Sarajevo was too far away. More authors have tried themselves in topics of medieval Bosnia, but I cannot remember any who were especially focused on the phenomenon of the stećak. We have today a kind of mimic, imitator of the epigraph on the stećak, which I believe not to be a positive phenomenon, even when they manage, mimicking the language and style of the stećak and when they manage to create a good poem, it seems to me that it is worse because they do not have command over the knowledge of authentic language, never mind that they have researched Slavonic language. When I first saw, on Facebook, kilometres-long poems without the signature of the author, which are posted and perceived by readers as authentic inscriptions taken from stećci, I reacted humorously. I said: if you find this stećak, on which this is written, it must be some kind of skyscraper, and those do not exist.

So, this is some sort of trendiness or some emergence of passion for research. However, it is never good to create an imitation in the spirit of an epigraph from a stećak or create literature after Mak Dizdar. Mak does not copy anything; he presented authentic epigraphs from stećci in the book Stari bosanski tekstovi, which was published in a cultural heritage edition. In this new age, it emerged that the phenomenon of the stećak has captured the interest of our cultural public to such an extent that writers who write in that way as also appeared.

What is learned with each passing day about the period which this book treatises, from Bato (about whom in our schools we also never heard a word) and some think that Bato is the most important historical figure from this region, so from Bato and Bato's revolt, until Ban Kulin (over 1000 years), such phenomenal things are revealed, that it is a life preserver for a man drowning, if our state in this epoch is the man drowning. All powers must be gathered and that must be entrusted to our humanity, who we are and what we are, and how far back our history reaches. It should also be noted that the entirety of the subject we are discussing is prone to political attacks, political manipulations, and I would even say, in some examples, political malversations. This book will, to some extent, do that as well, provide a small shield.

I can, as an amateur, cite a fresh example that in a book by a serious historian of these years, a concept is launched which until now in these medieval studies did not exist, and that is the concept of a "Hum stećak". So, there is an attempt to project the political narratives of today, according to which Bosnia is one thing, Herzegovina, another, according to which those stećci in Radimlja would no longer be what they were for 1000 years, a Bosnian stećak, and in the book of that historian, the term Hum stećak and Bosnian stećak is launched. That is a malicious fragmentation of the Bosnian being, cultural tradition and all. Along that line and in that plane, the authors Suad Haznadarević and Emir Medanhodžić provide a serious contribution to that which is the care, not about the past, but through the past, for the future, of our children, our homeland, and finally our philosophical existence.

Abdulah Sidran

BIBLIOGRAPHY

Lucius Cassius Dio Römische Geschichte

Smith, Dictionary of Greek and Roman Biography and Mythology. Archived June 7, 2008, at the Wayback Machine - He sent Bato to Ravenna.

Vučinić Stevo Prilozi proučavanju ljetopisa popa Dukljanina i ranosrednjovjekovne Duklje; Fakultet za crnogorski jezik i književnost Cetinje

Dubravko Lovrenović
http://www.prometej.ba/clanak/vijesti/predavanje-povodom-550-godina-od-pada-bosne-1137

Boškailo-Suljić Bisera, SRODNOSTI BOSANGICE SA GOTSKIM PISMOM Univerzitetska misao - časopis za nauku, kulturu i umjetnost, 2017.

Pašić Ibrahim : Predslavenski korijeni Bošnjaka; Mile I Moštre; Des Sarajevo 2009 "Libellus Gothorum" Ljetopis Popa Dukljanina; Matica Hrvatska Zagreb 1950.

Franz Glaser: Kirchenbau und Gotenherrschaft Auf den Spuren des Arianismus in Binnennorikum und in Rätien 1996.

Tamara Frömel, Karin Weseslindtner: Theoderich im Sagenkreis um Dietrich von Bern Theoderich der Große.

Suljić Boškailo Bisera; SRODNOSTI BOSANGICE SA GOTSKIM PISMOM Univerzitetska misao - časopis za nauku, kulturu i umjetnost, 2017.

Autor(en): Winckler, Katharina: Die ersten Christen in den Alpen, Januar 2012. ETH-Bibliothek, ETH Zürich

ISTORIJSKI INSTITUT CRNE GORE; Monumenta

Montenegrina; Volume II, Arhiepiskopije Duklja i Prevalitana; Scriptores ecclesiastici, Podgorica 2001. g.

Peter Borggraef. (1881) Der Codex Argenteus und die Gotenbibel des Bischofs Wulfila;

S. unter „Teja" XXXVII, 535, die Münzen, Urgeschichte I. Berlin. S. 300, die Kirchenlegenden, Könige III. 1866. S. 246, über das Schlachtfeld von Taginas die Karte bei Hodgkin, V. London 1885. p. 710.

Hans-Ulrich Wiemer, Theoderich der Große König der Goten – Herrscher der Römer Erschienen am 15. März 2018

Jordanes († nach 552): Getica (Bearbeitung und Fortführung von Cassiodors Gotengeschichte)

Pašić Ibrahim; Predslavenski korijeni Bošnjaka, Sarajevo, 2007. / Prerađena i dopunjena doktorska disertacija Predslavenski korijeni Bošnjaka s posebnim osvrtom na glasinačku ilirsku kulturu/

Ajnhardovi franački anali.

Ma Jesés Viguera und Federico Corriente der "Chronik des Kalifen Abdarrahman III An-Nansir zwischen den Jahren 912 und 942 (al-Muqtabis V)" von Ibn Hayyan von Cordoba.

Musca, Giosuè 1964: L'emirato di Bari, 847. –871. Università degli Studi di Bari Istituto di Storia Medievale e Moderna, 4. Dedalo Litostampa, Bari.

Krueger, Hilmar C. 1966: Review of L'emirato di Bari, 847–871, Giosuè Musca. Speculum

Kreutz, Barbara M. 1996: Before the Normans; Southern Italy in the Ninth and Tenth Centuries. University of Pennsylvania Press, Philadelphia.

Thomas, Arnold. Povjest islama, II izdanje, Sarajevo 1990.

Muhamed Hadžijahić ; Islam i muslimani Bosni i Hercegovini. Starješinstvo Islamske zajednice u SR Bosni i Hecegovini 1977.

Vjekoslav Klaić 1899: Povjest Hrvata, knj. I. srednji viek. L. Hartman (Kugli), Zagreb.

M. Warczakowski 2004: Slavs of Muslim Spain.

N. Ibrahimi 2007: Islam's first contacts with Balkan Nations, Prizren.

Lovrić Mihovil: Začetak i suton hrvatske pomorske baštine. Hrvatsko slovo, V / 220, Društvo hrvatskih književnika, Zagreb. 1999.

Pašić Ibrahim; Od stećka do nišana 16. Oktobar 2016.

ALIJA_NAMETAK_Islamski kulturni spomenici turskog perioda u Bosni i Hercegovini 1939. g.

Lovrić, Mihovil 2005: Gan-Veyãn (glossaries of Eastern Kvarner). Old- Croatian Medieval Archidioms vol. I: 1224 p. ITG - Zagreb,

Enes Ratkušić Tajna bosanskog štapa Narodna biblioteka, 2014

Reinhold F. Glei (Hrsg.) (1985): Schriften zum Islam/Petrus Venerabilis. (Corpus Islamo-Christianum, Series Latina, 1), Altenberge 1985.

Richard Gottheil (1898–1903): A Christian Bahira Legend. In: Zeitschrift für Assyriologie. 1898–1903 (bei Internet Archive)

Gernot Rotter (Übers.) (2004): Ibn Isḥāq. Das Leben des Propheten. Spohr, Kandern, 2004,

Krisztina Szilágyi: Muḥammad and the Monk: the Making of the Christian Baḥīrā Legend.In: Jerusalem Studies in Arabic and Islam (JSAI), 34 (2008), Chase F. Robinson: Waraḳa b. Nawfal. In: The Encyclopaedia of Islam. Second Edition. Bd. 11, 2002.

Thomas Prügl, Universität Wien; Vertrag an der Uni. Augsbur 17. Juli 2012 Petrus Venerabilis: Summa totius haeresis Saracenorum – Gesamtdarstellung der Häresie der Sarazenen.

Retso, J. (2003). The Arabs in Antiquity: Their History from the Assyrians to the Umayyads. Routledge.

Omerbašić, Šefko (1998) Najstariji arapski zapis o islamu i Muslimanima u Hrvatskoj, Behar, bošnjački časopis za kulturu i društvena pitanja, Zagreb, No. 37/1998.

Kalić, Jovanka Podaci o Abu Hamidu o prilikama u Južnoj Ugarskoj sredinom XII veka, në: Zbornik za istoriju, IV, Beograd, 1971.

Imamović Enver; Bosna i Hercegovina od najstarijih vremena do kraja Drugog svjetskog rata 2.izd. Sarajevo Bosanski kulturni centar, 1998.

Pohl Walter; Die Awaren, 11.09.2015 Verlag C.H.Beck

Lexikon des Mittelalters, Band 1, S. 1283 f; München [u.a.] (1980 - 1998) Falko Daim: Studien zur Archäologie der Awaren. 1984 ff.

Josef Deér: Karl der Große und der Untergang der Awaren. In: Karl der Große. Persönlichkeit und Geschichte. Hrsg. v. Helmut Beumann. Düsseldorf 1965, S. 719–791.

Eric Breuer: Byzanz an der Donau. Eine Einführung in Chronologie und Fundmaterial zur Archäologie im Frühmittelalter im mittleren Donau Raum.

Tettnang, 2005, (Neue Standardchronologie zur awarischen Archäologie.)

Harald Haartman; Artikel Awaren, in: Lexikon der untergegangenen Völker, München 2005.

Renate Rolle – Gold der Steppe. Archäologie der Ukraine (Schleswig 1991).

Wilfried Menghin – Germanen, Hunnen und Awaren. Schätze der Völkerwanderungszeit (Nürnberg 1987).

Walter Meier-Arendt – Awaren in Europa. Schätze eines asiatischen Reitervolkes (Frankfurt am Main 1985).

Gyula Laszlo – Steppenvölker und Germanen. Kunst der Völkerwanderungszeit (Wien und Budapest 1970).

Muhamed Hadžijahić – Bosna u IX. I X. vijeku, Preporod 2004.

Stjepan Krizin Sakać D. J. Pravo značenje naziva „bijela" i „crvena" Hrvatska

Ġakmak, Barbara ; Bizantsko-Karolinški utjecaj na području Hrvatske; University of Zagreb, University of Zagreb, Faculty of Humanities and Social Sciences / Sveučilište u Zagrebu, Filozofski fakultet

Stjepan Antoljak: Borna;

Esad Kurtović, Evelina Mihaljević UNIVERZITET U SAR AJEVU FILOZOFSKI FAKULTET ODSJEK ZA HISTORIJU: Ljudevit Posavski Sarajevo. maj, 2008

Đurđević, Josip; Karlo Veliki – ujedinitelj Europe 2011. Sveučilište Josipa Jurja Strossmayera u Osijeku, Filozofski fakultet, Odsjek za povijest

Aleksandar Radoman; Ko je naručilac dukljaninova kraljevstva slovena? MATICA, br. 65, proljeće 2016.

Tibor Živković; Gesta regum Sclavorum, tom II, Istorijski institut &Manastir Ostrog, Beograd, 2009.

Hadžijahić Muhamed: O vjerodostojnosti Sabora na Duvanjskom polju , ANUBiH

Kačić Miošić Andrija: „Razgovor ugodni naroda slovinskoga"

1756. g. Ljetopis Nikole Lašvanina , 1750. g. Glasnik Zemaljskog muzeja u Bosni i Hercegovini, g. 1914/1915, Sarajevo, 1916.

Ćirković, Sima (2008). The Serbs. Malden: Blackwell Publishing. Constantine Porphyrogenitus, De administrando imperio.

Curta, Florin (2006). Southeastern Europe in the Middle Ages, 500–1250. Cambridge: Cambridge University Press.

George Grote: History of Greece: I Legendary Greece. II Grecian history to the reign of Peisistratus at Athens, Vol 12, 1856 "...from the plain of Kossovo in modern Servia northward towards the Danube.

Chisholm, Hugh, ed. (1911). "Triballi". Encyclopædia Britannica. 27 (11th ed.). Cambridge University Press. p. 261.

John Wilkes. The Illiyans. Electronic version.

Zef Mirdita. Dardanci i Dardanija u antici. Hrvatski institut za povijest, Zagreb 2015.g.

Popovoć Marko. Tvrđava Ras, Arheološki institut, posebna izdanja ; volume 34, 1999.

Božidar Šekularac, Dukljanska država i povelje dukljanskih vladara

John V. A. Fine, The Late Medieval Balkans: A Critical Survey from the Late Twelfth Century to the Ottoman Conquest, The University of Michigan Press, 2009.

Živković T, Portreti srpskih vladara (IX - XII vek), Beograd 2006,

Frank Kämpfer: Nemanja, Stefan. In: Mathias Bernath, Karl Nehring (Hrsg.): Biographisches Lexikon zur Geschichte Südosteuropas. Band 3: L – P. Oldenbourg, München 1979,

Jireček Konstantin; Historija Srbije 1988. Beograd-Zemun

Pavle J. Šafarik, Prague, 1853. Žitije Svetog Simeuna : Pamatky drevniho jihoslovanskeho pismenistvi,

Andrejić Živojin R; Centar za mitološke studije Srbije; Schlumberger, 1884. Rački, Franjo, Documenta historiae Chroaticae periodum antiquam illustrantia, Zagreb 1877.

Aleksandar Solovjev, "Svedočanstva pravoslavnih izvora o bogomilstvu na Balkanu," GID,V, 1953.

Klaić Nada Srednjovjekovna Bosna 1989.

Pismo Vukana Nemanjića rimskom papi, from 1199. Fajrić Željko; „Sveta loza Stefana Nemanje", Šid 1998.

Radosavljević Nedeljko V. (2012). Joanikije, mitropolit raško-prizrenski B. Grafenauer, Proces doseljavanja Slovena na zapadni Balkan i u istočne Alpe, Simpozijum Predslavenski etnički elementi na Balkanu u etnogenezi južnih Slovena, Sarajevo 1969.

Pašić Ibrahim: O porijeklu vladarske titule "BAN" u srednjevjekovnoj Bosni Imamović Enver; PORIJEKLO I PRIPADNOST STANOVNIŠTVA BOSNE I

HERCEGOVINE Sarajevo 1998: National and University Library of Bosnia and Herzegovina, Sarajevo.

Dinić Mihajlo; Jugoslovenski historijski časopis I godina,

Škegro Ante; Hrvatski institut za povijest Akti crkvenih sabora održanih 530. i 533. u Saloni; Hrvatski institut za povijest.

T. Smićiklas CODEX DIPLOMATICUS diplomatički zbornik Hrvatske, Dalmacije i Slavonije, Volume three.

Ferdo Šišić, Povijest Hrvata prvi dio 600.–1526., pages

Imamović Mustafa; Bošnjačka zajednica kulture "Preporod", 1998. Historija Bošnjaka.

Imamović Enver: Porijeklo i pripadnost stanovništva Bosne i Hercegovine, National and University Library of Bosnia and Herzegovina, Sarajevo 1998. Rudolf Horvat; Povijest Hrvatske I, 1924.

T. Živkovič; Gesta Regnum Sclavorum Nikšić: Istorijski institut, Manastir Ostrog, 2006 Beograd.

Z. Bjelovučić; Hrvatska kruna u Stonu. Starohrvatska prosvjeta : glasilo Hrvatskoga starinarskog družtva u Kninu, 1928.

Klaić Nada; "Srednjovjekovna Bosna" Zagreb 1989, drugo izdanje 1994.

Klaić, Nada: Srednjovjekovna Bosna: politički položaj bosanskih vladara do Tvrtkove krunidbe, 1377. g.; "Grafički zavod Hrvatske", 1989.

Pejo Ćošković: Kulin. In: Hrvatski biografski leksikon. Lexikographisches Institut Miroslav Krleža, 2013.

Mustafa Imamović, Historija Bošnjaka. Bošnjačka zajednica kulture, Izdavačko preduzeće "Preporod" 1997.

Malcolm, Noel (1. listopada 1996) Bosna. Kratka povijest. London: New York University Press

Ćosoković Pejo: Kulin. In: Hrvatski biografski leksikon. Lexikographisches Institut Miroslav Krleža, 2013, accessed 13 January 2020;

Emir O. Filipović Bosansko kraljevstvo, Historija srednjovjekovne Bosne. Mladinska knjiga 2017.g. Imamović Enver; Kulin Ban i njegova Povelja.

Glasnika zemaljskog muzeja u Bosni i Hercegovini, XV, 1903, Ćiro Truhelka.

Bibanović E. Zoran; Prirodno i kulturno naslijeđe Sarajeva.

Marketinško informativni biro d.o.o. – MiB Sarajevo 2015.

Imamović, M. (2003.), Historija države i prava Bosne i Hercegovine, treće dopunjeno i redigirano izdanje, Magistrat, Sarajevo, 67.

Milaš, Nikodim (1901). Pravoslavna Dalmacija : istorijski pregled. Novi Sad: Izdavačka knjižarnica A. Pajevića.

Rudolf Kutzli, Die Bogumilen, Stuttgart 1977,

Mužić Ivan, Vjera crkve bosanske , Muzej hrvatskih arheoloških spomenika 2008.

Imamović, Mustafa. 1999. Historija države i prava Bosne i Hercegovine. M. Imamović.

www.ingramcontent.com/pod-product-compliance
Lightning Source LLC
Chambersburg PA
CBHW021143160426
43194CB00007B/667